# MANAGING AND RESOLVING WORKPLACE CONFLICT

# ADVANCES IN INDUSTRIAL AND LABOR RELATIONS

Series Editors: David Lewin and Paul J. Gollan

Recent Volumes:

ADVANCES IN INDUSTRIAL AND LABOR RELATIONS
VOLUME 22

# MANAGING AND RESOLVING WORKPLACE CONFLICT

EDITED BY

## DAVID B. LIPSKY
*Cornell University, Ithaca, NY, USA*

## ARIEL C. AVGAR
*University of Illinois at Urbana-Champaign, Champaign, IL, USA*

## J. RYAN LAMARE
*University of Illinois at Urbana-Champaign, Champaign, IL, USA*

Emerald

United Kingdom – North America – Japan
India – Malaysia – China

Emerald Group Publishing Limited
Howard House, Wagon Lane, Bingley BD16 1WA, UK

First edition 2016

Copyright © 2016 Emerald Group Publishing Limited

**Reprints and permissions service**
Contact: permissions@emeraldinsight.com

**British Library Cataloguing in Publication Data**
A catalogue record for this book is available from the British Library

ISBN: 978-1-78635-060-2
ISSN: 0742-6186 (Series)

Printed and bound by CPI Group (UK) Ltd, Croydon, CR0 4YY

ISOQAR certified
Management System,
awarded to Emerald
for adherence to
Environmental
standard
ISO 14001:2004.

Certificate Number 1985
ISO 14001

INVESTOR IN PEOPLE

# CONTENTS

# LIST OF CONTRIBUTORS

| | |
|---|---|
| *Ariel C. Avgar* | University of Illinois at Urbana Champaign, Champaign, IL, USA |
| *Alexander J. S. Colvin* | Cornell University, Ithaca, NY, USA |
| *Mark D. Gough* | Pennsylvania State University, State College, PA, USA |
| *Cynthia L. Gramm* | University of Alabama in Huntsville, Huntsville, AL, USA |
| *Colman Higgins* | Industrial Relations News, Dublin, Ireland |
| *J. Ryan Lamare* | University of Illinois at Urbana-Champaign, Champaign, IL, USA |
| *Paul L. Latreille* | University of Sheffield, Sheffield, UK |
| *David Lewin* | UCLA Anderson School of Management, Los Angeles, CA, USA |
| *David B. Lipsky* | Cornell University, Ithaca, NY, USA |
| *William K. Roche* | University College Dublin, Dublin, Ireland |
| *Richard Saundry* | Plymouth University, Plymouth, UK |
| *John F. Schnell* | University of Alabama in Huntsville, Huntsville, AL, USA |

# INTRODUCTION: NEW RESEARCH ON MANAGING AND RESOLVING WORKPLACE CONFLICT: SETTING THE STAGE

Original research by leading and emerging scholars of workplace conflict resolution fills this volume. To set the stage for the chapters that follow, this introduction discusses overarching societal and workplace changes that have likely influenced the nature of conflict in organizations and the manner in which it is resolved. In doing so, we review some of the lessons learned by previous research. Our chapter begins with an account of the nature of workplace conflict with a focus on the interpersonal, micro-organizational, and dyadic nature of most forms of conflict. We then proceed to a discussion of global forces, including international trade, immigration, and technological change that have influenced the nature of workplace conflict in the United States and most other countries. The focus then shifts to a set of societal forces, such as the growing inequality of income, the decline of the labor movement, and the movement from hierarchical organizations to team-based organizations that scholars believe are associated with the incidence of workplace conflict. We then turn specifically to the rise of alternative dispute resolution (ADR) in the United States and the movement beyond ADR to the adoption of conflict management systems. Taken together, we believe that this portrait of the diverse forces affecting conflict and its management in organizations helps to position the chapters in this special volume. The introduction ends with a summary of each of the subsequent chapters in the volume.

## THE NATURE OF WORKPLACE CONFLICT

Conflict, in all its forms and manifestations, is one of the major challenges of our era. The public usually focuses on conflicts that lead to major episodes of violence, whether they are mass school shootings in the United States or terrorist attacks in Paris or Brussels. It is perfectly understandable that the public — as well as the media — is preoccupied with these horrific occurrences. These days, workplace conflict only occasionally results in violent acts: According to the U.S. Bureau of Labor Statistics, of the 4,679 fatal workplace injuries that occurred in this country in 2014, only 403 were workplace homicides (U.S. Bureau of Labor Statistics, 2015). Nevertheless, despite its lower intensity level, workplace conflict is a much more common, everyday phenomenon than most other types of conflict. Scholars across different disciplines have defined this relational phenomenon differently. These differences are often a function of underlying assumptions about the level of intensity and formality required for a given episode to rise to the level of conflict. Thus, some scholars view conflict as a phenomenon related to incompatibility in goals and behaviors between at least two parties. Others have defined conflict as "a serious disagreement or argument, typically a protracted one." What is clear is that conflict arises in the workplace not only because of formal labor-management disagreements over wages, hours, and working conditions, or disputes between employees and their supervisors or coworkers, but more fundamentally because individuals differ in their values, interests, and beliefs. In addition, conflict is often a product of structural organizational features and work arrangements. As such, differences in the organization of work are likely to affect the dominant manifestations of conflict.

A comprehensive understanding of workplace conflict requires the bridging of insights across different disciplinary perspectives. As noted, some scholars are primarily interested in the formal expressions of workplace conflict, which include, among other things, labor-management and employment disputes, strikes, and lawsuits. Industrial relations and legal scholars tend to view conflict in this manner and ignore the informal and interpersonal conflict dynamics that take place underneath this formal layer. Nevertheless, alongside such formalized and easily recognizable episodes, workplace conflict may be entirely informal in nature and motivated by differences and frictions at the interpersonal level. Organizational behavior scholars focus on these informal types of conflict at the individual, dyadic, and team levels of analysis. While this disciplinary lens captures dimensions of conflict that are often less visible, it also tends to ignore its structural determinants.

Workplace conflict is the consequence of a variety of factors. Almost every adult spends the major part of his or her life at work, usually (but not always) in an organization, and conflict is a common characteristic of all organizations. Organizations are structured, to a greater or lesser degree, as hierarchies; in a hierarchy there are superiors and subordinates — managers, supervisors, and rank-and-file employees. These hierarchies are characterized by authority and status differentials. In a traditional organization, authority relationships can range from healthy and productive to toxic and pathological. Probably, the majority of supervisor-employee relationships are somewhere in the middle of that range: the parties are reasonably cordial on a day-to-day basis, but occasionally disagree over how to do a job, whether it needs to be done at all, or how soon it needs to be completed. Researchers have found that high-quality supervisor-employee relationships are characterized by mutual trust, respect, and open communication (Stringer, 2006). Unfortunately, this type of relationship is often the exception and not the rule. Instead, "armed truce" may be an accurate term for describing many of these relationships. When a truce turns to "war," an employee may quit or be discharged, file a formal complaint or a lawsuit, or join with other dissatisfied employees to engage in collective action, possibly through a union.

A Gallop poll in 2015 found that less than a third of American workers are "engaged" in their jobs in any given year — a finding that has remained consistent since 2000. Gallop defines engaged employees as "those who are involved in, enthusiastic about and committed to their work and workplace," and Gallop believes that "the majority of employees are indifferent, sleepwalking through their workday without regard for their performance or their organization's performance." The polling firm also found that half of the adults it had polled "had left their job to get away from their manager to improve their overall life at some point in their career" (Harter & Adkins, 2015). Of course ineffective supervisor-employee relationships are not the only source of workplace conflicts. Workers may find, for example, that their employer has not supplied them with the resources they need to do their jobs effectively. Some years ago, one of the authors of this chapter was retained by the New York State court system to study the sources of conflict among the employees of the system, many of whom were lawyers or other professionals. In the course of touring the civil, criminal, and family courts in Manhattan, he discovered that many of the professionals employed by the court system were crowded into very small offices and required to use out-of-date computers to handle stacks of files and paperwork (amazingly, in the 21st century, some of the staff did not even have computers and had to do all their work using pens, pencils, and typewriters). These conditions were quite obviously the source of considerable stress and tension on the job, led to dysfunctional relationships among these coworkers, soured their relations with their supervisors, and resulted in many formal complaints. This example highlights the structural and organizational sources of conflict. Had the taxpayers of New York State and their legislative representatives chosen to allocate sufficient tax dollars to the court system to provide these workers with adequate offices, up-to-date computers, and enough supplies and equipment to allow the staff to do their jobs, workplace conflict would have been reduced significantly.

Workplace conflict has real costs, both for employers and employees. In a careful study commissioned by CPP, Inc., a well-known consulting firm, it was found that in 2008 U.S. employees spent 2.8 hours per week dealing with conflict, which amounted to $359 billion in paid hours. The study also found that attempts to avoid conflict led to 25 percent of employees missing work because of illness and absenteeism, and that 10 percent of employees reported that conflict had resulted in failed projects (Lawler, 2010). The costs of conflict are not only monetary in nature but also of a character difficult to translate into monetary terms. The emotional toll on workers of on-the-job conflict can include stress and tension, and, in the extreme, physical and mental illness. Workplace conflicts often do serious damage to, or even destroy, personal relationships, and they can significantly affect not only the attitudes of the parties directly involved in the conflict but also those of the "innocent bystanders" who need to work side-by-side with coworkers directly involved in disputes.

> The collateral damage done by conflicts may be very grave indeed. The damage of wars, labor disputes, and the breakup of families are difficult to confine to the parties directly involved in the conflicts. Often civilians pay a heavier price than soldiers, customers lose more than employers and unions, and children are hurt more than their parents in these disputes. (Lipsky, Seeber, & Fincher, 2003, pp. xii–xiii)

Scholars have long been recognized, however, that workplace conflict can also have positive effects on employee performance and productivity (Baron, 1991; Cosier & Dalton, 1990; Tjosvold, 1985). Organizational behavior scholars in particular have distinguished between types of conflict and the effects that each is likely to have on individual and group level outcomes (Jehn, 1995). Thus, for example, conflict about work-related tasks can, under certain circumstances, have the potential to improve certain performance outcomes, while relationship-centered conflicts have been shown to have a negative effect on individual and group outcomes (Jehn & Mannix, 2001). Vigorous disagreements among coworkers that lead to open and honest discussions about how to do the work frequently result in the discovery of better, more efficient methods of designing, delegating, and completing the tasks at hand. Baron has pointed to evidence demonstrating that "successful organizations are often characterized, to a greater extent than less successful organizations, by open discussion of conflicting points of view. Apparently, this frank exchange of views increases flexibility and hence over-all performance or productivity" (Baron, 1991, p. 26; also see De Dreu, 2006; De Dreu & West, 2001)

Increasingly, scholars have come to realize that whether workplace conflict is a net plus or a net minus for an organization depends not only on whether the organization can successfully *resolve* conflict but, perhaps more importantly, also on whether the organization can effectively *manage* conflict. Workplace conflict that is not effectively managed and controlled can place a heavy tax — both in monetary and nonmonetary terms — on employers, employees, and their organizations. But workplace conflict that is properly channeled and effectively managed can lead to improved employee performance and better bottom-line results for organizations (Lipsky & Avgar, 2008; Lipsky et al., 2003; Roche, Teague, & Colvin, 2014). Managers, unions and their members, and policy makers have been searching for at least the last 30 years for the best mix of practices and policies that can be used to manage conflict, formal and informal, and thus maximize the positive dimensions of workplace conflict and minimize the negative ones.

# FORCES AFFECTING THE TRANSFORMATION OF THE WORKPLACE

The need to find an optimal mix of practices and policies to manage and resolve workplace conflict has been necessitated in the United States, the United Kingdom, Ireland, and other developed countries, by a historic set of forces that has transformed the economies, societies, and politics of these nations. One can acknowledge that the sources of workplace conflict can be found, in large part, in both interpersonal and intergroup (micro) relationships and organizational or inter-organizational (macro-organizational) relationships. But a full understanding of workplace conflict requires the recognition that the ultimate sources of conflict are rooted in larger forces that are typically beyond the control of individual managers and employees and require the intervention of key policymakers at the national and international level.

## *Globalization and Immigration*

It is probably not an overstatement to say that the major factor underlying the transformation in employer-employee relationships in recent decades has been the globalization of the world economy. Giddens provides a definition of the term: "Globalization can ... be defined as the intensification of world-wide social relations which link distant localities in such a way that local happenings are shaped by events occurring many miles away and vice versa" (Giddens, 1991, p. 64). For most of the 20th century it was ordinarily sufficient for key decision makers to concentrate on the national development of their own economies. Although international trade was a vital component of the economies of a handful of nations (e.g., Ireland), for the majority of developed nations international trade played an insignificant role in determining a nation's prosperity. In the United States, for example, at the start of the Great Depression exports and imports constituted about 3 percent of gross domestic product (GDP) (U.S. Department of Commerce, Bureau of Economic Analysis, 2007). Tariffs, quotas, and other barriers to trade were important factors limiting the U.S. role in the world economy. U.S. protectionism reached its peak in 1930 with the passage of the Smoot–Hawley Act, which imposed heavy tariffs and quotas on goods imported into the country. Another important factor was the mode of transportation. In an era before the common use of air transport, transportation by land or sea was time consuming and costly. A third factor was that significant barriers interrupted the flow of people from one nation to another. National rivalries served to seal the borders between one country and another.

After World War II, many of the barriers to international trade were reduced or eliminated. The Bretton Woods agreement of 1944, which established rules for the monetary relations among nations, set the stage for the rapid expansion of international commerce after World War II. Other trade liberalization agreements followed, notably including the General Agreement on Tariffs and Trade (GATT) in 1947; by 1990 more than 90 nations had become GATT signatories (U.S. Department of State, chapter 10, 2009, n.p.). The North American Free Trade Agreement (NAFTA), enacted by Canada, Mexico, and the United States on January 1, 1994, was from the start the cause of great controversy. On the one hand, the U.S. Chamber of Commerce credited NAFTA with increasing U.S. trade in goods and services with Canada and Mexico from $337 billion in 1993 to $1.2 trillion in 2011(U.S. Chamber of Commerce, 2014). On the other hand, the AFL-CIO maintains that NAFTA "allowed companies to move labor intensive components of their operations to locations with weak [labor] laws and lax enforcement.... This dynamic undermined organizing and bargaining efforts even in areas with relatively robust labor laws" (AFL-CIO, March 2014, p. 4). By 2010 international trade constituted nearly one-quarter of U.S. GDP; for the United Kingdom international trade was 30 percent of GDP while for

Ireland it was 95 percent (Organization for Economic Cooperation and Development [OECD], 2009). For these nations and many others, most (but not all) economists believe that trade liberalization has been essential to the prosperity of their economies.

In October 2015, the United States and 11 other Pacific Rim countries signed an agreement establishing the Trans-Pacific Partnership (TPP). The TPP agreement is a complex one, but essentially it calls for the elimination or reduction of tariffs and other trade barriers among the pact's signatory nations (Office of the United States Trade Representative, 2015). Implementing the agreement became a major objective of the Obama administration, but the TPP became the subject of intense debate. Prominent American economists, such as Joseph Stiglitz and Jeffrey Sachs, opposed ratification of the agreement (see Amy Goodman's interview with Stiglitz at Democracy Now, October 27, 2015; Sachs, 2015). In the Presidential campaign of 2016, Hillary Clinton opposed the TPP, and Donald Trump strongly opposed not only the TPP but also trade deals in general.

The liberalization of trade continues to be the source of significant conflict not only in the political arena but also between employers and their employees and unions, especially in industries that have been hard hit by the loss of jobs, such as apparel, textiles, appliances, and automobiles. The evidence suggests that U.S. corporations shifted millions of jobs overseas over the last decade or so. The Center for American Progress reported that "the big brand-name companies that employ a fifth of all American workers ... cut their work forces in the U.S. by 2.9 million during the 2000s while increasing employment overseas by 2.4 million" (Lach, 2012). The Economic Policy Institute reported that the U.S.'s expanded trade deficit with China cost the country 3.2 million jobs between 2001 and 2013 (Kimball & Scott, 2014).

Similarly, in the decades after World War II the barriers to the movement of people across borders fell significantly. Hollifield, Martin, and Orrenius have written that "the increasing international mobility of workers and their dependents has had a dramatic effect on international relations." They continue, "The end of the Cold War contributed to this sea change in international relations by increasing the movement of populations from east to west, without slowing or stopping south-to-north migrations flows" (Hollifield, Martin, & Orrenius, 2014, p. 6). The growing mobility across borders of workers and their families, along with the nearly free flow of capital from one economy to another, were defining characteristics of the globalization of the world economy.

## Technological Change

Technological change also drove the transformation of the world's economies. Computerization and the rise of the Internet dramatically altered the nature of work and employee relations. It has been estimated that technological innovation has accounted for 80 percent of the productivity growth of U.S. workers (Johnson, 1991, p. 2). The effect of technological change on job loss and unemployment has been vigorously debated by historians and economists since the dawn of the industrial age. On the one hand, some scholars point out that over the past several decades millions of new jobs have been created in computer and electronic manufacturing as well as those parts of retail trade and the service sector that deal with computers and electronic products. Moreover, technological change has lifted the burden of grueling physical labor for scores of workers and made work a more satisfying endeavor. "New technologies augment human and physical capital and enable firms to automate routine tasks previously performed by middle-rank workers" (Autor, Dorn, & Hanson, 2015, p. 621). Although the question has been debated over many decades, a general consensus among scholars has been that technological innovation does not cause a net loss of jobs for an economy.

On the other hand, in recent years the scholarly pendulum may have started to swing in the opposite direction. "Economists long argued that, just as buggy-makers gave way to car factories, technology would create as many jobs as it destroyed. Now many are not so sure" (Miller, 2014). In part this is because the effects of technological change are no longer confined to blue-collar jobs but are increasingly affecting high-skilled white-collar jobs. Lawrence Summers, the former Secretary of the Treasury and a Harvard economist, has stated that he no longer believes that technological innovation would always create new jobs: "This isn't some hypothetical future possibility. This is something that's emerging before us right now" (Quoted in Miller). Robots, self-driving cars, artificial intelligence, and two-way, interactive video teleconferencing are only some of the recent or emerging innovations that are threatening the livelihoods of taxi drivers, sales agents, telemarketers, and even college professors.

In sum, globalization, international trade, immigration, and technological change are major factors destabilizing employer-employee relations in the United States and elsewhere and seeding the roots of workplace conflict.

# THE SEGMENTATION OF THE WORKFORCE

## *The Changing Workforce and Lagging Wages*

In the wake of these tectonic forces, the structure of the workforce has changed considerably over the last 40 years. On the one hand, the forces of change have led to the need for higher skilled, better educated workers. By 2014, the educational attainment of American workers was at an all-time high and a majority — 51 percent — of the labor force consisted of professional, managerial, and technical workers (AFL-CIO, Department of Professional Employees, 2016). About 85 percent of this segment of the workforce had full-time work and median earnings of over $50,000 a year.

On the other hand, a significant proportion of the new jobs created in recent years, especially in retail trade and the services, has been low-wage jobs. Appelbaum and her co-authors reported that in 2006 nearly 28 million U.S. workers — nearly a quarter of the workforce — earned less than $8.70 an hour, "which was not enough to keep a family of four out of poverty, even working full-time year round" (Appelbaum, Burnhardt, & Murnane, 2006). For decades, the link between earnings and productivity went hand-in-hand. The more the workers produced, the more they earned. But in the United States, the historic link between yearly productivity gains and increases in average wages was apparently broken in the early 1970s. Between 1973 and 2014 the real (i.e., inflation-adjusted) average hourly compensation of American workers increased by only 9 percent, while their average hourly productivity increased by over 72 percent (Economic Policy Institute, 2015). Stagnant wages are not a recent phenomenon; they date from the Carter administration. "This means that although American workers are working more productively than ever, the fruits of their labors have primarily accrued to managers and executives at the top of the pay scale and to corporate profits" (Economic Policy Institute, 2015).

## *The Decline of the Labor Movement*

Some scholars associate stagnant U.S. wages to the decline of the labor movement. Unionism in the United States reached a peak of 35 percent of total payroll in 1954. Union membership as a proportion of the workforce (often referred to as union density) has steadily declined for nearly 60 years.

By 2015, only 11.1 percent of the workforce were union members. Although the proportion of public sector workers that belonged to unions was 35.2 percent, the proportion of private sector workers had fallen to 6.7 percent. What caused this significant decline in union density in the United States? The decline is partially related to the transformation of the U.S. economy. Historically, union membership had been concentrated in the smokestack industries — the industries hit hardest by globalization and international competition. In addition, the labor force over time became increasingly diversified: a growing number of women, immigrants, and minorities joined the workforce. The shift from a manufacturing to an information economy brought an increase in the white-collar, service, and professional segments of the workforce. Unions found it difficult to organize a more diversified workforce that was increasingly concentrated outside manufacturing.

Also, management opposition to unions and collective bargaining increased after World War II. The U.S. political climate became significantly more conservative after President Reagan took office. It became more and more acceptable for managers to express their anti-union attitudes in the public arena. Still another factor leading to the decline of the labor movement was the weakness of U.S. labor law. The statutory framework for labor relations that had been put in place during the Great Depression became more and more incompatible with the transformation from a manufacturing to an information-based economy. Political polarization prevented serious consideration of labor law reform (Lipsky et al., 2003, pp. 63−65).

### The Decline of Hierarchy and the Rise of Teams

There has been over the course of several decades a movement away from hierarchical, top-down workplace structures and toward team-based approaches to the organization of work that allow for more employee participation in decision making. Both employers and employees have benefited from this transformation to more participative organizations. Employees generally have higher levels of job satisfaction when they have greater autonomy and more influence over how they perform their jobs. Moreover, employers realize that having empowered teams result in a benefit of improved performance and efficiency, even if those teams occasionally disagree about the way the work needs to be done (Appelbaum & Batt,

1994; Cohen & Bailey, 1997; Mathieu, Maynard, Rapp, & Gilson, 2008; Mohrman, Cohen, & Mohrman, 1995).

It remains the case, however, that a majority of American workers continue to be employed by traditional organizations. They work under supervisors — in factories, offices, and shops — who continue to exercise principal authority to direct their lives on the job. In addition, there is a growing number of U.S. individuals who are "contingent workers" — those who do not have an implicit or explicit contract for ongoing employment. They may work as independent contractors, temporary workers, or on-call employees (U.S. Department of Labor, Office of the Secretary, 1999). Some of these workers are in the so-called "gig economy," where they work in "a series of short-termed jobs coordinated through a mobile app"; the transportation companies Uber and Lyft are two examples of employers in the new gig economy (Irwin, 2016, p. A3). The number of workers in alternative work arrangements has soared in recent years, increasing by 9.4 million over the last decade and reaching 15.8 percent of the U.S. workforce in 2015 (Katz & Krueger, 2016).

A major consequence of the segmentation of the U.S. workforce is a growing gap between the haves and the have-nots. From the depths of the Great Depression in the 1930s through the 1970s, income inequality in this country steadily declined. Over the last 40 years, however, income inequality has increased dramatically, both in the United States and around the world. These global trends have been meticulously documented by Thomas Piketty in his landmark book (Piketty, 2013). If inequality is worsening around the world, as Piketty and other scholars have documented, the trend does not bode well for the future of workplace conflict — or indeed, for the future of democratic institutions.

## THE RISE OF ADR

Alongside these significant societal and workplace changes, a quiet revolution has been occurring in the system of justice in the United States and other developed countries for the past four decades: a dramatic growth in the use of ADR to resolve disputes that might otherwise have to be handled through litigation. ADR techniques (arbitration, mediation, and so forth) probably have their roots in antiquity. According to Riskin and Westbrook, "Arbitration has an ancient lineage and an active present. King Solomon, Phillip II of Macedon and George Washington employed arbitration. Commercial arbitration has been used in England and the United States for hundreds of years" (Riskin & Westbrook, 1987)

Although ADR has had a long history, the contemporary growth in its use developed as a consequence of increasing dissatisfaction with the U.S. judicial system in the 1960s and 1970s. Complaints about the excessive costs and delays associated with litigation are not new, of course. Charles Dickens included a vivid depiction of the never-ending civil suit *Jarndyce v. Jarndyce* in *Bleak House*. A seminal event in the more recent development of ADR, though, was the Pound Conference on "The Causes of Popular Dissatisfaction with the Administration of Justice" held in April 1976. At that conference, attended by more than 200 judges, scholars, and leaders of the bar, Chief Justice Warren Burger called for the development of informal dispute resolution processes (Burger, 1976),

Many observers believe that the so-called "litigation explosion," which they believe started in the 1960s and may be continuing today, was widely perceived as a principal cause of the rise of ADR. Over a 30-year period, from 1963 to 1993, Congress passed at least two dozen major statutes regulating employment conditions, including the Civil Rights Act of 1964, the Occupational Safety and Health Act in 1970, the Employee Retirement Income Security Act in 1974, the Americans with Disabilities Act in 1990, the Civil Rights Act of 1991, and the Family and Medical Leave Act of 1993. These statutes gave rise to new areas of litigation, ranging from sexual harassment and accommodation of the disabled to age discrimination and wrongful termination. More and more dimensions of the employment relationship were brought under the scrutiny of the court system and of a multitude of regulatory agencies (Dunlop & Zack, 1997; U.S. Department of Labor, 1994).

Over time, litigants (especially employers) expressed increasing frustration with the legal system because of the long delays in resolving disputes, the expenses associated with the delays, and the often unsatisfactory outcomes. Increasingly they turned to ADR as a means of avoiding these costs and delays. As critical actors in this changing milieu, corporations began to promote the use of ADR in a wide range of conflicts with businesses, clients, customers, and their own employees. The time and cost associated with traditional litigation in each of these areas have been important factors pushing corporations toward the growing use of ADR processes (Dunlop & Zack, 1997; Harwell & Weinzierl, 1995; U.S. Department of Labor, 1994).

Other scholars have linked the rise of ADR to the decline of the labor movement. The growing use of ADR to resolve workplace disputes over the last 40 years occurred simultaneously with the decline in union density. As many workers lost the protection of collective bargaining, they needed to turn to enforcing their employment rights through litigation. But as employers faced the growing burden of litigation, they turned to the introduction of ADR to resolve employee rights disputes. It is also commonly recognized that many employers have introduced ADR policies and procedures as a means of avoiding the unionization of their employees. Although union avoidance clearly is an important motivation for some employers (WalMart would be one example), recent empirical evidence suggests that it is not a major motivation for the majority of U.S. employers (Avgar, Lipsky, Lamare, & Gupta, 2013).

From its inception, ADR has been controversial. On the one hand, it has been embraced by a coterie of champions who have always believed that its advantages over litigation were so obvious and compelling that it would only be a matter of time before it was adopted universally. These champions have also been missionaries, proselytizing their faith in all quarters and making numerous converts. Like all true believers, ADR champions cannot understand why others have not yet "got the faith" (Lipsky et al., 2003, pp. 135–137). On the other hand, there has always been a group of ADR opponents who believe ADR undercuts our system of justice and must be resisted (Sternlight, 2001; Stone, 1996). ADR champions believe in the inevitability of ADR, while ADR opponents believe the movement to ADR can be stopped and even reversed.

## The Advantages of ADR

Compared to litigation, the use of ADR has the great advantage of providing a faster, cheaper, and more efficient means of resolving disputes. The parties in a conventional court proceeding often invest considerable funds and energy from the time of the initial filings in court, through interrogatories, depositions, and preparation for the trial itself and then, 90 percent of the time, negotiate a settlement on the courthouse steps or in the judge's chambers (Galanter & Cahill, 1994). So the costs of litigation include not only the awards or settlements themselves but also the so-called "transaction costs" of inside and outside legal counsel, expert witnesses, gathering documents and engaging in discovery, and so forth. In the United States, the transaction costs of litigation are often two or three times greater than the settlements themselves. Moreover, this calculation does not include the value of the time saved as a consequence of resolving disputes quickly. Reducing these "opportunity costs" may be the largest benefit of using ADR (Lipsky & Seeber, 1998).

In theory, ADR is a means of circumventing the expensive, time-consuming features of conventional litigation. ADR processes are not usually confined by the legal rules that govern court proceedings, such as those regarding the admissibility of evidence and the examination of witnesses. Arbitrators, for example, may conduct expedited hearings, dispense with pre- or post-hearing briefs, consider hearsay evidence, and allow advocates to lead their witnesses. Discovery is almost never a part of the mediation process and is used only slightly more often in arbitration, usually when the parties request it. The parties have significantly more control over the ADR process than they would over a court proceeding. Within broad limits, they can design the ADR procedure themselves. Because the disputants often jointly select the neutral, they are likely to have more trust and confidence in the neutral's ability than they would in a judge assigned to hear the case. Moreover, compliance with the eventual settlement is less likely to be a problem when the disputants have controlled the process that produced that outcome (Ponte & Cavenagh, 1998; Trachte-Huber & Huber, 1996).

### The Disadvantages of ADR

Although there are many advantages in using ADR, some observers contend that it poses a substantial threat to the system of justice in the United States. In effect, ADR transfers the dispute resolution function from public forums (e.g., the courts or regulatory agencies) to private ones. Typically, ADR proceedings are private and confidential. In contrast to court decisions, arbitration decisions are seldom published because they are considered the property of the disputants. Proponents of ADR view the private and confidential nature of various ADR procedures as advantageous, but opponents worry that critical employment matters, often involving statutory claims and matters of public rights, are being resolved behind closed doors, beyond the scrutiny of public authority (Lipsky & Seeber, 1998, pp. 15–19).

Critics also dislike arbitration because arbitrators' decisions are difficult to appeal. Courts will defer to an arbitrator's award as long as the arbitrator holds a full and fair hearing, is impartial and unbiased, and issues a decision that is consistent with relevant statutes. If these conditions are met, arbitrators' decisions are truly final and binding. Although many employers believe the finality of arbitration is one of its advantages, over half of the respondents in our Fortune 1000 survey criticized arbitration because of the difficulty of appealing arbitrators' decisions (Lipsky & Seeber, 1998, pp. 24–29).

Critics are also concerned about the difficulty of achieving a level playing field when ADR techniques are used. In fact, an increasing number of employers are requiring their employees, *as a condition of continued employment*, to waive their right to sue and to accept arbitration as a substitute means of resolving future disputes. In a nutshell, ADR opponents maintain that there is an imbalance of power between employers and most employees, so employees have little choice but to accept a mandatory arbitration provision even if they would prefer not to. Stone has called mandatory pre-dispute arbitration the "yellow dog contract" of contemporary employment relations (Stone, 1996; U.S. Department of Labor, 1994).

Another concern revolves around the question of representation in ADR proceedings. In arbitration and mediation cases, employees are not necessarily represented by attorneys or advocates of their own choosing. Employers, on the other hand, are almost always represented by experienced attorneys and skilled professionals. Many employees cannot afford to hire attorneys, while most employers can. Even if an employee can retain an attorney, critics purport, the quality of their representation is likely to be inferior to the quality of the representation on the employer's side of the table. Furthermore, critics say, employers have more experience and skill in selecting their legal counsel than do employees (Dunlop & Zack, 1997).

One line of research on employment arbitration has focused on the so-called repeat-player effect. For example, Bingham analyzed a large sample of employment arbitration awards and discovered that employers who made repeated use of arbitration won the great majority of their cases, while employers who used arbitration only once lost most of their cases. Her research raises the possibility that repeat players — normally employers — have advantages in ADR because of their experience and expertise that one-shot players — normally employees — lack. Bingham's research has been highly controversial, but if she is right, the repeat-player phenomenon makes it all the more difficult to achieve a level playing field in employment ADR (Bingham, 1998; Bingham & Chachere, 1999). According to ADR critics, the increasing privatization of the U.S. system of justice poses serious challenges for the guarantees of due process and equality under the law (Lipsky et al., 2003, pp. 331–339).

## *Integrated Conflict Management Systems*

Over the last 15 years, the editors of this volume have conducted research on the use of ADR by major American corporations (see, e.g., Avgar et al.,

2013; Lipsky & Avgar, 2008; Lipsky, Avgar, & Lamare, 2013, 2016; Lipsky et al., 2003). In our research, we discovered that an increasing number of American corporations are moving beyond ADR to the adoption of so-called "integrated conflict management systems" (ICMSs). Although considerable research on the operation of various ADR procedures exists, very little has been done on the formation of conflict management strategies, including the use of conflict management systems (Costantino & Merchant, 1996; Slaikeu & Hasson, 1996; Ury, Brett, & Goldberg, 1988).

In 2011, the Scheinman Institute on Conflict Resolution at Cornell completed a comprehensive survey of the use of ADR by Fortune 1000 firms. The survey was cosponsored by the International Institute for Conflict Prevention and Resolution (CPR) and the Straus Institute for Dispute Resolution at Pepperdine University. Cornell had conducted a similar survey in 1997 that had documented the emergence of a new phenomenon, namely, conflict management systems. The 1997 survey was the first to provide empirical evidence on the emergence of conflict management systems in U.S. corporations. On the basis of the 1997 survey, Lipsky, Seeber, and Fincher estimated that about 17 percent of Fortune 1000 companies had implemented a conflict management system (Lipsky et al., 2003, p. 147).

The 2011 survey was able to identify corporations that had either all or most of the characteristics of an authentic ICMS. The researchers conducting the survey estimated that roughly one-third of the corporations at the time of the survey had some version of a conflict management system, but not necessarily an *integrated* conflict management system. The researchers' confidence in this estimate was buttressed by the identity of the corporations that met the criteria used to define a conflict management system. That list included corporations that were well known among scholars and practitioners for having sophisticated ADR programs: Coca Cola, General Electric, Eaton, Macy's, Harman International, Prudential, Werner Enterprises, and others (Lipsky, 2014, pp. 34–36).

## NEW EMPIRICAL AND CONCEPTUAL INSIGHTS: CHAPTERS IN THIS VOLUME

This special issue seeks to contribute to the existing conflict resolution literature by providing novel empirical and conceptual insights that will help to inform and advance our field. The eight chapters contained here address a wide array of research questions applying different disciplinary lenses and focusing on a range of societal and organizational actors. We believe that this volume serves as another building block in the continued development of conflict resolution research in a manner consistent with the changing nature of conflict in the 21st century workplace.

Alexander J. S. Colvin grapples in his chapter with the conflict resolution implications associated with the decline of unions and collective representation. Colvin proposes a conceptual model designed to outline the role that dispute resolution procedures play given the rise of individual employment rights as an alternative to collective representation. In doing so, Colvin presents a framework through which to understand the effects that this new rights regime has on employees, employers, and the employment relationship generally. The chapter makes an important contribution by positioning internal organizational practices in the context of a broader employment rights transformation.

David Lewin's chapter shines a light on an important and central mechanism for resolving workplace disputes that is more often than not absent from this literature – litigation. Lewin argues that conflict resolution scholars have devoted much of their attention to the analysis of internal conflict management practices and systems, with far less consideration regarding the substantive role that litigation plays as a vehicle to resolve workplace disputes. The author focuses on disputes related to employee misclassification, no-poaching, and executive compensation disputes and assesses the extent to which each of these could be addressed using internal conflict resolution practices as opposed to litigation.

Cynthia L. Gramm and John F. Schnell's chapter tackles the relationship between internal organizational factors and litigation. Specifically, the authors examine the extent to which the similarity or dissimilarity between managers and employees affects the tactics used by employees who have been mistreated at work. Gramm and Schnell explore the effects that gender and race similarity and dissimilarity have on the likelihood that a mistreated employee will initiate a legal action, use organizational mechanisms, or decide to exit the organization. They find that gender and race similarity and dissimilarity affect employee responses to mistreatment in very different ways. This chapter provides important evidence on the relationship between a dyadic level factor within the organization – manager and employee similarity – and a number of potential employee responses to mistreatment.

Mark D. Gough's chapter provides another lens through which to understand the relationship between external factors and internal organizational conflict resolution. Gough presents new survey data documenting the perceptions that employment plaintiff's attorneys have regarding the nature and adequacy of pre-dispute mandatory employment arbitration.

The author also explores the relationship between the perceptions these actors have regarding this form of arbitration and their willingness to accept new clients covered by agreements to arbitrate their employment disputes. Gough contributes to the heated debate around pre-dispute mandatory employment arbitration agreements and their implications for employee access to justice by documenting plaintiff attorney objections to this procedure and, more importantly, their reluctance to accept a case when an employee has signed such an agreement.

Also examining the question of procedural fairness as it relates to employment arbitration, J. Ryan Lamare's chapter presents novel empirical evidence from the securities industry on a central phenomenon known as the repeat-player effect. Lamare analyzes all employment arbitration awards within the securities industry from the inception of its arbitration system through 2008, analyzing the extent to which employer, arbitrator, and attorney experience with this process affects the nature of the award that is handed down. He contributes to the literature on the repeat-player effect by distinguishing between within-group and between-group experience with arbitration. Utilizing this distinction alongside regression modeling not previously applied to this phenomenon, Lamare is able to point more accurately to the nature of the repeat-player effect in the context of the securities industry's arbitration program.

This special volume also includes two chapters that provide important and novel evidence regarding conflict management innovations from other countries. William K. Roche and Colman Higgins' chapter reports on the use of network-based dispute resolution in Ireland. Roche and Higgins paint a detailed portrait of this ADR model, which seeks to involve disputants' professional and personal networks as vehicles through which to reach a resolution or to find an appropriate forum in which to do so. The authors focus on the role that one particular industrial relations institution — the National Implementation Body — plays in mobilizing disputant networks to resolve workplace disputes. Their chapter contributes to the literature in two meaningful ways. First, the authors shed light on an alternative, underexplored dispute resolution approach. Second, the chapter adds a comparative lens to the study of workplace conflict management.

Paul L. Latreille and Richard Saundry's chapter details the experiences of a state-owned healthcare organization's efforts to adopt an integrated conflict management system in the United Kingdom. Utilizing a mixed methods case study, the authors explore the process by which a strategic conflict management approach becomes embedded as part of the organizational culture. They highlight sources of resistance to the restructuring especially as it pertains to frontline managers. Since the use of integrated conflict management systems has only recently begun to take hold in the United Kingdom, Latrielle and Saundry's study is one of the first comprehensive analyses of the inner workings of a conflict management system using U.K. data.

Finally, Ariel C. Avgar's chapter examines the adoption of a conflict management system in another healthcare context. His chapter documents the experience of one large U.S. teaching hospital in designing, implementing, and utilizing such a workplace. Employing a case study methodology, Avgar describes the pressures that led to the system's adoption and analyzes the individual and organizational outcomes for the hospital and its multiple stakeholders. In doing so, he highlights variation in the drivers that likely lead to the adoption and implementation of a conflict management system and in the outcomes delivered across the organization.

# ACKNOWLEDGMENTS

The editors would like to thank Elaine Goldberg for her superb editing of all the chapters in this volume. We would also like to thank Missy Harrington for her excellent assistance in preparing this volume. We are grateful to Zoe Morris, the publisher of Emerald Publishing Company, for her guidance and advice. Our thanks also to Louise Lister, the publishing editor at Emerald. We are indebted to David Lewin and Paul Gollan for inviting us to serve as co-editors of this special volume and for their encouragement in its preparation. A portion of this chapter has been adapted from chapter 3 of Lipsky et al. (2003, pp. 75–80) (Copyright © by John Wiley & Sons, Inc.). Permission to use the material is gratefully acknowledged.

David B. Lipsky
Ariel C. Avgar
J. Ryan Lamare
*Editors*

# REFERENCES

AFL-CIO. (2014, March). *NAFTA at 20*, p. 4. Link to the report. Retrieved from http://www. aflcio.org/Issues/Trade/NAFTA/NAFTA-at-20

AFL-CIO, Department of Professional Employees. (2016, April 9). AFL-CIO, Department of Professional Employees, *The Professional and Technical Workforce*. Retrieved from http://dpeaflcio.org/programs-publications/issue-fact-sheets/the-professional-and-technical-workforce/

Appelbaum, E., & Batt, R. (1994). *The new American workplace: Transforming work systems in the United States*. Ithaca, NY: ILR Press.

Appelbaum, E., Burnhardt, A., & Murnane, R. (2006). *Low-wage America: How employers are reshaping opportunity in the workplace*. New York, NY: Russell Sage Foundation.

Autor, D. H., Dorn, D., & Hanson, G. H. (2015, May). Untangling trade and technology: Evidence from local labour markets. *The Economic Journal*, *125*(584), 621−646.

Avgar, A. C., Lipsky, D. B., Lamare, J. R., & Gupta, A. (2013). Unions and ADR: The relationship between labor unions and workplace dispute resolution in U.S. corporations. *Ohio State Journal on Dispute Resolution*, *28*(1), 63−106.

Baron, R. A. (1991). Positive effects of conflict: A cognitive perspective. *Employee Responsibilities and Rights Journal*, *4*(1), 25−36.

Bingham, L. B. (1998). On repeat players, adhesive contracts, and the use of statistics and judicial review of arbitration awards. *McGeorge Law Review*, *29*, 222−260.

Bingham, L. B., & Chachere, D. R. (1999). Dispute resolution in employment: The need for research. In A. E. Eaton & J. H. Keefe (Eds.), *Employment dispute resolution and worker rights in the changing workplace* (pp. 95−135). Champaign, IL: Industrial Relations Research Association.

Burger, W. (1976, April). Agenda for 2000 A.D. Presentation at the Pound Conference on the Causes of Popular Dissatisfaction with the Administration of Justice.

Cohen, S. G., & Bailey, D. E. (1997). What makes teams work: Group effectiveness research from the shop floor to the executive suite. *Journal of Management*, *23*(3), 239−290.

Cosier, R. A., & Dalton, D. R. (1990). Positive effects of conflict: A field assessment. *International Journal of Conflict Management*, *1*(1), 81−92.

Costantino, C. A., & Merchant, C. S. (1996). *Designing conflict management systems*. San Francisco, CA: Jossey-Bass.

De Dreu, C. K. W. (2006). When too little or too much hurts: Evidence for a curvilinear relationship between task conflict and innovation in teams. *Journal of Management*, *32*(1), 8107.

De Dreu, C. K. W., & West, M. A. (2001). Minority dissent and team innovation: The importance of participation in decision-making. *Journal of Applied Psychology*, *86*(6), 1191−1201.

Democracy Now. (2015, October 27). Retrieved from http://www.democracynow.org/2015/10/27/joseph_stiglitz_under_tpp_polluters_could

Dunlop, J. T., & Zack, A. M. (1997). *Mediation and arbitration of employment disputes*. San Francisco, CA: Jossey-Bass.

Economic Policy Institute. (2015, December 17). *The Top Charts of 2015*. p. 3b. Retrieved from http://www.epi.org/publication/the-top-charts-of-2015/

Galanter, M., & Cahill, M. (1994, July). 'Most cases settle': Judicial promotion and regulation of settlements. *Stanford Law Review*, *46*(6), 1339−1391.

Giddens, A. (1991). *Modernity and self-identity: Self and identity in the late modern age.* Cambridge, UK: Polity.

Harter, J., & Adkins, A. (2015). Employees want a lot more from their managers. *Business Journal*, April 8. Retrieved from http://www.gallup.com/businessjournal/182321/employees-lot-managers.aspx

Harwell, D. W., & Weinzierl, M. E. (1995, October–December). Alternatives to business lawsuits. *Business and Economic Review, 40.*

Hollifield, J., Martin, P., & Orrenius, P. (2014). *Controlling immigration: A global perspective.* Palo Alto, CA: Stanford University Press.

Irwin, N. (2016, March 31). Job growth in past decade was in temp and contract. *New York Times*, p. A3.

Jehn, K. A. (1995). A multimethod examination of the benefits and detriments of intragroup conflict. *Administrative Science Quarterly, 40*(2), 256–282.

Jehn, K. A., & Mannix, E. A. (2001). The dynamic nature of conflict: A longitudinal study of intragroup conflict and group performance. *Academy of Management Journal, 44*(2), 238–251.

Johnson, S. (1991). Productivity, the workforce, and technology education. *Journal of Technology Education, 2*(2), 2. Retrieved from https://scholar.lib.vt.edu/ejournals/JTE/v2n2/html/johnson.html

Katz, L. F., & Krueger, A. B. (2016, March 29). *The rise and nature of alternative work arrangements in the United States, 1995–2015.* Unpublished paper, National Bureau of Economic Research.

Kimball, W., & Scott, R. E. (2014, December 11). *China trade, outsourcing and jobs: Growing U.S. trade deficit with China cost 3.2 million jobs between 2001 and 2013, with job losses in every state.* Washington, DC: Economic Policy Institute. Retrieved from http://www.epi.org/publication/china-trade-outsourcing-and-jobs/

Lach, A. (2012, July 9). *5 facts about overseas outsourcing: Trend continues to grow as American workers suffer.* Washington, DC: Center for American Progress. Retrieved from https://www.americanprogress.org/issues/labor/news/2012/07/09/11898/5-facts-about-overseas-outsourcing/

Lawler, J. (2010, June 21). *The real costs of workplace conflict.* Retrieved from http://www.entrepreneur.com/article/207196

Lipsky, D. B. (2014). The evolution of conflict management systems. In J. W. Waks, N. L. Vanderlip, & D. B. Lipsky (Eds.), *Cutting edge advances in resolving workplace disputes* (pp. 25–43). New York, NY: The International Institute for Conflict Prevention and Resolution.

Lipsky, D. B., & Avgar, A. C. (2008). Toward a strategic theory of workplace conflict management. *Ohio State Journal on Dispute Resolution, 24*(1), 143–190.

Lipsky, D. B., Avgar, A. C., & Lamare, J. R. (2013). Conflict resolution in the United States. In W. K. Roche, P. Teague, & A. J. S. Colvin (Eds.), *Oxford Handbook on conflict management in organizations.* Oxford, UK: Oxford University Press.

Lipsky, D. B., Avgar, A. C., & Lamare, J. R. (2016). The evolution of conflict management policies in U.S. corporations: From reactive to strategic. In R. Saundry & P. Latrielle (Eds.), *Reframing resolution: Innovation and change in the management of workplace conflict* (pp. 307–329). London: Palgrave Macmillan.

Lipsky, D. B., & Seeber, R. L. (1998). *The appropriate resolution of corporate disputes: A report on the growing use of ADR by U.S. corporations.* Ithaca, NY: Institute on Conflict Resolution.

Lipsky, D. B., Seeber, R. L., & Fincher, R. D. (2003). *Emerging systems for managing work-place conflict: Lessons from American corporations for managers and dispute resolution professionals*. San Francisco, CA: Jossey-Bass.

Mathieu, J. M., Maynard, T., Rapp, T., & Gilson, L. (2008). Team effectiveness 1997−2007: A review of recent advancements and a glimpse into the future. *Journal of Management, 34*(3), 410−476.

Miller, C. C. (2014). As Robots grow smarter, American workers struggle to keep up. *New York Times*, December 15. Retrieved from http://www.nytimes.com/2014/12/16/upshot/as-robots-grow-smarter-american-workers-struggle-to-keep-up.html

Mohrman, S. A., Cohen, S. G., & Mohrman, A. M., Jr. (1995). *Designing team-based organizations: New forms for knowledge work*. San Francisco, CA: Jossey-Bass.

Office of the United States Trade Representative. (2015). *The trans-pacific partnership: Leveling the playing field for American workers & American businesses*. Executive Office of the President. Washington, DC. Retrieved from https://ustr.gov/tpp/

Organization for Economic Cooperation and Development. (2009). *ITCS: International trade by commodity statistics*. Paris, France. Retrieved from http://www.oecd.org/std/its/itc-sinternationaltradebycommoditystatistics.htm

Piketty, T. (2013). *Capital in the twenty-first century*. Cambridge, MA: Belknap Press.

Ponte, L. M., & Cavenagh, T. D. (1998). *Alternative dispute resolution in business*. Dublin: Dame Publishing.

Riskin, L. L., & Westbrook, J. E. (1987). *Dispute resolution and lawyers*. St. Paul, MN: West Publishing.

Roche, W. K., Teague, P., & Colvin, A. J. S. (Eds.). (2014). *The Oxford handbook of conflict management in organizations*. Oxford, UK: Oxford University Press.

Sachs, J. (2015). Why the TPP is too flawed for a 'yes' vote in congress. *The World Post*, November 11. Retrieved from http://www.huffingtonpost.com/jeffrey-sachs/tpp-flawed-vote-congress_b_8534286.html

Slaikeu, K. A., & Hasson, R. H. (1996). *Controlling the costs of conflict: How to design a system for your organization*. San Francisco, CA: Jossey-Bass.

Sternlight, J. R. (2001). Mandatory binding arbitration and the demise of the seventh amendment right to a jury trial. *Ohio State Journal on Dispute Resolution, 16*, 669−733.

Stone, K. V. W. (1996). Mandatory arbitration of individual employment rights: The yellow dog contract of the 1990s. *Denver University Law Review, 73*, 1017−1050.

Stringer, L. (2006). The link between the quality of the supervisor-employee relationship and the level of the employee's job satisfaction, *Public Organization Review, 6*(2), 125−142.

Tjosvold, D. (1985). Implications of controversy research for management. *Journal of Management, 11*(3), 21−37.

Trachte-Huber, E. W., & Huber, S. K. (Eds.). (1996). *Alternative dispute resolution: Strategies for law and business*. Cincinnati, OH: Anderson Publishing Company.

Ury, W. L., Brett, J. M., & Goldberg, S. B. (1988). *Getting disputes resolved: Designing systems to cut the cost of conflict*. San Francisco, CA: Jossey-Bass.

U.S. Bureau of Labor Statistics. (2015). *Census of fatal occupational injuries summary, 2014*. September 17. Retrieved from http://www.bls.gov/news.release/cfoi.nr0.htm

U.S. Chamber of Commerce. (2014). *NAFTA triumphant: Assessing two decades of gains in trade, growth, and jobs*. Washington, DC: U.S. Chamber of Commerce. Retrieved from https://www.google.com/?gfe_rd = ssl&ei = JQUNV5muIYuu-AX28aBw#q = U.S. + Chamber + of + Commerce + NAFTA

U.S. Department of Commerce, Bureau of Economic Analysis. (2007). *Industry economic accounts information guide*. Retrieved from http://www.bea.gov/industry/iedguide.htm. Accessed on March 16, 2016.

U.S. Department of Labor. (1994). *Report and recommendations: The commission on the future of worker-management relations*. Washington, DC: U.S. Government Printing Office.

U.S. Department of Labor, Office of the Secretary. (1999). *Future work—Trends and challenges for work in the 21st century*. Retrieved from http://www.dol.gov/dol/aboutdol/history/herman/reports/futurework/report.htm

U.S. Department of State. (2009). *Outline of the U.S. economy*. Retrieved from http://usa.usembassy.de/etexts/oecon/chap10.htm

# CONFLICT AND EMPLOYMENT RELATIONS IN THE INDIVIDUAL RIGHTS ERA

Alexander J. S. Colvin

## ABSTRACT

Purpose — *The decline of collective representation and rise of individual employment rights is a transformative shift in employment relations that has changed the landscape of workplace dispute resolution. I propose a model that seeks to provide a new approach to understanding how workplace dispute resolution functions in the era of individual employment rights.*

Methodology/approach — *The model I propose focuses the analysis on the elements that connect the structure of rights that are enacted to the patterns of employment practices in the workplace.*

Findings — *My argument is that the systems for enforcement of individual employment rights and the mechanisms of representation for the employees affected are as important as the substantive rights themselves in determining the impact of the individual rights regime. These three elements combine to determine the degree to which the individual employment rights*

Managing and Resolving Workplace Conflict
Advances in Industrial and Labor Relations, Volume 22, 1–30
ISSN: 0742-6186/doi:10.1108/S0742-618620160000022002

*serve as an effective source of power for employees in relation to their employers.*

Research implications — *The establishment of these sources of power is what then results in the individual rights regime producing an effect on the employers' patterns of practices in the workplace and ultimately determining the nature and character of the employment relationship.*

**Keywords:** Conflict resolution; dispute resolution; industrial relations; labor relations; employment law; individual rights

The field of industrial relations has undergone a fundamental transformation in recent decades. Collective bargaining and union representation, which traditionally lay at the heart of this field of study, have experienced widespread disruption and decline. This trend has been particularly strong in the liberal economies of the Anglo-American world (Colvin & Darbishire, 2013). Following the conservative revolution of the elections of Thatcher and Reagan, public policy in the United Kingdom and the United States shifted sharply away from support for collective bargaining, encouraging rising employer efforts to avoid unions that led to a contraction of union representation and weakened bargaining power for the unions that remained. The epic public policy battles over industrial relations system reform in Australia and New Zealand resulted in the disruption of the formerly centralized Award systems and a much more narrowly confined role for unions. Meanwhile the coordinated market economies of continental Europe no longer represent the unchallenged union strongholds that they once were. Notably Germany, the traditional exemplar of union centered industrial relations, has begun to shift dramatically with declining levels of collective agreement coverage, more decentralized arrangements, and a rapidly growing secondary labor market of lower paid workers on precarious contracts (Doellgast & Greer, 2007). Looking at the great arc of history, collective bargaining, and industrial relations with it, appears to be clearly on a downward trajectory.

Yet when we take a broader perspective on employment relations, the judgment of history seems less clear. This same period of declining collective representation is also the era of the individual rights revolution in employment relations. If we go back a half century to when industrial relations was in its heyday and the lions of the field could hopefully project the worldwide expansion of collective bargaining (Kerr, Dunlop, Harbison, & Myers, 1964), the field of individual employment rights was largely an afterthought relevant mainly to police the relatively small segment of employers competing on the lower margins of the labor market. From the 1960s onward, however, it was individual employment rights not collective bargaining that steadily expanded and became an increasingly widespread mechanism for structuring the employment relationship. In the United States, this individual rights revolution focused particularly on the area of employment discrimination, beginning with the landmark Civil Rights Act of 1964, extending through additional anti-discrimination legislation and blossoming into the current complex system of employment litigation (Colvin, 2012). In the United Kingdom, there were the beginnings of an individual rights-based system with the introduction of legal protections against unfair dismissal in 1971 enforced through the Employment Tribunals system. More recently it is striking that the return of the Labour Party to power in 1997 produced little if any revival in union fortunes, but did produce the UK's first minimum wage law, strengthen employment standards, and bring forth rising numbers of individual employment rights disputes (Dix, Sisson, & Forth, 2009). In Australia and New Zealand, as well, the decline in union representation has been accompanied by an expansion of minimum employment standards (Colvin & Darbishire, 2013). Even in Germany, there has been a large increase in the numbers of individual employment disputes in that country's labor courts, paralleling the similar growth in numbers of cases in the employment tribunals and courts of the United Kingdom and United States (Schneider, 2001). Looking again at the great arc of historical change, unlike collective bargaining, individual employment rights are clearly on an upward trajectory.

Although industrial relations researchers have begun to investigate the new areas of individual employment rights (e.g., Colvin, 2003a, 2003b; Colvin & Gough, 2015; Currie & Teague, 2016; Lipsky, Seeber, & Fincher, 2003; Roche & Teague, 2012a; Roche, Teague, & Colvin, 2014; Wheeler, Klaas, & Mahony, 2004), the field's more general theories and models have not caught up with the shifting nature of employment relations. The foundational work in the industrial relations field, notably that of Commons and the Webbs, was framed in a setting where unions and collective bargaining were being established as institutions to govern employment relations, leading them to address such important questions of that era as what led unions to expand (Commons, 1909) and what types of strategies organized labor used to advance worker interests (Webb & Webb, 1897). In the mid-20th century period of ascendency of the industrial relations field, the leading theories focused even more intensely on collective bargaining (Kaufman, 1993). In the United States, the foremost theoretical model put forward by Dunlop (1958) presented the idea of an industrial relations system operating with unions and employers as its key actors. Similarly in the United Kingdom, much of the leading industrial relations research of the 1960s and 1970s, whether from pluralist or radical perspectives, sought to understand and explain the features of the then dominant world of union-management relations and its central processes of collective bargaining, strikes, and shop-floor labor relations (e.g., Clegg, 1970; Flanders, 1970; Fox & Flanders, 1969; Hyman, 1972). More recently, the Transformation theory advanced by Kochan, Katz, and McKersie (1986) provided a more dynamic perspective on change in industrial relations systems, but focused on understanding the decline in collective bargaining and did not address the rise of individual employment rights. Similarly, Kelly's (1998) theory of social movements provided us insights into newer forms of collective action, but did not help us understand the nature of individual rights-based employment relations.

The danger, as Piore and Safford (2006) have observed, is that the field of industrial relations in its focus on collective representation is failing to adequately address a transformation in employment relations that has already occurred with the rise of individual employment rights. To speak to the major problems and concerns of our times, as a field industrial relations needs to develop theories and analyses that help us understand how employment relations operate in the setting where most employees are not represented by unions and where individual employment rights and not collective bargaining is the major influence on their employment.

In this chapter, I will propose an approach to theorizing employment relations in the current era and apply it to analyze individual employment rights conflicts and their impact on employment relations. My focal examples will draw on the experiences in the United States, which provides the leading-edge exemplar of an individualized, rights-based system of employment relations, but I will also contrast this with parallel developments in other countries.

The model I am proposing includes three components that capture the institutional framework for how individual rights are enacted and realized. First, there is a structure of substantive employment rights — the formal employment protections typically enacted through statutes and regulations and enunciated in court decisions. Second, there is a system of enforcement,

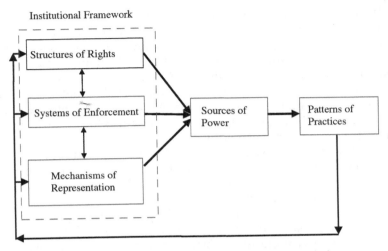

*Fig. 1.* Model of Individual Rights Employment Relations.

the set of procedures and practices through which employment rights and rules are enforced and implemented. Third, there is a mechanism of representation — the process by which employee interests are articulated and realized. Together these three components of the institutional framework combine to provide the source of employee power, which is the fourth component of the model. Employee power is a key intermediary construct in this model, serving as the conduit through which individual employment rights influence employment outcomes. The last component of the model is the patterns of employer practices that are the focal outcome. This model is illustrated in Fig. 1. As shown in the figure, I will also describe recursive paths in the model, where structures of rights, systems of enforcement, and mechanisms of representation are also influenced by and respond to the patterns of practices produced by the interactions in the model.

# CONCEPTUALIZING INDIVIDUAL RIGHTS ERA EMPLOYMENT RELATIONS

If we are to develop an approach to understanding individual rights era employment relations, what insights can we draw from past industrial relations theory and research that can be adapted to this new setting? In my view there are three touchstones to an industrial relations-based approach that we should build upon: institutions, power, and conflict.

First, recognizing the importance of institutions, not just as a constraint on the behavior of actors and markets but rather as foundational elements structuring the nature of employment relations, has been a central contribution of industrial relations research. In the individual rights setting, this suggests the importance of going beyond the formal enunciated set of enacted laws or rights to analyze how the new institutions structure and reshape the employment relationship.

Second, endemic imbalances of bargaining power between employers and employees provided a focal concern for the development of the industrial relations field. In the heyday of collective bargaining and union strength in the mid-20th century, contests of bargaining power were often more evenly balanced between organized labor and management, arguably shifting the emphasis of theory and research away from issues of unequal power. In the present era of heightened employer power and diminished union strength, a central concern to be addressed is to what degree individual employment rights provide a new source of employee power in the employment relationship.

Third, the industrial relations perspective has traditionally seen conflict as inherent in the nature of the employment relationship. For understanding individual employment rights, this means that rather than view conflicts over rights as something residual that occurs in marginal cases of employer deviance, we should view conflict in the individual employment rights era as inherent in employment relations in this setting. We should see it as a central process through which the individual employment relationship is shaped.

The approach I am proposing here is one that is clearly rooted in the institutionalist research tradition. However that tradition, particularly in its American Dunlopian variant, has been criticized, in my view rightly, from more critical perspectives for failing to take sufficient account of issues of power and conflict (e.g., Godard, 2014, chapter 2; Hyman, 1975). By bringing conflict and power more centrally into the analysis of the role of institutions, the perspective that I am proposing is one of critical institutionalism.

Using these starting points, how should we approach analyzing individual rights era employment relations? I will argue there are five important components of how individual employment rights operate and that their combined operations characterize the nature of employment relations in this era.

The first component is the *structure of rights* that employees have. This includes the substantive employment rights and standards enacted under employment laws. But it also includes the structure of who is entitled to the protections of these rights and what is the process for determining coverage of the laws.

The second component is the *system of enforcement* of employment rights. Absent an effective process to enforce employment rights, they will remain laws on the books rather than laws in practice. These systems vary by country and include the activities of government investigators, specialized labor courts and employment tribunals, and in some countries the general court system. They may also include private arbitration and other alternative dispute resolution procedures in some countries. They can include both rights-based processes, such as litigation and arbitration, and interest-based processes, such as mediation. They may also include multistage procedures and combinations of rights-based and interest-based options that operate together as a system to provide for more effective realization and enforcement of employment rights.

The third component is the *mechanism of representation* for employees. To effectively articulate and enforce individual employment rights it is critical that there be some well-functioning mechanism for providing representation for employees. One of the strengths of collective bargaining systems is that unions provide an effective mechanism for representation through organizing collective action and, depending on the system, financing of representation through union dues and other sources of union finances. In the context of individual employment rights, organizing and financing individual employee representation is a much greater challenge and can undermine the operation of the system.

The fourth component is the *sources of power* available to employees. In the traditional industrial relations realm of collective bargaining, the strike weapon, either explicitly or implicitly, served as the source of countervailing collective power for labor in dealing with employers. In the individual employment rights realm, the threat of legal and other sanctions for violation of employee rights serves a parallel function as a source of countervailing employee power checking the workplace authority and power of management.

The fifth component is the *pattern of practices* of employment within organizations. An effective individual employment rights system does not operate at a level removed from the workplace, but rather by altering employment relations practices and behavior within organizations. This can consist of individual practices, such as how an employer handles core human resource functions of selecting, training, compensating, or disciplining employees. These individual employment practices and decisions can be subject to the influence of individual employment rights. But it also includes the broader patterns of practices found outside a specific work environment but within work and employment systems in general.

The relationships among these five components are illustrated in Fig. 1. The combination of the structure of rights, the system of enforcement, and the mechanism of representation provide the basis for the sources of power for employees. These sources of power operate together to influence the pattern of practices within organizations, which is the key outcome of the system. These patterns of practices reflecting the employment system of the workplace then in turn help determine the degree to which individual employment rights are respected and incorporated into the employment relationship for individual workers.

# ELABORATION AND APPLICATION OF THE MODEL

In this section I will elaborate on the model and apply it to analyze the state of individual rights era employment relations. Although I will compare the situation in different countries, I will focus on the experience of the United States as providing the paradigmatic example for employment relations focusing on individual employment rights. The United States is the country that has seen the longest and deepest deterioration of collective representation and correspondingly the greatest shift over to an individualized model of employment relations. Given its role as an exemplar of a liberalized labor market in worldwide debates on labor relations reform, it is particularly important to understand how its individual employment rights-based system functions as an alternative. In order to provide a more generalizable model, I will also discuss the American model in comparative perspective and attempt to identify from the differences between it and other countries how the distinctive features of the individual employment rights system in the United States drive the nature of its employment relations.

## Structures of Rights

If we want to understand the individual employment rights system, we need to begin with the substantive rights it offers employees. Different national systems offer different types of substantive rights protections and varying extents of entitlements within these rights. These differences in the structure of substantive rights also extend into the scope of coverage of employees by these rights.

In the United States, it is employment discrimination laws that are the crown jewels of the individual employment rights system. Beginning with the landmark Civil Rights Act of 1964, which sought to end institutionalized segregation in America, employment discrimination laws have been a central focus of employment rights legislation (Estlund, 2010). Initially, Title VII of the Civil Rights Act began with prohibitions on discrimination in employment based on race, color, sex, religion, and national origin. This was extended to include areas such as age discrimination, pregnancy discrimination, and sexual harassment. Even following the 1980s conservative shift in American politics, the early 1990s saw the extension of employment rights to include protections against disability discrimination and the substantial strengthening of the Civil Rights Act through a comprehensive set of amendments in 1991. In subsequent years, continued extension of the individual employment rights regime has mostly been at the state level, with a number of states adding protections against discrimination in areas such as sexual orientation, non-work lifestyles, and "smokers' rights."

Discrimination law is an area where the United States has been a leader with many other countries following its example in introducing employment discrimination statutes from the 1960s onward. None provide the same levels of sanctions for discrimination in employment as does American law, however. By contrast, in other areas of individual employment rights, the United States is more of an outlier in the limited extent of its employment protections.

In the area of employment standards laws, there has been an increasing convergence across countries in recent years, particularly in the Anglo-American world (Colvin & Darbishire, 2013). We now see a common basket of minimum standards protections entitling employees to minimum wages, standard holidays, annual vacations, and parental leaves, among other items. The convergence in this area in recent years is noteworthy, including such changes as the adoption of minimum wage laws in the United Kingdom in the late 1990s and of paid parental leave in Australia.

The package of basic employment standards is now remarkably similar across the Anglo-American countries. The one major outlier is the United States, which continues to lack basic entitlements to sick leave, annual vacation, and paid parental leave. Interestingly, though, this is an area where we have begun to see decentralized change with limited paid parental leave schemes being introduced at the state level in California, New Jersey, Washington, and Rhode Island and paid sick days being required at the municipal level in San Francisco and New York (Befort & Budd, 2009). In addition, debates over employment issues in the United States have increasingly focused on enhancing general standards, such as the minimum wage, while prospects for labor law reform have faded after the defeat of the Employee Free Choice Act advocated by the union movement.

The other area where the United States continues to be an outlier is in its adherence to the employment-at-will rule barring any legal protection against wrongful dismissal or any entitlement to severance pay. There was some thought in the 1980s that the American courts were gradually moving away from this doctrine as they began to craft a number of exceptions to it (Weiler, 1990). This proved a false dawn for just-cause protection for American workers, however, as the exceptions were narrowly interpreted and courts allowed organizations to reaffirm the at-will status of employees through declarations of this status in employee handbooks and other employment policies and documents (Befort & Budd, 2009). The result is that when we talk about employment litigation in the United States, we continue to be mainly discussing employment discrimination litigation, which constitutes the majority of claims brought by employees through the courts.

So far I have considered the structure of rights in regard to the substantive protections and rights accorded to employees. Equally important in analyzing the structure of rights, though, is the question of which employees are covered by the laws in question. Employment statutes often limit the employees covered based on various criteria (Befort & Budd, 2009). Sometimes exclusions are based on number of hours worked. For example, the Family and Medical Leave Act (FMLA), which provides limited unpaid leave for American workers, applies only if the employee has worked 1,250 or more hours for that employer over the past 12 months, excluding large number of part-time workers. Another common exclusion of coverage is of small employers. Title VII of the Civil Rights Act excludes employers with fewer than 15 employees. The FMLA includes an even broader small-enterprise exclusion, only covering employers who have at least 50 employees within a 75-mile radius.

Another important coverage issue is whether the worker meets the criteria for being considered an employee. Growing number of workers are either classified as independent contractors instead of employees or are classified as the employees of subcontractors or temp agencies rather than the organization where they do their primary work. If workers are not classified as employees of the organization, they are typically not protected by individual employment rights. Thus, the legal definition of employment becomes a major contested aspect of employment relations in the individual rights era. This was illustrated by the classic dispute in the lawsuit *Microsoft v. Vizcaino*, where a group of "perma-temps" who had worked for Microsoft at the company's own facilities for years sued to be covered by the provisions of the Employee Retirement Income Security Act (ERISA), which would entitle them to benefits similar to the regular Microsoft employees who worked alongside them (Van Jaarsveld, 2004). This dispute was ultimately settled on favorable terms for the workers, but battles over employment status continue to be a central feature of individual employment rights law.

The structure of rights in the individual employment rights system provides general sets of entitlements to workers. Yet it is also the case that the degree of protection varies widely. This is certainly the case in differences between national systems, but also importantly within countries. Within country inequality in the structure of rights is driven by differences in who is covered on both the employer and the employee side. As the next section will discuss, similar differences are also evident in the processes for enforcement of employment rights.

### System of Enforcement

Individual employment rights on the books will mean little in the absence of a process to enforce them in case of violations. The way in which enforcement systems operate varies widely, with implications for how these rights are implemented in the workplace.

One major distinction is between inspection-based enforcement processes and adjudicatory-based enforcement processes. In inspection-based processes, some government agency is given the authority to inspect workplaces for compliance with employment standards and rights. These inspections can be routine, conducted according to some plan of inspection of workplaces, or complaint-driven, conducted in response to particular concerns about a particular workplace. Inspection-based processes tend to be used in the context of particular statutory schemes. For example, in the United States, which tends to have a more adjudicatory-based process for most statutes, the Occupational Safety and Health Act (OSHA) operates through an inspection-based system (Weil, 1996). Some countries, particularly in Southern Europe and Latin America, primarily have inspection-based systems for the full range of individual employment rights (Piore & Schrank, 2008). The key to these systems is that they bring the authority of the state to bear on the workplace through the office of the inspector engaged in the investigation. These systems can have advantages in their coverage of workplaces and their ability to integrate different employment rights into a more holistic evaluation of employment relations in the workplace. At the same time, they are vulnerable to underfunding of government agencies and lack of inspector expertise or resources to effectively monitor large number of workplaces (Amengual, 2014).

Adjudicatory processes, by contrast, are primarily driven by the filing of complaints against non-compliant employers and the adjudication of these complaints through a neutral adjudicatory forum. The key to the effectiveness of these processes is that they provide a fair process for determining whether individual employment rights violations have occurred and the imposition of sanctions by the adjudicating body in the event that there is liability. Complaints in an adjudicatory process can be brought by either public or private actors, depending on the specific process. Where these processes involve private parties bringing complaints, this can have the advantage of mobilizing private resources and broader sets of decentralized actors in enforcing employment rights. In the United States, for example, although employment discrimination complaints can be brought to court by either the public Equal Employment Opportunity Commission (EEOC) or by private parties, in practice the EEOC is able to bring only a few cases each year and around 96–98 percent of employment discrimination cases in the federal courts are brought by private parties (Equal Employment Opportunities Commission [EEOC], 2014). Although this leads to a much broader set of complaints being adjudicated, it also raises the problem that not all employees are equally able to bring complaints as private parties due to limited resources or lack of knowledge or experience with the law.

Among adjudicatory processes we also see variation in the types of bodies adjudicating cases. One major divide is between specialized tribunals and general courts. There is a long tradition of using specialized tribunals in the labor and employment area, reflecting the perceived need for specialized expertise in knowledge in this area as well as the advantages of tribunals designed to be accessible to the needs of employees. The British system of Employment Tribunals is a good example of this type of adjudicatory body. In the North American setting, these types of specialized tribunals have been used primarily for specific pieces of legislation, such as the Canadian system of Human Rights Tribunals that handle employment discrimination cases or the American system of workers compensation and unemployment insurance tribunals. In other areas of employment law, however, the general court system plays an important role. In Canada, employees can bring wrongful dismissal claims through the general court system, sometimes under expedited hearing procedures, and are typically able to recover substantially larger damages than provided for in statutory minimum severance pay (Colvin, 2006). In the United States, employment discrimination cases are heard through the general court system and typically tried before juries (Clermont & Schwab, 2004). The United Kingdom also allows employees to opt to bring cases through the general courts rather than the employment tribunals, thereby avoiding the damage caps on the tribunals, albeit at the cost of the greater procedural complexity and expense of the courts, which thus tends to be an option utilized more often by relatively high-income employees.

Another variation is a distinctively American one, the substitution of private adjudication for the public courts. In North America there is a long-standing and well-developed system of labor arbitration for resolving disputes between unions and management regarding the enforcement of the terms of collective agreements. Over the last two decades there has been a parallel but very different development of the use of arbitration in the non-union sector to resolve individual employment rights claims. This type of employment arbitration is something employers can require nonunion employees to agree to as a term and condition of employment, leading to it being commonly referred to as mandatory arbitration. Mandatory arbitration is a private process, not publicly regulated, and forecloses access by the employee to the courts. Although of recent origin, it is likely that mandatory arbitration now covers more workers in the United States than are represented by unions (Colvin, 2007). This is a very controversial development in the United States, which I will discuss further below.

An additional distinction in enforcement systems is between rights-based and interest-based processes. Whereas the adjudicatory processes of litigation and arbitration focus on determination of employment rights, interest-based systems such as mediation focus on producing consensual resolution of conflicts over these rights as well as the satisfaction of other interests of the parties. Mediation as an interest-based process is classically used to supplement and provide an alternative to the adjudicatory rights-based processes of litigation and arbitration. However, where effectively implemented, mediation can resolve a large proportion of conflicts and become a primary mechanism for dispute resolution (Ury, Brett, & Goldberg, 1988). Conflict management systems theory suggests that enforcement systems will be most effective when they incorporate a combination of both rights-based and interest-based processes that are accessible to employees for resolving conflict (Constantino & Merchant, 1996; Lipsky et al., 2003).

## Mechanisms of Representation

Establishment of an effective mechanism for representation of employees is important for ensuring the effectiveness of enforcement of individual rights and also for providing employee voice in the system. In the traditional collective bargaining-based industrial relations system, unions served this dual role of providing the ability to negotiate and enforce agreements protecting worker interests, as well as serving as a mechanism to give voice to workers' views and concerns. Put alternatively, representation by unions serves the interests of both equity and voice (Budd, 2004).

In addition to continuing to serve their direct representational role for workers who are covered by collective bargaining, unions are playing an additional role as a mechanism of representation for individual employment rights. Union-negotiated collective agreements themselves may provide strengthened protections against discrimination and other rights violations and union dispute resolution procedures like the American system of labor arbitration can provide an accessible and effective process for enforcing those rights. For workers not covered directly by collective bargaining, unions in various countries have made some efforts to represent employees in individual rights conflicts. In the United Kingdom, unions provide representation in some cases before the Employment Tribunals. In Germany, unions provide a form of legal representation insurance to their members, with representation of individual employees in cases before that country's public labor arbitration tribunals being provided by outside legal service firms retained by the unions for that purpose (Schneider, 2001). Meanwhile in Japan some new community-based unions provide representation in that country's new labor tribunal system to employees not covered by collective bargaining (Benson, 2012; Nakamura & Nitta, 2013, chapter 14). Australian unions provide another interesting example of activity and expertise in this area with their more legally focused historical role under the old Award system (Colvin & Darbishire, 2013).

Despite these various examples, the overall picture is not one in which unions provide the predominant mechanism of representation for individual employment rights in any of these countries. Why has the union role here been limited? One issue is financial. It is a cost for unions to provide this type of representation and so unions cannot afford to provide it on a widespread basis without some source of revenue. For that reason, we most often see unions providing these services to members who pay dues and not to the larger groups of nonunion employees. A system in which employees who are not covered by collective bargaining pay smaller than typical dues to unions in exchange for legal representation in the event of an individual rights dispute might have significant promise. However, there may be limitations to this model. For example, the community-based unions in Japan that have tried this approach have run into the problem that employees take out membership in the union only when they start running into an individual rights conflict at work and then proceed to drop membership once the conflict is resolved (Benson, 2012; Nakamura & Nitta, 2013). A bigger problem to date has been a lack of sufficient interest by unions themselves in trying this model. This may be understandable given the various immediate pressure unions are under in many countries, but it is not promising for the longer term.

Other types of collective actors like worker centers and Non-Governmental Organizations (NGOs) hold some potential as mechanisms of representation for individual employment rights. Worker centers have expanded in the United States in recent years and proven effective in addressing a number of employment law and immigration-related issues (Fine, 2006). Fine's leading study of worker centers in America shows many promising examples of how worker centers have been able to mobilize collective action in support of individual employee rights. Yet her comprehensive study of U.S. worker centers also reveals their limitations. Although there are over a hundred worker centers now established, the vast majority of them are focused on representing the interests of immigrant worker groups and emphasize dealing with issues around the nexus of employment and immigration issues. This is an important set of issues and the workers served represent a significant and disadvantaged minority group in the United States. However, the mechanism of workers centers with a few notable exceptions has not expanded to serve the larger population of American employees. Although it might be desirable to think about encouraging the establishment of a widespread system of worker centers that could represent all types of employees, we have not yet seen that type of system emerging.

A mechanism of representation that does have widespread reach is that provided by government agencies focused on employee rights. We do not typically think of the government or public agencies as providing representation, but I would argue that in practice they do serve this function in a number of respects. Certainly in investigating and prosecuting cases against employers that violate individual employment rights, government agencies represent the collective public interest in ensuring that employee rights are respected. But they also serve a more specific representational role in individual cases in pursuing justice on behalf of the individual employees involved. For example, in the United States the EEOC in pursuing individual employment discrimination cases both furthers the public interest in ensuring respect for the civil rights statutes and obtains specific damages and other remedies that are received by the individual employee claimants. This representational role of public agencies may be enhanced in investigator type systems such as those in Latin America where labor inspectors have a broad ambit to address a range of workplace concerns and different types of labor rights (Piore & Schrank, 2008). In the Anglo-American countries, there is the potential for an expanded and more effective mechanism of representation to be provided by the recent advent of integrated public agencies in the employment area. The leading examples of this are the Australian Fair Work Commission and the Irish Workplace Relations Commission. Both of these examples are noteworthy for having a broad ambit of types of labor and employment rights that they cover and for being able to use a range of approaches to encourage respect for and implementation of these rights.

It is also important to recognize the limitations of government agencies as mechanisms of representation. One is the financial limitations that often plague public agencies. The reach of a public employment agency is often proscribed by the budget it is provided with. For example in the United States, the EEOC has only the resources to prosecute some 200–400 cases each year, whereas there are now over 100,000 complaints filed with the agency annually of which around 20,000 result in lawsuits being filed in the federal courts (EEOC, 2014). Countries and governments vary in their willingness to provide the resources to public employment agencies to fulfill their mission and extend their reach across the workforce, but the limits of their resources are a much more common theme than their breadth. A more fundamental limitation of public agencies as a mechanism of representation is their limited ability to provide authentic employee voice. Public agencies may stand in for the employee interest, but they do not directly represent employees in the same way that unions as the collective representative of employees do. In the individual employment rights realm, it is worth recognizing the traditional industrial relations insight that voice has an inherent value to employees (Budd, 2004). Processes for resolving individual rights conflict may be fair and provide equitable outcomes but still fall short if they do not provide employees with voice in ensuring their own rights are recognized and in shaping their own employment relationship (Budd & Colvin, 2008).

Some type of legal representation of individual employees is an important mechanism for providing the widespread representation that other mechanisms lack. Lawyers provide representation for employees with individual employment rights disputes in all types of countries and different legal settings. The expertise provided by legal representation enhances employees' ability to enforce individual employment rights and successfully win cases against employers. Representation by lawyers has so far received relatively little attention in industrial relations research, reflecting the field's focus on collective representation. However, lawyers are much more important actors in employment relations in the individual employment rights era, and research and theories need to address their role more directly.

Despite the effectiveness of expert legal representation, a major barrier to the widespread provision of legal services is the cost of financing it. Individual lawyers in most countries charge substantial fees, reflecting their professional training and the complexity of legal procedures and requisite knowledge to navigate them. As a result, retaining and paying for a personal legal representative is often the preserve of relatively high-income employees. Charity or pro bono legal services can supplement this for lower or middle income employees, but are not plausible as a widespread mechanism available for the majority of employees in need of representation. One alternative is the use of an insurance model to pay for representation given that most employees will only rarely need legal representation and might reasonably be willing to pay some small amount on an ongoing basis to ensure against this risk. The provision of legal services to members by German unions, discussed above, is a version of this. Collective labor efforts to fill this social insurance function for workers would be an example of one of the original forms of labor action identified by the Webbs over a century ago (Webb & Webb, 1897), and its revival could provide an important role for unions in the individual rights era.

Another mechanism for financing legal representation that plays an important role in the United States is the use of contingency-fee arrangements. Under a standard contingency-fee arrangement, the employee seeking representation does not have to pay upfront or ongoing hourly fees to the lawyer. Instead the lawyer receives a percentage, typically 30−40 percent, of the damages in the event the case is successful. In essence the cost of financing the case is shifted from the employee to the lawyer, who then also bears the financial risk of losing. Part of what makes this system effective is that the employment lawyer will typically be handling a number of cases at the same time. Even if only a portion of those cases are successful, the payoff over the full set of cases is sufficient to justify handling all the cases, including the ones where the employee loses and there are no damages to provide compensation for the lawyer. In this way, the middle or lower income employees who otherwise would be unable to afford legal representation are able to get a lawyer to handle their cases at no charge. The limitation, however, is that the lawyer's willingness to accept a case under a contingency-fee arrangement will be dependent on the prospects for success and 'the likely damages that will result. In the United States, the current situation is that most employment rights cases are handled by plaintiff lawyers on contingency-fee arrangements. However this system only functions to the degree that there are reasonable prospects of employees' winning cases and that there are relatively large damages available in cases.

## Sources of Power

The three elements discussed so far, the structure of rights, the process of enforcement, and the mechanism of representation, provide the institutional framework of the individual employment rights system. However, it is also necessary to consider how this framework translates into changes in employer practices and how it affects the terms of the employment relationship. To analyze this issue, I draw on the traditional industrial relations concept of bargaining power, but translate it to address the nature of employee power in the individual employment rights system.

In collective negotiations, the bargaining leverage of unions derives from their theoretical or actual strike power (Katz, Kochan, & Colvin, 2007). It is the threat of the economic costs imposed by a strike that creates the pressure and incentive for the employer to accede to union demands at the bargaining table. Thus union bargaining power is a function of the union's ability through a strike to impose costs on the employer by disrupting production, reducing sales, and ultimately affecting the employer's profits. Union bargaining power is also enhanced by the pressures on managers of having to deal with the consequences of a strike and especially the uncertainties inherent in a strike situation. The threat of union strike power then alters the decisions and behavior of management to the workers' advantage.

When we turn to employment relations in the individual employment rights era, the potential effects of legal claims can have a similar effect of providing a source of employee power that alters the decisions and behavior of managers to the advantage of employees. The characteristics of the individual employment rights system will influence the strength of this source of power and the degree to which it is likely to shift management behavior. I will explore this concept using the paradigmatic example of the U.S. litigation-based system for enforcing individual employment rights.

A key feature of the U.S.-based individual employment rights system is that although the structure of rights protected is relatively narrow, being largely restricted to employment discrimination, the litigation-based process of enforcement of these rights produces relatively large damage awards and substantial risks and costs for employers in attempting to defend claims. The damages awarded in American employment litigation are strikingly large compared to those in other countries. One study of employment discrimination cases in the federal courts decided in 1999 found a mean award of $336,291 and a median of $150,500, with employees winning 36.4 percent of cases that went to trial (Eisenberg & Hill, 2003). Another study of wrongful dismissal cases in the California state courts found a median award of $296,991, with employees winning 59 percent of trials (Oppenheimer, 2003). These relatively large damage awards represent the results of employees who were able to get a verdict at trial. Typically, American employment litigation is a long drawn-out process with extensive pre-trial discovery and preliminary motions that result in the dismissal of many cases before trial (Clermont & Schwab, 2004). Although these preliminary proceedings provide a level of protection to employers against the most negative results to them of litigation, they also introduce a high level of procedural complexity into the system that substantially increases the costs for employers of defending cases. The uncertainty and costs of defending cases are exacerbated by the impact on individual managers who may have to devote substantial time to providing discovery of company files and documents, as well as being subject to extended interrogation by opposing plaintiff counsel in pre-trial discovery hearings where there are few limitations on the questions that a manager can be asked. Taken together it is unsurprising that while this litigation system is complex, unwieldy, and often difficult for employees to access, it nonetheless strikes fear in the hearts of American managers and motivates them to take strong actions to reduce the risk of litigation.

Much as bargaining power varies across groups of unionized workers, the strength of litigation power varies across different employees in the individual rights system. Litigation power will be a function of the employees' ability to bring claims forward and the outcomes if they do so. To the extent that individual employment rights laws provide protections for disadvantaged groups through prohibitions on discrimination or the provision of basic minimum standards, then there will be an inequality-reducing effect as these legal rights provide a source of power for otherwise disadvantaged groups. At the same time, if already advantaged, higher income employees are better able to access the legal system due to superior knowledge and resources for obtaining representation, then they will have greater litigation power, increasing their existing advantages and reinforcing existing inequalities.

We can see evidence of the influence of the American litigation system as a source of power in comparative research on how employers respond to legal threats and pressures. Simply looking at the extent of substantive legal protections, the United States appears as a particularly weak individual rights system with its continued adherence to the employment-at-will doctrine compared to just-cause protections in other countries. Nevertheless, the nature of the high risk–high reward employment litigation system complicates the picture. In an interesting case study of dismissal practices in a multi-national company operating in Canada and the United States, Nielsen (1999) found a surprisingly similarity across the two countries. Although Canadian employment law requires substantial severance pay or notice for dismissal in the absence of just cause compared to the at-will rule in the United States, the company she studied actually spent similar amounts of time and resources in dealing with dismissals in both countries. While the company could have taken advantage of the at-will rule in the United States, in practice it was sufficiently concerned about the potential for employment litigation, including discrimination claims, that it devoted substantial managerial and legal resources to vetting dismissal decisions to avoid potential liability. In a larger scale quantitative survey, I compared the concerns over legal pressures and resulting impacts on hiring and firing decisions among establishments in Ontario in Canada and Pennsylvania in the United States (Colvin, 2006). An unexpected finding was that the managers of the establishments in the United States perceived greater pressures from the legal system than did their Canadian counterparts and these perceptions reflected a reality that their establishments were significantly more likely to have been subject to a legal claim or government agency investigation in the previous two years. What this suggests is that the litigation system-based source of power for employees in the United States may be mitigating the apparent employer advantage from the formal at-will rule.

## Patterns of Practices

Individual employment rights will only have limited impact on employment relations unless they can alter the facts on the ground of the workplace by affecting the pattern of practices engaged in by employers. The public policy objective of declaring sexual harassment to be illegal, for example, is not simply to make a statement of principle, however worthwhile that is, but to get organizations to take concrete steps to prevent harassment of employees and to correct and remedy any instances of harassment that do occur. So to understand the nature of the individual employment rights regime, we need to analyze how it shapes the pattern of practices within the workplace.

In the paradigmatic example of the United States, as a result of employer concerns over the strengths of legal pressures, there has been widespread use of defensive human resource practices to attempt to reduce the risks of legal liability. Nonunion organizations began adopting internal grievance procedures in increasing numbers through the 1970s and 1980s as employer concerns grew about this new litigation-based source of employee power (Edelman, 1990; Sutton, Dobbin, Meyer, & Scott, 1994). This trend has continued and we now see American firms offering a wide range of dispute resolution procedures and advanced conflict management systems to respond to the concerns and complaints of their nonunion employees (Colvin, 2003a; Lipsky et al., 2003). Although not providing as elaborate a set of employment rights and due process protections as the strong grievance arbitration procedures used in American unionized workplaces, they nevertheless are mechanisms that allow significant number of workers to challenge unfair decisions in the workplace, and they represent an enhanced recognition of employee rights compared to the alternative of unchecked managerial authority (Colvin, 2003b).

The more general coverage of individual employment rights across the workforce allows this source of power to have a broader effect on employer practices than the more limited set of workers who benefit from collective representation by unions. The threat of union organizing does lead to better treatment of a segment of nonunion workers (Colvin, 2003a), but for the large segments of the economy where union organizing is no longer a significant threat to employers, the threat of litigation is the primary source of employee power likely to affect employer practices. In a study I conducted of the adoption of alternative dispute resolution procedures among nonunion employers, I found that strength of concerns about union organizing were a strong predictor of adopting more advanced ADR procedures, such as peer-review panels to review discipline and dismissal decisions (Colvin, 2003a). I was unable to find a similar relationship for a parallel set of questions about employer perceptions of the threat of litigation; however, for the simple reason that most employers had a uniformly high perception of the level of this threat and the importance of responding to it. In essence, virtually all employers were worried about litigation and taking steps to protect themselves against it.

The impact of litigation pressures on employer practices is also evident in comparative employment relations research findings. As discussed in the previous section, my own research comparing organizations in the United States and Canada found that despite the existence of just-cause protection in Canada compared to the at-will rule in the United States, American employers perceived greater legal pressures than their Canadian counterparts. This American employer perception of a greater threat from the litigation sources of power results in a pattern of employment practices that alters the common perception of very lightly regulated American employment relations. I found that in practice the complexity of decision-making in the hiring and firing processes were similar between American and Canadian organizations (Colvin, 2006). American employers do not always behave like the unconstrained managers they are sometimes ascribed to be, and their concerns over litigation threats and pressures provide a compelling explanation for this behavior.

In recognizing the impact of individual employment rights as a source of power that alters employer patterns of practices, it is also important to acknowledge that not all employers will react the same way to these pressures and that these differences can also be a significant source of inequality in the experiences of workplace justice of different employees. Employers have a realm of freedom to make strategic choices about the set of practices or employment systems they want to adopt in managing their workforces (Kochan et al., 1986). This general observation about work and employment practices also holds true for the set of practices implicated in and affected by individual employment rights. For example, when we consider an area like employment discrimination law, these laws generally provide a set of rights against a certain category of adverse decisions by employers rather than a set of positive structures about what the employer practices and decisions have to be (Edelman, 1990). Similarly, employment standards laws are in most instances, particularly now in the Anglo-American countries, framed as minimum standards allowing substantial room for employer variation above these minima (Colvin & Darbishire, 2013).

Structuring individual employment rights to allow a good degree of employer discretion and choice has advantages in promoting flexibility of employment practices and encouraging experimentation in best practices. There is a danger, though, that placing too much of the authority on the employer to determine the nature of employment practices will produce excessive emphasis on the organization as the primary determinant of employment rights and result in inequality in justice across workplaces. This phenomenon, which I call organizational primacy (Colvin, 2013, chapter 11), has the potential to undermine the generality of individual employment rights. The danger of organizational primacy can be seen most acutely in the system of mandatory arbitration of employment rights that has become a major new practice in American employment relations.

### Applications of the Model

How can this model help in analyzing issues relating to individual employment rights? I will illustrate its application by using it to analyze two different major phenomena in the resolution of individual employment rights disputes: the rise of mandatory arbitration of employment disputes and the use of integrated conflict management systems in organizations. Each of these examples will illustrate an additional feature of the model – the existence of feedback loops between different components. In this sense the model shows the operation of the interconnected components as parts of a general individual employment rights *system*. However, I am using the term system here as a descriptive and analytical term, rather than in the normative sense that it was used historically in industrial relations theory by Dunlop (1958) or more recently in discussions of conflict management systems (Constantino & Merchant, 1996; Lipsky et al., 2003).

The first application is the rise of mandatory arbitration. As I described earlier, under mandatory arbitration employers can require employees to agree to arbitrate any statutory or other legal claim against the employer through a private arbitration procedure designated in the contract drafted by the employer. Following a series of decisions of the U.S. Supreme Court,[1] these mandatory arbitration procedures are enforceable and preclude access to the courts for resolving any claim covered by the arbitration agreement (Colvin, 2012). Although arbitration has a long and successful history of use in labor relations, the particular institutional structure of mandatory arbitration with its unilateral implementation at the choice of the employer has resulted in a process that tends to produce favorable results for employers. Whereas employees on average win some 37 percent of trials in federal courts and 57 percent of trials in state courts (Eisenberg & Hill, 2003), employees win only 21 percent of hearings in mandatory arbitration (Colvin, 2011). Damage amounts are also substantially lower with a median award of only $36,500 in mandatory arbitration compared to a median of $150,500 in federal courts and $296,991 in California state courts (Colvin, 2011). These lower prospects of success and reduced damages make it much harder for employment lawyers to justify accepting cases under mandatory arbitration because it limits the potential payoff under contingency-fee arrangements used to finance cases on behalf of lower and middle income employees who are unable to afford hourly fees for legal services. Recently the Supreme Court has further enhanced the value of mandatory arbitration to employers by holding that these arbitration agreements can require claims to be brought individually, effectively barring the use of class actions by employees covered by these procedures.[2] The result is that mandatory arbitration serves as a strong shield for employers against being subject to the risk and pressures of litigation.

Mandatory arbitration is a signal example of organizational primacy in individual employment rights since it allows the employer to determine the process of enforcement through which individual rights are pursued by employees. The resulting undermining of the mechanism of representation for lower income employees and diminution of the litigation-based sources of power result in reduced pressure on employers to alter their employment practices to respect individual employment rights. This is obviously a very specific American phenomenon that is a product of U.S. Supreme Court decisions that are reframing the uniquely American system of individual employment rights litigation. However, it also has broader lessons for employment relations theory and policy. From a research and theory standpoint, what it shows is the importance of the interconnections amongst the different elements of the individual employment rights-based system in the model that I have outlined. From a policy standpoint it shows the importance of understanding and addressing the specific features of the individual employment rights system, because these features can have profound effects on the nature of employment relations in the individual rights era.

The second phenomenon to consider in applying the model is the adoption of conflict management systems by organizations. Early innovations in the area of alternative dispute resolution looked at the impact of specific practices and procedures, such as the adoption of arbitration, mediation, or ombudspersons. By contrast the conflict management systems approach suggests that more effective resolution of conflict will occur where there are a combination of different procedures and practices used in conjunction with one another (Constantino & Merchant, 1996). Lipsky et al. (2003) argue that effective systems, which they term integrated conflict management systems, will include five characteristics: a broad scope, covering all employees and types of problems; a culture that welcomes dissent and encourages resolution of conflict through negotiation; multiple access points to the system; multiple options for resolution, including both rights-based and interest-based options; and support structures for the system. In another version of the conflict management systems argument, Bendersky (2003) suggests that effective systems should include three elements: rights-based processes; negotiated processes; and interest-based neutrals.

The idea of conflict management systems has been a popular normative concept for thinking about organizational approaches to conflict resolution design. However, there has been only a small amount of empirical work systematically examining its impact, notably Bendersky's (2007) study of a Canadian government agency and Roche and Teague's (2012b) study of conflict management systems in Irish firms (see generally Roche & Teague, 2014, chapter 12). Despite the limited empirical evidence to date, the strong consensus in the dispute resolution field is that conflict management systems provide a best practice model for organizations to follow. Yet a common theme among case studies of conflict management systems is their fragility and lack of sustainability. In their leading work in this area, Lipsky et al. (2003) noted the importance of having an organizational ADR champion to encourage the adoption and operation of integrated conflict management systems. In the absence of or following the departure of this ADR champion, these systems tended to fall into disuse and abandonment. But why should conflict management systems be so dependent on an individual champion if they are indeed effective systems for dealing with employment rights disputes?

Applying the model developed in this chapter, the key problem with conflict management systems developed at the organizational level is that they represent innovation in only part of a broader system. An organizational conflict management system can emerge as an innovation in organizational employment practices in response to pressures from employment conflicts. This organizational innovation then provides a new enforcement system for employees with employment rights disputes, but these types of organizational systems are often lacking in effective mechanisms of representation. Many are introduced in nonunion settings lacking collective representation from unions. Because they are internal systems, participation in them by outsider lawyers is generally unwelcome. The result is that the institutional framework of organizational conflict management systems is not one well suited to the production of sources of power for employees. It may be that these systems are sustainable for some period of time based on internal support for the principle of effective conflict management led by an ADR champion. However, the employee sources of power are necessary over time for most organizations to pressure employers to adopt practices that are responsive to individual employee rights.


# CONCLUSIONS

There are two general themes that can be drawn from the discussion presented here. The first relates to the role of organizations in individual rights employment relations. Individual employment rights are typically enacted as laws providing rights to employees across the whole economy not particular to any individual employer – in contrast for example to an organizational or enterprise level collective agreement. Some researchers have also questioned the importance of the individual employer in an era where long-term standard employment relationships have broken down and organizational forms have become increasingly complex and intertwined into network structures and production chains that often span the globe. I am suggesting that the institutional structure of the individual employment rights system has actually empowered organizations as the central actors in the system and the key parties who determine the nature of employment relations that workers experience. This is a consequence of both the variation in pressure exerted on different employers from individual employment rights conflict and the variation in employer responses in terms of adopting different patterns of employment practices.

The second general theme concerns the growth of inequality in justice in employment. There has rightly been much attention to the growth of income inequality and the problems it poses for societies and economies. My argument is that along with this trend, there is a growing inequality in access to justice in the workplace. Rather than individual employment rights providing a universal structure of rights and fair treatment, accessible to all workers, there is great variation in practice in the protections and fairness accorded to workers. This inequality is not inherent or accidental, but rather a product of the institutional structure of the individual employment rights system as currently constituted.

I began with a call for industrial relations research and theory to more fully address the issues and implications posed by the rise of the individual employment rights era in employment relations. The model I have proposed seeks to provide an approach to understanding how individual employment rights affect employment relations. It focuses the analysis on the elements that connect the structure of rights that are enacted to the patterns of employment practices in the workplace. My argument is that the systems for enforcement of these rights and the mechanisms of representation for the employees affected are as important as the substantive rights themselves in determining the impact of the individual rights regime. These three elements combine to determine the degree to which the individual employment rights serve as an effective source of power for employees in relation to their employers. The establishment of these sources of power is what then results in the individual rights regime producing an effect on the employers' patterns of practices in the workplace and ultimately determining the nature and character of the employment relationship.

For industrial relations to remain relevant and thrive as a field it is important that it takes on the new issues of work and employment such as those posed by the rise of individual employment rights. This does not mean abandoning the basic insights of our field, because, as I have argued here, our foundational concepts and focus on analyzing institutions, conflict, and power remain relevant and yield insights in understanding the nature of employment relations in the individual rights era. Rather, our task going forward is to take these tools and ideas and use them to address the problems of the new world of work that confronts us.

## NOTES

1. The key decision enabling mandatory arbitration to be used for disputes involving statutory employment rights was *Gilmer v. Interstate/Johnson Lane* (1991). For a more detailed recent discussion of the law in this area see: Stone and Colvin (2015).
2. *AT&T v. Concepcion* (2011).

## REFERENCES

Amengual, M. (2014). Pathways to enforcement: Labor inspectors leveraging linkages with society in Argentina. *Industrial and Labor Relations Review, 67*(1), 3–33.

AT&T v. Concepcion, 563 U.S. 333 (2011).

Befort, S. F., & Budd, J. W. (2009). *Invisible hands, invisible objectives: Bringing workplace law & public policy into focus.* Stanford, CA: Stanford University Press.

Bendersky, C. (2003). Organizational dispute resolution systems: A complementarities model. *Academy of Management Review, 28*(4), 643–656.

Bendersky, C. (2007). Complementarities in organizational dispute resolution systems: How system characteristics affect individuals' conflict experiences. *Industrial and Labor Relations Review*, *60*(2), 204–224.

Benson, J. (2012). Alternative dispute resolution in Japan: The rise of individualism. *International Journal of Human Resource Management*, *23*(3), 511–527.

Budd, J. W. (2004). *Employment with a human face: Balancing efficiency, equity, and voice*. Ithaca, NY: ILR Press.

Budd, J. W., & Colvin, A. J. S. (2008). Improved metrics for workplace dispute resolution procedures: Efficiency, equity, and voice. *Industrial Relations*, *47*(3), 460–479.

Clegg, H. A. (1970). *The system of industrial relations in Great Britain*. Oxford: Blackwell.

Clermont, K. M., & Schwab, S. J. (2004). How employment discrimination plaintiffs fare in federal court. *Journal of Empirical Legal Studies*, *1*(2), 429–458.

Colvin, A. J. S. (2003a). Institutional pressures, human resource strategies and the rise of nonunion dispute resolution procedures. *Industrial and Labor Relations Review*, *56*(3), 375–392.

Colvin, A. J. S. (2003b). The dual transformation of workplace dispute resolution. *Industrial Relations*, *52*(4), 712–735.

Colvin, A. J. S. (2006). Flexibility and fairness in liberal market economies: The comparative impact of the legal environment and high performance work systems. *British Journal of Industrial Relations*, *44*(1), 73–97.

Colvin, A. J. S. (2007). Empirical research on employment arbitration: Clarity amidst the sound and fury? *Employee Rights and Employment Policy Journal*, *11*(2), 405–447.

Colvin, A. J. S. (2011). An empirical study of employment arbitration: Case outcomes and processes. *Journal of Empirical Legal Studies*, *8*(1), 1–23.

Colvin, A. J. S. (2012). American workplace dispute resolution in the individual rights era. *International Journal of Human Resource Management*, *23*(3–4), 459–475.

Colvin, A. J. S. (2013). Organizational primacy after the demise of the organizational career: Employment conflict in a post-standard contract world. In H. Arthurs & K. Stone (Eds.), *Employment regulation after the demise of the standard employment contract: Innovations in regulatory design* (pp. 194–210). New York, NY: Russell Sage.

Colvin, A. J. S., & Darbishire, O. (2013). Convergence in industrial relations institutions: The emerging Anglo-American model? *Industrial and Labor Relations Review*, *66*(5), 1045–1075.

Colvin, A. J. S., & Gough, M. D. (2015). Individual employment rights arbitration in the United States: Actors and outcomes. *Industrial and Labor Relations Review*, *68*(5), 1019–1042.

Commons, J. R. (1909). American shoemakers, 1648–1895. *Quarterly Journal of Economics*, *24*(4), 39–83.

Constantino, C. A., & Merchant, C. S. (1996). *Designing conflict management systems*. San Francisco, CA: Jossey-Bass.

Currie, D., & Teague, P. (2016). Economic citizenship and workplace conflict in Anglo-American industrial relations systems. *British Journal of Industrial Relations*, *54*(2): 358–384.

Dix, G., Sisson, K., & Forth, J. (2009). Conflict at work: The changing pattern of disputes. In W. Brown, A. Bryson, J. Forth, & K. Whitfield (Eds.), *The evolution of the modern workplace* (pp. 176–200). Cambridge: Cambridge University Press.

Doellgast, V., & Greer, I. (2007). Vertical disintegration and the disorganization of German industrial relations. *British Journal of Industrial Relations*, *45*(1), 55–76.

Dunlop, J. T. (1958). *Industrial relations systems.* New York, NY: Holt.

Edelman, L. B. (1990). Legal environments and organizational governance: The expansion of due process in the American workplace. *American Journal of Sociology, 95,* 1401–1440.

Eisenberg, T., & Hill, E. (2003). Arbitration and litigation of employment claims: An empirical comparison. *Dispute Resolution Journal, 58*(4), 44–55.

Equal Employment Opportunities Commission (EEOC). (2014). *Enforcement and litigation statistics.* Retrieved from http://www.eeoc.gov/eeoc/statistics/enforcement/index.cfm. Accessed on January 10, 2014.

Estlund, C. (2010). *Regoverning the workplace.* New Haven, CT: Yale University Press.

Fine, J. (2006). *Worker centers: Organizing communities at the edge of the dream.* Ithaca, NY: Cornell University Press.

Flanders, A. (1970). *Management and unions: The theory and reform of industrial relations.* London: Faber.

Fox, A., & Flanders, A. (1969). The reform of collective bargaining: From Donovan to Durkheim. *British Journal of Industrial Relations, 7*(2), 151–180.

Gilmer v. Interstate/Johnson Lane, 500 U.S. 20 (1991).

Godard, J. (2014). Labor-management conflict. In W. K. Roche, P. Teague, & A. J. S. Colvin (Eds.), *The Oxford handbook of conflict management in organizations.* Oxford: Oxford University Press.

Hyman, R. (1972). *Strikes.* London: Fontana.

Hyman, R. (1975). *Industrial relations: A Marxist introduction.* London: Macmillan.

Katz, H. C., Kochan, T. A., & Colvin, A. J. S. (2007). *An introduction to collective bargaining and industrial relations* (4th ed.). New York, NY: McGraw Hill Irwin.

Kaufman, B. (1993). *The origins and evolution of the field of industrial relations.* Ithaca, NY: ILR Press.

Kelly, J. (1998). *Rethinking industrial relations: Mobilization, collectivism, and long waves.* London: Routledge.

Kerr, C., Dunlop, J., Harbison, F., & Myers, C. (1964). *Industrialism and industrial man.* Cambridge, MA: Harvard University Press.

Kochan, T. A., Katz, H. C., & McKersie, R. B. (1986). *The transformation of American industrial relations.* New York, NY: Basic Books.

Lipsky, D. B., Seeber, R. L., & Fincher, R. D. (2003). *Emerging systems for managing workplace conflict: Lessons from American corporations for managers and dispute resolution professionals.* San Francisco, CA: Jossey-Bass.

Nakamura, K., & Nitta, M. (2013). Organizing nonstandard workers in Japan: Old players and new players. In K. V. W. Stone & H. Arthurs (Eds.), *Rethinking workplace regulation: Beyond the standard contract of employment* (pp. 253–270). New York, NY: Russell Sage.

Nielsen, L. B. (1999). Paying workers or paying lawyers: Employee termination practices in the United States and Canada. *Law & Policy, 21*(3), 247–282.

Oppenheimer, D. B. (2003). Verdicts matter: An empirical study of California employment discrimination and wrongful discharge jury verdicts reveals low success rates for women and minorities. *U.C. Davis Law Review, 37,* 511–566.

Piore, M., & Safford, S. (2006). Changing regimes of workplace governance, shifting axes of social mobilization, and the challenge to industrial relations theory. *Industrial Relations, 45*(3), 299–325.

Piore, M., & Schrank, A. (2008). Toward managed flexibility: The revival of labor inspection in the Latin world. *International Labour Review, 147,* 1–23.

Roche, W. K., & Teague, P. (2012a). The growing importance of workplace ADR. *International Journal of Human Resource Management, 23*(3), 447–458.

Roche, W. K., & Teague, P. (2012b). Do conflict management systems matter? *Human Resource Management, 51*(2), 231–258.

Roche, W. K., & Teague, P. (2014). Conflict management systems. In W. K. Roche, P. Teague, & A. J. S. Colvin (Eds.), *The Oxford handbook of conflict management in organizations* (pp. 250–272). Oxford: Oxford University Press.

Roche, W. K., Teague, P., & Colvin, A. J. S. (Eds.). (2014). *The Oxford handbook of conflict management in organizations.* Oxford: Oxford University Press.

Schneider, M. (2001). Employment litigation on the rise? Comparing British employment tribunals and German labor courts. *Comparative Labor Law & Policy Journal, 22,* 261–280.

Stone, K. V. W., & Colvin, A. J. S. (2015). *The arbitration epidemic: The use of mandatory arbitration to deprive consumers and workers of their rights.* Washington, DC: Economic Policy Institute (EPI). EPI Briefing Paper #414.

Sutton, J. R., Dobbin, F., Meyer, J., & Scott, W. R. (1994). The legalization of the workplace. *American Journal of Sociology, 99,* 944–971.

Ury, W. L., Brett, J. M., & Goldberg, S. B. (1988). *Getting disputes resolved: Designing systems to cut the costs of conflict.* San Francisco, CA: Jossey-Bass.

Van Jaarsveld, D. D. (2004). Collective representation among high-tech workers at Microsoft and beyond: Lessons from WashTech/CWA. *Industrial Relations, 43*(2), 364–385.

Webb, S., & Webb, B. (1897). *Industrial democracy.* London: Longmans, Green and Co.

Weil, D. (1996). If OSHA is so bad, why is compliance so good? *Rand Journal of Economics, 27*(3), 618–640.

Weiler, P. C. (1990). *Governing the workplace: The future of labor and employment law.* Cambridge, MA: Harvard University Press.

Wheeler, H. N., Klaas, B. S., & Mahony, D. M. (2004). *Workplace justice without unions.* Kalamazoo, MI: W.E. Upjohn Institute.

# RESOLVING WORKPLACE CONFLICTS THROUGH LITIGATION: EVIDENCE, ANALYSIS, AND IMPLICATIONS

David Lewin

## ABSTRACT

Purpose — *Industrial relations, organizational behavior, and human resource management scholars have studied numerous aspects of internal workplace conflict resolution, ranging from the design of conflict resolution systems to the processes used for resolving conflicts to the outcomes of the systems. Scholars from these specialties, however, have paid considerably less attention to external workplace conflict resolution through litigation. This chapter analyzes certain areas of such litigation, focusing specifically on workplace conflicts involving issues of managerial and employee misclassification, independent contractor versus employee status, no-poaching agreements, and executive compensation.*

Methodology/approach — *Leading recent cases involving these issues are examined, with particular attention given to the question of whether the conflicts reflected therein could have been resolved internally or*

Managing and Resolving Workplace Conflict
Advances in Industrial and Labor Relations, Volume 22, 31–67
ISSN: 0742-6186/doi:10.1108/S0742-618620160000022003

*through alternative dispute resolution (ADR) methods rather than through litigation.*

Practical implications — *Implications of this analysis are drawn for workplace conflict resolution theory and practice. In doing so, I conclude that misclassification disputes could likely be resolved internally or through ADR rather than through litigation, but that no-poaching and executive compensation disputes could very likely not be resolved internally or through ADR.*

Originality/value — *The chapter draws on and offers an integrated analysis of particular types of workplace conflict that are typically treated separately by scholars and practitioners. These include misclassification conflicts, no poaching and labor market competition conflicts, and executive compensation conflicts. The originality and value of this chapter are to show that despite their different contexts and particular issues, the attempted resolution through litigation of these types of workplace conflicts has certain common, systematic characteristics.*

**Keywords:** Workplace; conflict resolution; litigation; misclassification; no poaching; executive compensation

Scholars from a variety of disciplines and specialized fields have studied workplace conflict resolution. For several decades industrial relations scholars in particular concentrated their research on unionized employment relationships featuring written collective bargaining agreements that included formal grievance procedures to resolve disputes that arose during the duration of those agreements (Budd, 2013; Kuhn, 1961; Lewin & Peterson, 1988, 1999). As the incidence of unionism and collective bargaining declined in the United States and other nations, though, this research focused increasingly on non-union employment relationships, individual employer-employee agreements, and alternative dispute resolution (ADR) (Eaton & Keefe, 1999; Lipsky, Seeber, & Fincher, 2003; Colvin, 2003). This latter focus attracted human resource management and organizational behavior scholars in particular (Kaufman, Lewin, & Fossum, 2000; MacDuffie, 1995; Pfeffer, 1998).

As a whole, this research features a strong emphasis on positive workplace conflict resolution. For industrial relations scholars, this emphasis is reflected in such phrases as integrative bargaining and mutual gains negotiations (Lewin, 2010; Walton & McKersie, 1965). For human resource management scholars, it is reflected in such phrases as high involvement management and employee engagement (Albrecht, 2010; Cotton, 1993). For organizational behavior scholars, it is reflected in such phrases as organizational citizenship (Bateman & Organ, 1983) and restorative justice (Braithwaite, 2002). This is not to say that scholars in these areas are unmindful of, or ignore, negative workplace conflict resolution. To the contrary, industrial relations scholars' studies have attempted to explain factors associated with adversarial employment relationships (Chamberlain & Kuhn, 1965; Katz & Keefe, 1992). Human resource management scholars' studies have attempted to explain factors associated with high employee turnover (Huselid, 1995) and low employee morale (Sanborn & Oehler, 2013). Organizational behavior scholars' studies have attempted to explain factors associated with intragroup and intergroup conflict (Alper, Tjosvold, & Law, 2000; Jehn & Bendersky, 2003). Nonetheless, most of this research focuses on how the direct parties to workplace conflict, that is, employees and managers, their representatives and agents, can resolve conflict internally through one or more processes, mechanisms, or methods.[1]

By contrast, the focus of this chapter is on external workplace conflict resolution, that is, workplace conflicts that are not resolved internally but, instead, become the subject of litigation. The specific issues taken up in such litigation are many and varied, although most of them fall under the heading of "labor and employment." These include wages and hours, specifically alleged failure to pay minimum wage, misclassification, off-the-clock work, missed meal and rest breaks, and excess waiting time to receive end-of-employment pay; independent contracting versus employee status, which is also a particular form of misclassification; and employment discrimination on the basis of age, gender, race, national origin, disability, or religion. Other issues involving workplace conflict do not fall (or fall neatly) under the labor and employment rubric. Conflicts over wrongful termination, for example, are pursued through claims of violation of public policy, sometimes in conjunction with claims of discrimination; conflicts over hiring and labor market competition are pursued through antitrust law; and conflicts over executive compensation are pursued through laws pertaining to fraud, bankruptcy, merger and acquisition, and securities transactions.

All of these otherwise varied workplace conflict issues have been pursued externally through litigation. Because the litigation (i.e., judicial) system followed in the United States (and many other nations) is based on the principle of adversarialism, workplace conflicts that proceed all the way through litigation to trial verdicts yield clear winners and losers. Often, however, the parties reach negotiated settlements prior to trial or during trial prior to a verdict. Such settlements suggest the possibility that some workplace conflicts could have been settled internally or via ADR rather than externally through litigation.

This chapter explores this possibility by analyzing several main types of workplace conflict in which resolution has been pursued through litigation. It focuses on litigation involving managerial and employee misclassification, independent contractor versus employee status, no-poaching agreements and labor market competition, and the reasonableness of executive compensation.

## LABOR AND EMPLOYMENT LITIGATION: WAGES AND HOURS

In the United States, labor and employment litigation may be pursued under a wide variety of federal laws, including the National Labor Relations Act (NLRA), the Labor-Management Reporting and Disclosure Act (LMRDA), the Railway Labor Act (RLA), the Employee Retirement Income Security Act (ERISA), the Fair Labor Standards Act (FLSA), the Equal Pay Act (EPA), the Civil Rights Act (as amended), the Age Discrimination in Employment Act (ADEA), the Family and Medical Leave Act (FMLA), the Americans With Disabilities Act (ADA), and the Occupational Safety and Health Act (OSHA). It may also be pursued under similar state and local government laws, where, in fact, most of it originates. A portion of this state or local litigation may subsequently proceed to the federal level or be filed simultaneously under federal laws.

Especially in an era of "big data," one expects the volume of labor and employment-related litigation that occurs annually or during a particular time period to be well documented and systematically incorporated into extant databases. This is apparently not the case, however. Extensive Google, LexisNexis, Westlaw, U.S. Department of Labor (DOL), U.S. General Accounting Office (GAO), Federal Judicial Center, and Factiva searches yielded only piecemeal data in this regard, as did searches of academic and professional journal articles. Consequently, it is not possible precisely to determine the overall volume, issue composition, level of government, or other characteristics of contemporary labor and employment-related litigation.

The most systematic available data in this regard pertain to the FLSA and are shown in Fig. 1.[2] Between 1990 and 2015, the annual volume of FLSA cases filed in U.S. federal courts increased about 10-fold, from 888 in 1990 to 8,954 in 2015 (PACER, 2016).[3] This happened while employment in the United States increased by about 31 percent (USDOL, BLS, 2016).[4] Furthermore, these case filing data tell only part of the story because they do not include state-level filings under state FLSA-like statutes (McGillivary & Mechak, n.d.). All but a handful of U.S. states have their own wage and hour laws, and it is likely that thousands of cases alleging violations of those laws were also filed during the 1990—2015 period. While California is often considered to be the hotbed of FLSA-related litigation, Florida and New York have consistently been the "leaders" in this regard. Between 2005 and 2012, for example, these two states accounted for about half of all FLSA lawsuits filed in federal courts

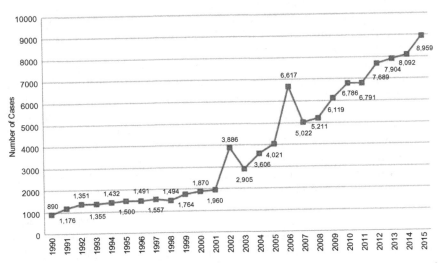

*Fig. 1.* FLSA Cases Filed by Calendar Year. *Notes*: Pacer Case Locator was used to compile these statistics by selecting the "Civil" tab and searching by nature of suit "710 Labor: Fair Standards," which returns all FLSA cases. Each search was limited to one year increments. *Source*: Pacer Case Locator-Civil-Nature of Suit (NOS) Labor: Fair Standards — FLSA per year.

(USGAO, 2014).[5] In these lawsuits, moreover, both current and former employees may be and typically are represented.[6]

The FLSA and similar state laws are particularly wide-ranging in terms of the aspects of employment relationships they regulate. These include minimum wages, overtime, meal and rest breaks, waiting time (among others), and child labor. The most frequently alleged violation of the FLSA involves overtime, with employee plaintiffs claiming that they were not paid at one and half times their regular pay rate when they worked beyond 40 hours in a week.[7] A detailed analysis of 2012 FLSA lawsuits conducted by the United States General Accounting Office (USGAO) estimated that 95 percent of these lawsuits contained alleged violations of the overtime pay provision (USGAO, 2014). This percentage far outpaced the proximately one-third of 2012 lawsuits that contained alleged violations of the FLSA's minimum wage provision. Notably, about 30 percent of the lawsuits alleged that employees were required to work "off-the-clock" and therefore were not paid at all for such work. In addition, about 20 percent of these lawsuits contained allegations of misclassification.[8] The main such allegation was that employees were mistakenly classified as exempt from the FLSA when they should have been classified as non-exempt from (i.e., covered by) the law. The other such allegation was that independent contractors were mistakenly excluded from FLSA coverage because they were in fact employees rather than contractors.

FLSA lawsuits have been concentrated in four industries, namely, accommodations and food services, manufacturing, construction, and other services, which include laundry services, domestic work, and nail salons (USGAO, 2014).[9] Employees who worked in accommodations and food services, which include hotels, restaurants, and bars, filed about 23 percent of FLSA lawsuits in 2012. Employees in manufacturing filed another 20 percent: most of these, however, were employees in automobile manufacturing who filed individually in the State of Alabama where they were originally part of two class action lawsuits in which the classes were later decertified.[10]

In this regard, it is especially notable that under the FLSA, "an action may be brought by any one or more employees for and on behalf of himself or themselves and other employees similarly situated."[11] During the last quarter century and especially during the 21st century to date, class action lawsuits as a percentage of all FLSA lawsuits have risen markedly.[12] By 2012, fully 40 percent of FLSA lawsuits were class actions or, in the parlance of the USGAO, "collective actions."[13] An additional 16 percent of such lawsuits were individual actions "originating from a decertified collective action."[14] It is interesting that employee use of collective action through unionization and collective bargaining declined substantially during this very same period.[15] This means that relatively fewer workplace disputes were settled internally through the negotiation of collective agreements and the use of grievance procedures contained in those agreements, and that relatively more disputes were settled externally through litigation. In such litigation, moreover, individual employees are always represented by an agent (i.e., an attorney rather than a union official), and employees frequently form a collective — that is, a class — that is also represented by an agent. This is a leading example of how private sector representation in employment relations in the United States has shifted markedly from internally oriented unionization and collective bargaining to externally oriented litigation.

But a decline in unionization and collective bargaining does not necessarily mean that workplace disputes cannot be resolved internally or through ADR. To the contrary, internal non-union employment dispute procedures have become quite common, even pervasive; these procedures increasingly include arbitration as a specific ADR method; and there is evidence that these procedures are actually used, that is, are not simply available (Colvin, 2013; Colvin, Klaas, & Mahoney, 2006; Lewin, 2008, 2014). If this is so, then why aren't these internal procedures or ADR methods used to take up and resolve issues of off-the-clock work, failure to pay for overtime hours worked, misclassification, and the like? Why is it that disputes involving these matters are pursued and resolved through litigation? Analysis of two main types of misclassification over which lawsuits are filed may be helpful in developing answers to these interrelated questions. In doing so, I focus on litigation involving relatively large companies that typically have both a formal human resource (HR) staff function (or department) and an internal conflict resolution system. Such litigation encompasses far more employees (and former employees) than the relatively more numerous lawsuits filed against smaller companies that typically do not have either a formal HR staff function or an internal conflict resolution system.[16]

# MANAGER AND EMPLOYEE MISCLASSIFICATION

The first type of misclassification litigation features the claim that some employees are incorrectly classified as exempt from the FLSA and should be reclassified as non-exempt. On its face, the FLSA contains certain exemptions from coverage, including those for executive, administrative, professional, outside sales, and computer employees (USDOL, 2008). The law also exempts from coverage employees who earn above a specified annual income. Currently, this income level is $100,000 (USGAO, 2014).[17] Nonetheless, the stated exemptions from FLSA coverage become considerably less straightforward and considerably more contentious in practice (USGAO, 2013).

Let me illustrate. A common type of misclassification claim is one made on behalf of individuals holding managerial positions. These are typically first-line or front-line positions, such as store or location managers in large, chain type big box retailers, supermarkets, restaurants, and car rental agencies. In such businesses, most front-line managers have been promoted through the ranks, are paid an annual salary rather than (as previously) an hourly wage, and have bonus potential, meaning that they may qualify to receive an annual or periodic bonus based on their performance or the business's performance (Levine & Lewin, 2006).

The key question that arises in these types of managerial misclassification lawsuits is whether and to what extent front-line managers actually perform managerial work as distinct from or instead of non-managerial, that is, employee work. Extant research indicates that when businesses are relatively young, small, and in the early stages of their organizational life cycles, front-line managers do perform largely managerial work (Lewin, 2012). In retail store businesses with these characteristics, for example, store managers decide or participate in deciding hours of operations, product prices, product displays, and inventory. They also choose or play a role in choosing vendors and negotiating prices and other terms with vendors. They play a lead role in hiring, staffing, deploying, evaluating and, when necessary, disciplining employees.

When such businesses grow larger and especially when they become national (or even international) chain type enterprises, however, the decision-making role and exercise of managerial duties by front-line store managers decline substantially. This is due to such factors as the adoption by these enterprises of standard operating procedures, workplace replication, supply chain optimization, and nationally focused marketing and branding initiatives. These factors, in turn, lead these enterprises to adopt more centralized decision-making, often by creating new internal regional and district units headed by upper level managers as well as by expanding corporate staff units. As a result, the extent to which front-line store managers actually perform managerial work declines markedly (Levine & Lewin, 2006).

Furthermore, the non-managerial work performed by front-line store managers may also increase, perhaps considerably, because of the way in which they are compensated. As noted earlier, store managers are paid base salaries and are also bonus eligible. Bonuses paid to front-line store managers are based either on store profitability or the extent to which actual store operating costs are lower than budgeted. One of the main components of store operating costs is labor cost, which is commonly considered to be a controllable cost. Hence, bonuses for front-line store managers often are determined by the extent to which actual store labor costs are below budgeted labor costs. In any event, by substituting his or her own labor for some of the work that would otherwise be performed by hourly paid employees that these managers ostensibly supervise and manage, a store manager increases the likelihood of achieving the business's or store's particular profit or cost objective and thus of receiving a bonus. The fact that, unlike employees, store managers are not eligible for overtime pay provides additional incentive for such managers to substitute their labor for that of employees (Levine & Lewin, 2006).

In light of these developments, it is not surprising that store managers have increasingly filed lawsuits – class action lawsuits – claiming that they are or were managers in name only, that they should be reclassified as non-exempt from the FLSA (and state wage and hour laws), and that they should receive overtime pay for all the overtime hours they worked during certain prior years (known as the class period). Some of these lawsuits, especially the larger ones, have included front-line managers at different levels, for example, store manager, associate manager and assistant manager or department manager. Notably, many businesses that have faced such litigation subsequently classified or reclassified their assistant and associate managers – but not store managers – as non-exempt employees and thereby made them eligible for overtime pay.[18] Also notable is the fact that class action managerial misclassification lawsuits almost always include both currently employed managers and formerly employed managers.

While claims of managerial misclassification appear to be especially prevalent in retail type businesses, they have also been made in other settings. Local location managers of a California-based moving and relocation company, for example, sued that company, claiming that they mainly performed non-managerial duties and therefore should have been reclassified as non-exempt and made eligible for overtime pay. This lawsuit was unusual in that it proceeded all the way through a jury trial, which in 2001 resulted in a verdict for plaintiffs/location managers. The jury concluded that the local

location managers were managers in name only and that they largely performed employee type work.[19]

Other employees, that is, non-managerial employees, have also made
claims of misclassification. For example, the U.S.-based sales representatives of a large international pharmaceutical company sued that company,
claiming that they were non-exempt from the FLSA and therefore should
have been reclassified and deemed eligible for overtime pay. In 2009, a
Federal District Court judge ruled in favor of those plaintiffs/sales representatives on the ground that despite their title they did not actually con-
summate sales to hospitals, doctors, and other health care professionals.[20]
As a result of this decision, the pharmaceutical company reclassified their
sales representatives as non-exempt from the FLSA and began to record
the amount of time those sales representatives spent performing
their work.

In yet another example, claim adjusters of a large national insurance
company sued that company, alleging that they were misclassified as
exempt from the coverage of Illinois State law and the FLSA. In particular,
the adjusters alleged that they did not exercise sufficient independent judgment and discretion in performing their work to warrant exempt status
under the laws. A substantial amount of testimony about the content of
claim adjusters' jobs was presented during the trial in this matter. At the
conclusion of the trial in July 2010, the Circuit Court of Cook County,
Illinois, decided in favor of the defendant insurance company.[21] In May
2012, an Illinois Appellate Court upheld that decision.[22] In all of these class
action cases, the plaintiffs included both current and former employees.

Returning to the question posed earlier, why is it that misclassification
disputes involving a wide range of employees are pursued and eventually
resolved externally through litigation rather than internally through grievance, appeal, complaint, ADR or related procedures? Answering this
question requires consideration of several factors. First, in the case of
front-line managers who claim to be misclassified, a union does not represent them in collective bargaining even if the employees they supervise are
unionized and bargain collectively with the employer. In this circumstance,
the terms and conditions of front-line managers' employment are determined unilaterally by the employer and are not subject to challenge by
front-line managers exercising their voice through a collectively bargained
grievance procedure. The same is true of the aforementioned sales representatives and insurance claims adjusters, who were also not unionized or
represented in collective bargaining with their respective employers.
Furthermore, both current and former employees are represented in class

action misclassification litigation whereas only current employees are (or would be) represented in collective bargaining.[23]

In non-union businesses that have grievance or grievance-like systems and processes for their employees, the scope of employee coverage is typically broader than in unionized businesses; it often includes supervisors and front-line managers. In this circumstance, front-line managers apparently have a voice mechanism available to them for pursuing their claims — grievances — about misclassification. However, availability is different from use, and some empirical studies find that managers are statistically less likely to use available grievance procedures than non-managerial employees (Lewin & Boroff, 1996). In particular, managers are significantly more likely than non-managerial employees to fear retaliation for filing grievances and exercising voice under a non-union grievance procedure (Boroff & Lewin, 1997). Moreover, formerly employed managers are not eligible to use non-union grievance systems, but they can be and often are represented in misclassification and other types of wage and hour litigation.

Another characteristic of these non-union grievance procedures is that the scope of issue or topic coverage is determined by the employer rather than jointly between the employer and front-line managers or a representative of those managers. The topic of job classification is not included in such procedures, and front-line managers therefore cannot exercise voice about misclassification by using these procedures. Furthermore, even if an employer is aware of a reduction in managerial work and an increase in non-managerial work performed by front-line managers, it is likely to be in the economic interest of the employer not to reclassify such managers. In this regard, the employer weighs the economic gain from not having to incur overtime pay costs for salaried managers against the probability that such managers will file a misclassification lawsuit and the probability of the employer losing such a lawsuit.

These same factors apply to the resolution of non-managerial employee claims of misclassification. Salespersons, computer technicians, professional employees, and others (such as insurance claims adjusters) who believe that they are mistakenly classified as exempt from the FLSA and state wage and hour laws are no more likely than managerial employees to be able to exercise voice about this matter through internal grievance or grievance-like procedures. If they attempt to exercise such voice or do in fact exercise it, such as by talking with their immediate supervisors or managers or with employment relations or human resource management staff, it is unlikely to result in an employer decision to reclassify them. This helps us

understand why both managerial and non-managerial employees who
believe that they are misclassified have increasingly turned to external litigation in attempting to resolve this particular type of workplace conflict.[24]

Could such conflict be resolved through mediation, arbitration, or other
third-party methods? In theory, yes, it could, but this would require the
parties agreeing to the establishment of a process they would actually use
and to being bound by the results or outcomes the process created. For
employers, their aforementioned reluctance to include job classification
(and alleged misclassification) as a matter falling within the scope of internal conflict resolution systems contrasts with their strong support for and
use of arbitration as a final, binding alternative to litigation in the resolution of conflicts with consumers and in the resolution of conflicts with
employees over matters other than classification. It would therefore be a
relatively modest, incremental change for them to agree to include job classification as a matter subject to arbitration, either in a modified internal
conflict resolution system practice or as a stand-alone practice. For employees, including but not limited to those who might challenge their employers'
decisions about job classification, they too would have to agree a priori to
the use of binding arbitration as a conflict resolution procedure.
Furthermore, both employers and employees could agree to a job classification conflict resolution process in which mediation is the first and potentially final step of the process. Thus, workplace conflict resolution through
ADR processes of mediation and arbitration is conceptually plausible.

# INDEPENDENT CONTRACTOR VERSUS
# EMPLOYEE STATUS

The second main type of misclassification issue over which lawsuits are filed
concerns independent contractor versus employee status. By definition,
independent contractors are not employees and therefore are not covered
by the provisions of the FLSA, state wage and hour laws, and other federal
and state "labor" legislation. Accordingly, an independent contractor can
be viewed as just another vendor or service provider. If it can be shown,
however, that an independent contractor is basically an employee, then the
coverage and related provisions of the FLSA and state wage and hour laws
will apply. Hence, the key question in this regard is whether and to what
extent independent contractors are in fact independent.

To answer this question, consider the "economic realities" factors specified in the FLSA for application to this issue. These factors are (1) the extent to which the work is an integral part of the employer's business, (2) the extent to which the worker's management skill affects that work's opportunity for profit or loss, (3) the extent to which the worker's relative investment compares to the employer's investment, (4) the extent to which the work performed requires special skill and initiative, (5) the extent to which the relationship between the worker and the employer is permanent or indefinite, and (6) the nature and degree of the employer's control over the work performed.[25] As with the specified exemptions from FLSA coverage, however, application of these economic realities factors becomes considerably less straightforward and considerably more contentious in practice.

A leading example in this regard involves FedEx, specifically FedEx Ground Package System, Inc. (hereafter, "FedEx Ground"), a business that has been the defendant in numerous lawsuits filed during the 21st century. In those lawsuits, delivery drivers for FedEx Ground claim that they are FedEx employees rather than independent contractors. While certain state courts have decided some of these lawsuits individually, about three dozen of the lawsuits that were originally filed in 26 states were combined into multidistrict legislation (MDL) and assigned to the U.S. District Court for the Northern District of Indiana. In December 2010, that court applied the aforementioned economic realities factors as well individual state factors to the MDL and ruled that the delivery drivers were independent contractors to FedEx Ground in 23 states and employees of FedEx Ground in three other states.[26]

Numerous appeals were then filed in this matter, and in August 2014 the Ninth Circuit Court of Appeals issued decisions reversing the lower court rulings regarding California and Oregon. In those states, said the appeals court, FedEx Ground delivery drivers were employees rather than independent contractors.[27] In the court's judgment, the extent of control that FedEx maintained over its delivery drivers was such that it met the California and Oregon laws' "right of control" tests for determining that such drivers were in fact employees. The court gave substantial weight to the fact that, in the operating agreement between FedEx and the delivery drivers, FedEx retained the right to control the physical appearance of drivers, the physical appearance of vehicles, drivers' use of vehicles when not delivering FedEx packages, drivers' workloads, and the reconfiguration of drivers' territories. One year after this decision, FedEx settled the California lawsuit for $228 million. Similarly and also in 2014, the Seventh Circuit Court of Appeals issued a decision that concurred with the findings of the Kansas Supreme Court that "Given the undisputed facts presented to the district court in this case, the plaintiff drivers are employees of FedEx Ground Package System, Inc. as a matter of law under the Kansas Wage Payment Act ... and a plaintiff driver does not lose his or her employee status by acquiring another route for which that plaintiff is not the driver."[28]

Returning once more to the question posed earlier, could the independent contractor versus employee status cases involving FedEx Ground have been resolved internally through grievance-like procedures rather than externally through litigation? The answer may seem to be "no" because whereas in the type of misclassification disputes analyzed earlier all of the plaintiffs unquestionably were employees of the defendant employers, in the FedEx Ground cases the fundamental dispute was over whether delivery drivers were or were not employees. A "no" answer, however, may be premature or even wrong. Consider, for example, that FedEx Corporation is in essence a holding company composed of several businesses (often referred to as strategic business units or SBUs). FedEx Ground is one of these units but so, too, is FedEx Express. FedEx Ground is a "B to C" business that delivers packages and related items to residences, mainly homes and apartments. FedEx Express is a "B to B" business that delivers packages and related items to companies' and other organizations' offices and field locations. These two FedEx businesses provide virtually identical services and their delivery drivers perform virtually identical functions. Yet, in FedEx Ground these delivery drivers are (or have been) independent contractors whereas in FedEx Express these delivery drivers are employees.

How can this be? How can two such different arrangements for delivery drivers performing essentially identical work co-exist in the same company? They can do so because FedEx's Corporation's strategy and related organizational structure provide considerable decision-making autonomy to its SBUs. As long as the general managers of those businesses achieve the strategic objectives set for them by FedEx Corporation (sometimes referred to as P&L objectives), they are more or less free to manage their respective business as they choose. FedEx Ground's general managers chose to have its delivery drivers operate as independent contractors, while FedEx Express's general managers chose to have its delivery drivers operate as employees. Hence, from both a business perspective and an independent contractor versus employee status perspective, FedEx is not a single, undifferentiated company.

However, some FedEx Corporation policies and practices are uniform or companywide, meaning that they do not vary by business unit. One of these is the Guaranteed Fair Treatment Procedure (GFTP), which dates to the company's founding in 1973. The GFTP is a multi-step process that in some respects closely resembles a unionized grievance procedure. It is formal, contains provisions for putting complaints in writing, and specifies time limits for employee filing and management responses at each step of the process.[29] In other respects, the GFTP does not closely resemble a unionized grievance procedure: the scope of employees and the scope of issues covered by this procedure are broader than in a typical unionized grievance procedure.[30] All FedEx employees except executives and senior managers are eligible to use the GFTP, meaning that about 90 percent of the company's workforce across its various business units is eligible to file complaints under the GFTP. They may do so over a wide range of issues, including traditional issues such as pay, work schedules, and discipline, but also such nontraditional issues as performance appraisals, workflow, technological change, and delivery schedules.

These characteristics of the GFTP are consistent with FedEx's founders' beliefs that employees were its most important constituency, that FedEx should have a strong organization culture, and therefore that employees should have a mechanism through which they could express their voice to senior management.[31] This reasoning is consistent with concepts of organizational citizenship, mutual gains, integrative bargaining, and problem-solving type employer-employee relations. It is not at all consistent with the adversarial, fixed-sum, win-lose nature of the litigation involving FedEx Ground delivery drivers. As noted earlier, the FedEx litigation has been voluminous, long standing, and resulted in judicial decisions against FedEx Ground that require this business to reclassify its delivery drivers as employees in most states. Given the existence of the GFTP for FedEx employees, it is conceivable that FedEx Corporation could have adopted a similar procedure for independent contractors, such as delivery drivers at FedEx Ground.

Disputes over independent contractor versus employee status have also occurred in other industries, including insurance. To illustrate, Allstate Insurance Company has been the defendant in class action lawsuits filed by insurance agents who were converted from employees to independent contractors beginning in 1999. Those insurance agents claimed that the company violated the terms of their employment agreements and that the change from employment to independent contractor was motivated by the company's desire to increase profitability by reducing labor costs, especially fringe benefit costs. This long-standing litigation is multifaceted, features several relatively small class action lawsuits, and continues to be adjudicated.[32]

Farmers Insurance Company has also been a defendant in misclassification lawsuits, which have been filed by individual district managers as well as by individual insurance agents or classes of agents. In the district manager lawsuits, former district managers claim that they did not perform management functions or exercise independent judgment and discretion while ostensibly serving in management roles. Therefore, these plaintiffs contend that they should be reclassified as non-exempt from the FLSA and state laws and should be awarded retroactive overtime pay for all of the overtime hours they worked for the company. The courts have typically ruled against plaintiffs in this litigation, finding that the district managers did indeed perform such management functions as planning, organizing, staffing, directing, and controlling.[33]

Other disputes over the independent contractor versus employee status issue feature newer, younger companies than FedEx, Allstate, and Farmers, especially companies that have emerged as part of the "gig" economy. Two of these companies are Uber and Lyft, which are both in the "on demand" limousine and car service portion of the transportation industry. Uber has faced class action misclassification lawsuits in states that include California, Texas, New York, Arizona, Pennsylvania, and Florida. In the California litigation, a federal district court ruled in December 2015 that arbitration clauses contained in the drivers' agreements with Uber were unenforceable. Had they been enforceable, those agreements would have prevented drivers from participating in a class action and required them to bring individual claims against Uber if they had any such claims.[34] The court also ruled that the drivers could proceed with a class action seeking reimbursement by Uber of the costs that drivers incurred while operating their vehicles for Uber-related business. This includes transportation and cell phone costs and entitlement to the full amount of all tips that drivers receive from customers.[35]

In a class action misclassification lawsuit filed against Lyft by the company's California-based drivers, a federal court judge rejected Lyft's argument that the lawsuit should be dismissed. That decision, rendered in March 2015, also concluded that the question of whether Lyft's drivers were independent contractors, as the company claimed they were, or employees, as the drivers claimed they were, should be decided in a jury trial. Subsequently, in January 2016, Lyft paid $12.25 million to its drivers to settle this lawsuit and also agreed to limit the grounds on which it could terminate its relationships with drivers.[36]

In another closely related example, Amazon has been sued by drivers in California and Arizona who deliver its products to the company's "on-demand" customers within one or two hours of being ordered to do so through Amazon's Prime Now app. In the Arizona litigation, the drivers claim that both Amazon and Courier Logistics Services, LLC, a company that provides delivery services for Amazon, have misclassified them as independent contractors. The drivers allege that they (a) are entitled to unpaid minimum wage and overtime compensation, (b) are prohibited from accepting tips even though the Prime Now app suggests a $5.00 tip per trip for drivers, (c) are scheduled to work fixed shifts, (d) cannot reject work assignments or request particular geographical area assignments, (e) are required to wear clothing bearing the Amazon Prime Now logo, (f) receive substantial training in making Amazon Prime Now deliveries, (g) must check in with a dispatcher prior to the start of a shift, (h) are tracked while making deliveries, (i) receive fees that are unilaterally determined by the defendants, and (j) are required to use their own vehicles without reimbursement by the defendants. In short, these drivers claim that they are not "independent" and that they are highly controlled by Amazon and Courier Logistics Services.[37]

These particular examples of current litigation over the independent contractor versus employee status issue illustrate how the modern economy and advanced technology have in essence converted what once would have been employment relations or workplace conflict into a form of vendor or service provider conflict. Indeed, this is a main difference between this type of conflict and the employee misclassification conflict analyzed previously. In conflict over independent contractor versus employee status, there is no employment relationship and therefore no employer — such as FedEx, Uber, Lyft, and Amazon — at least not according to defendants. The plaintiff service providers, whether drivers or others, are seeking to establish employment relationships through conversion of the independent contractor relationship. In theory, a company such as Uber or Amazon could seek to have this particular type of dispute resolved internally, either on an ad hoc basis or by establishing a standing process or method for doing so. The company might respond to a claim by its drivers that they are not really independent in the work they perform or the service they provide by analyzing that work or service using certain established criteria and then reaching a conclusion in this regard. This is basically a process of job analysis, which has a long history and is well documented (Brannick, Levine, & Morgeson, 2007). If this type of analysis led to the conclusion that the drivers were not independent, then the company could decide to reclassify those drivers so that they become employees.

Another approach to this type of conflict could be for a company to establish a third-party dispute resolution ADR procedure, providing for mediation, arbitration, or both. Analytically, this would be comparable to performing a contractor job analysis, but a third-party mediator would assist in doing so and a third-party arbitrator would decide whether or not the results of the job analysis warranted a decision to convert independent contractors to employees. This approach would also be consistent with the widely adopted use of arbitration (but not mediation) by non-union companies for workplace disputes involving their employees.

Set against these analytical approaches, however, is the cost saving that accrues to a company when independent contractors rather than employees perform some of its work. The main saving in this regard stems from not having to pay for overtime work or provide fringe benefits or incur payroll taxes for them. Especially if such savings are substantial, an employer not only has a strong incentive to continue to have certain types of work performed by independent contractors rather than employees, but also to convert additional work from that performed by employees to that performed by contractors. This incentive appears to be strongly prevalent among businesses in portions of both the gig and the more traditional economy.

## LABOR MARKET COMPETITION AND "NO POACHING"

Another type of workplace conflict for which resolution is pursued through litigation rather than internally involves alleged restrictions on labor market competition or, in popular parlance, "no poaching." Unlike litigation on other workplace conflict matters that is initiated under one or another labor law, this litigation is initiated under antitrust law, that is, the Sherman Act. The leading example in this regard is a case known as the High Tech Employee Antitrust Litigation (HTEAL), which was originally filed in September 2011 with the Federal District Court of Northern California.[38] In that lawsuit, current and former employees of seven Silicon Valley-based high-tech companies claimed that their pay had been suppressed over several years due to no-poaching agreements reached by the Chief Executive Officers (CEOs) of those companies. The plaintiffs claimed that in effect these companies engaged in cartel arrangements that had the effect of restraining trade (competition) in the labor market and therefore violated the Sherman Act.[39] This lawsuit was filed shortly after the completion of a U.S. Department of Justice investigation of the same allegation against the same companies. That year and an half-long investigation concluded without charges being filed against the companies, but also with the companies signing a cease-and-desist order.[40]

Initially, more than 100,000 employees of the seven companies constituted the proposed class in the HTEAL. During the first two years of this litigation, plaintiffs and defendants filed numerous motions with the court in attempting to receive rulings favorable to their respective positions. The court's responses to these motions tended to concur with plaintiffs' positions in some instances and with defendants' positions in others in what was basically a form of three-party negotiations. Substantial intra-organizational negotiations also occurred among both the plaintiffs and the defendants. As a result, in late 2012 plaintiffs employed by three of the companies, namely, Pixar, Lucasfilm, and Intuit, reached settlements that were later approved by the court. This left Adobe, Apple, Google, and Intel as the four remaining defendants. In October 2013, the court issued a decision certifying a class of 64,625 technical, creative, and research and development employees of these companies as the plaintiffs in the continuing litigation.[41]

The no-poaching agreements that plaintiffs claimed existed in this matter were not contained or expressed in formal written documents or contracts but, rather, in email messages and other communications exchanged among CEOs of the four companies. Plaintiffs contended that during 2005–2009 (a) these agreements cut off the flow of information about job vacancies that existed in the companies other than the ones at which individual class members were employed, (b) members of the class would have applied for those jobs at the other companies had they known about them, and (c) members of the class would have been hired into those jobs at higher rates of compensation than they were receiving at the time from their individual employers.[42] The ultimate result of these agreements, claimed the plaintiffs, was to restrict labor market competition and thereby suppress their pay during the entire period for which these agreements were in effect, that is, 2005–2009. In sum, said the plaintiffs, the total amount of this pay suppression was $3.1 billion. Had the plaintiffs prevailed at trial in this matter — that is, won their case — the treble damages provision of the Sherman Act would have been applied, thereby resulting in an award of $9.3 billion.

Analytically, these 64,625 employees constituted a collective that was represented by counsel that, in turn, retained several experts to support its position in this matter. Although separate counsel represented each of the four defendant companies and each company retained one or more experts to support its particular position, the four companies also constituted a collective in this matter.[43] The two collectives engaged in episodic negotiations that appeared to be largely adversarial in nature during 2012–2013, but that became relatively more cooperative later on. The case was scheduled for trial in May 2014 in San Francisco. About 10 days prior to the trial start date, however, the parties submitted a proposed settlement of $324 million to the court. The court subsequently rejected it. Shortly thereafter, defendants requested that the U.S. Court of Appeals for the Ninth Circuit overturn the lower court's rejection of the settlement.[44] Meanwhile, the parties to the dispute continued to negotiate with each other, and in December 2014 submitted a new proposed settlement of $415 million to the court. That settlement was subsequently approved by the court and thereby brought this landmark case to its end.[45]

Returning to the focal question posed earlier, could these employees' claims of pay suppression have been settled internally? After all, the defendant companies are widely known and admired (including for the quality of their human capital), are considered to have leading-edge human resource management policies and practices, and are often ranked among the best places to work.[46] With such characteristics, one might expect that an employee or group of employees in any one of these companies who believed that their pay was being suppressed due to no-poaching agreements would bring this matter to their own management's attention and would exercise voice in their employment relationships.

There is no evidence, however, that this occurred in the companies that were party to the HTEAL litigation. Instead, plaintiffs appear to have voiced their concerns to each other on a within-company and across-company basis, largely through internet-based social networks. Furthermore, the complaint in this matter included the actual names of only five of the plaintiffs, which implies that at least initially the allegations about the effects of no-poaching arrangements on plaintiffs' compensation were concentrated among a few employees. It was these named plaintiffs who sought and eventually retained legal counsel to pursue their claim.[47]

Moreover, the allegation in this matter did not involve explicit company policies or sets of codified practices that might otherwise be the subject of grievances. Instead, it involved actions allegedly taken and agreements reached informally by those at the very top of the defendant companies, which could not be grieved or complained about through internal workplace dispute resolution systems or processes. In this regard, it appears that in the defendant companies the heads and senior staffs of functional units that are typically involved in internal workplace conflict resolution, namely, human resources and legal, were unaware of the alleged no-poaching agreements that their CEOs had initiated or agreed upon with their counterparts.[48] Hence, these agreements were outside the formal scope of the issues over which employees of the defendant companies could exercise internal voice.

Similarly, it is highly unlikely that employees' claims of pay suppression in this matter could have been resolved through mediation, arbitration, or other ADR methods. To do so would have required the parties (or their representatives) either to establish a process that included one or more ADR methods or to adopt one or more such methods on an ad hoc basis. But the very nature of this dispute, which at its core involved the behavior of CEOs, mitigates the potential use of ADR methods to resolve the dispute. Ironically, the litigation of this dispute ultimately featured what may plausibly be characterized as a combination of mediation and arbitration (med-arb) undertaken by the judge in the case, who rejected the parties' first proposed settlement of $324 million but accepted the parties' second proposed settlement of $415 million. This is a particularly redolent example of workplace dispute resolution through litigation rather than through the use of ADR methods, per se.

Although the HTEAL has concluded, other cases involving the same type of no-poaching and wage suppression allegations have been filed against various companies, including Sony, Disney, and DreamWorks. Animators employed by these companies and by Pixar and Lucasfilm, two of the original defendants in the HTEAL, have brought their own class action lawsuit against these companies and have requested that they be provided class certification documents and expert reports from the HTEAL.[49] In a separate matter, a group of former account managers at Oracle Corporation sued the company, claiming that it had no-poaching agreements with Google and other companies that resulted in suppressing the account managers' pay.[50] In a related matter that is notable for being outside of the high-tech sector, an assistant professor of radiology at Duke University who sought a similar position at the University of North Carolina filed a class action lawsuit in June 2015 against both universities alleging that they had a no-hire agreement that suppressed competition and employee wages, thereby violating the Sherman Act (and state law).[51] In sum, it appears that there is a new wave of labor and employment litigation that involves challenges by current and former employees to the anticompetitive behavior of companies (and other employers) in the labor market, challenges that do not seem amenable to internal workplace dispute resolution.

# EXECUTIVE COMPENSATION

Most labor and employment litigation involves employees and former employees who work or worked in lower level, mid-level, or upper level jobs in companies. Some of this litigation, especially concerning wages and hours, features class actions. Litigation over executive compensation, however, involves those at the top levels in companies and rarely features class actions. Yet this, too, is an active and apparently growing area of contemporary labor and employment litigation.

In disputes over executive compensation, one or more parties typically contend that the compensation received by one or more executives is or was "unreasonable," that is, excessive. The objective of such litigation appears to be recouping or clawing back excessive executive compensation. Disputes over executive compensation may arise because shareholders of a public company believe that a severance package granted to an outgoing CEO was excessive or because creditors of a bankrupt company that is reorganizing believe that a new incentive plan designed to retain top officers is "too rich" or because a trustee of a defunct financial services company seeks to recover fraudulently obtained monies from top executives or because a non-officer co-owner of a family-owned business believes that the co-owner family member officers are overpaid.[52]

Let me illustrate. After Hewlett-Packard's board of directors fired CEO Carleton Fiorina in February 2005, a group of shareholders sued the company, the board, and Fiorina claiming that her severance package of approximately $42 million was excessive. According to these shareholders, the board violated its own policy (adopted in 2003) that a departing executive's severance payments would be limited to 2.99 times that executive's annual salary and bonus. Therefore, the severance package should have been $16.7 million instead of $42 million. The excess amount, said the shareholders, should be returned to the company.[53]

An example of a dispute involving compensation for the executives of a bankrupt enterprise is Molycorp, a mining company that produces rare earths used in electric cars and wind turbines. The company filed for Chapter 11 bankruptcy in June 2015 and subsequently filed a reorganization plan with the court.[54] That plan included a proposed key employee incentive plan (or KEIP) that was intended to retain top executives of the company and motivate them to perform well during reorganization. Essentially, the KEIP specified cash payments to be made to these executives as a replacement for their "under water" stock shares in the bankrupt company. The exact amount of the payments depended in part on the achievement of certain reorganization milestones. The contending parties are the creditors and debtors of the company, respectively, with the executives being among the debtors. The dispute is over the amount of the cash payments to be made under the KEIP, with the creditors filing periodic objections claiming that these payments are (or will be) excessive, and the debtors claiming that they are necessary and proper. The Bankruptcy Court is charged with deciding this matter. KEIPs are commonly included in bankrupt companies' reorganization plans, meaning that disputes between creditors and debtors over proposed incentive or replacement compensation for executives are quite common; this case constitutes but one example.

A leading example of a dispute over executive compensation in which a trustee of a defunct company seeks to recover fraudulently obtained monies is that involving Bernard L. Madoff Investment Securities, LLC (BLMIS). Mr. Madoff, the company's founder and owner, became famous — notorious — for running a major, far-reaching Ponzi scheme for which he was convicted and sentenced to a long prison term (Henriques, 2009). The particular executive compensation matter of concern to the trustee involves Mr. Madoff's two sons, Andrew and Mark, who served as Co-Directors of the Proprietary Trading Division of BLMIS during 2000–2008.[55] If it can be shown that their compensation was unreasonable, that is, excessive, the excess will be clawed back (recouped) by the trustee. The trustee retained an expert to determine whether and to what extent reasonable executive compensation was paid in this matter. (More will be said below about the criteria for determining such reasonableness).[56]

An example of a dispute over executive compensation that involves a non-officer co-owner of a family-owned business who believes that his officer co-owner family members' compensation is unreasonable — meaning that they are overpaid — is World Oil Company, a privately owned firm based in Los Angeles. The company is co-owned by three brothers, two of whom serve as the top officers of the company. The other brother is not an officer or employee of the company and is therefore not paid a salary or bonus or any other type of compensation. However, he and his two brothers share equally in the returns on their invested capital in the company or, in other words, they each receive one-third of the return annually. This has not stopped the non-officer brother from periodically filing lawsuits claiming that his two brothers are excessively compensated.[57] The court must then make a determination about the reasonableness of such compensation. This type of dispute is basically a family feud, and this particular example is hardly an isolated one in the realm of executive compensation litigation.

Despite their different characteristics and circumstances, these examples of litigation over executive compensation all involve claims that one or more executives' compensation was unreasonable. To resolve such claims requires a standard of or criteria for or an approach to determining reasonableness. Probably the most well-established and surely the most single-minded approach to determining the reasonableness of executive compensation is the independent investor test in which the relevant consideration, in question form, is "would an independent investor would be willing to compensate the employee as he was compensated?"[58] While some courts have adopted this test in adjudicating disputes over executive compensation, the more widely used approaches in this regard are known, respectively, as the 12-factor test and the 9-factor test.[59]

The 12-factor test is made up of the following: (1) the employee's qualifications, (2) the nature and scope of the employee's work, (3) the size and complexity of the business, (4) general economic conditions, (5) the employer's financial condition, (6) a comparison of salaries paid with sales and net income, (7) distributions to shareholders and retained earnings, (8) whether the employee and employer dealt at arm's length and, if not, whether an independent investor would have approved the compensation, (9) the employer's compensation policy for all employees, (10) the prevailing rate of compensation for comparable positions in comparable companies, (11) compensation paid in prior years, and (12) whether the employee guaranteed the employer's debt. The 9-factor test is narrower but similar and is made up of the following: (1) the employee's qualifications, (2) the nature, extent and scope of the employee's work, (3) the size and complexities of the business, (4) a comparison of salaries paid with gross income and net income, (5) the prevailing economic conditions, (6) a comparison of salaries with distributions to shareholders, (7) the prevailing rates of compensation for comparable positions in comparable companies, (8) the salary policy of the taxpayer as to all employees, and (9) in the case of small corporations with a limited number of officers, the amount of compensation paid to the particular employee in previous years. Whether these complex tests are actually helpful in adjudicating lawsuits over the reasonableness of executive compensation is unclear, but they nonetheless illustrate how the courts are searching for an operational definition of reasonableness.

Returning to the focal question posed earlier, could any of these (and similar types of) litigated disputes over executive compensation have been resolved internally through one or another conflict resolution system or process or through ADR? Perhaps yes in certain disputes, but probably no in most. In the aforementioned shareholder dispute with Hewlett-Packard over the "excessive" severance package granted to its former CEO and in other disputes like it, it is conceivable that a corporate governance system would be in place through which such a dispute would be heard, deliberated, and resolved without resort to litigation but with the potential use of mediation and/or arbitration. In order to do so, however, the dispute would have to be aired early on, that is, prior to finalization of the decision about the amount of severance pay to be awarded to a CEO or other executive — and perhaps even prior to the decision to fire such an executive. The corporate governance responsibility would most likely rest with the board of directors or one of its subcommittees, meaning that the board would be attempting to fulfill the dual and in this instance likely conflicting roles of judge (deciding to fire an executive and the amount of severance pay for that executive) and mediator (among corporate constituents). Yet, this is what corporate boards of directors have increasingly been called upon to do, as is reflected in the "say on pay" movement.[60] Hence, a combination of shareholder activism and more fulsome corporate governance with selective use of ADR methods may lead to more internally based resolution of certain types of conflicts over (the reasonableness of) executive compensation.

In other circumstances, however, such as the bankruptcy, fraud, and family feud examples provided earlier, the internal resolution of conflicts over executive compensation or the use of ADR methods are most unlikely to occur. A bankrupt firm by definition has gone almost all the way through its organizational life cycle and may not re-emerge under a reorganization plan. Opposition to a proposal to pay additional monies to executives of such a firm under a KEIP constitutes a conflict that cannot be resolved internally or through ADR methods. A firm that has experienced organizational death due to the fraudulent activities of one or more of its owners or top executives and in which a post-death attempt is made to recoup excess compensation paid to the firms' executives also constitutes a conflict that cannot be resolved internally or through ADR, but even more so than in a bankrupt (but still existing) firm. In the case of a firm in which there is deep-seated intra-family conflict over executive compensation, an internal organizational grievance-like procedure would also not be well suited to resolving the conflict. Indeed, in this particular circumstance the parties to the conflict typically do not want to deal directly with one another and do not want to participate in mediation or arbitration or other ADR methods, preferring instead to be represented by counsel in a third-party litigation process. In sum, these various types of conflict over executive compensation are ones for which resolution is much more likely to be pursued through litigation.

## IMPLICATIONS FOR WORKPLACE CONFLICT RESOLUTION THEORY AND PRACTICE

A long history of research into workplace conflict resolution emphasizes and strongly favors the use of internal grievance, grievance-like, and ADR procedures, but many such disputes are not settled internally. Instead, they are pursued and settled externally through litigation. Determining the extent to which such litigation occurs, however, turns out to be considerably more difficult than might be thought, partially due to the fact that some of it is pursued under antitrust, bankruptcy, securities, fraud, and other laws rather than under traditional labor laws.

The most systematic data about this litigation are those pertaining to the FLSA, for which it is possible to trace the volume of lawsuits filed and the issues they covered. These data show a 10-fold increase in such litigation — popularly known as wage and hour litigation — during 1990–2015, with the sharpest increases occurring during the last few years of this period. It appears that state-level wage and hour litigation simultaneously also increased substantially. Among the leading wage and hour issues litigated are those involving misclassification, which in some instances pertains to employees, including managerial employees, and in others to independent contractors.

Most of this litigation features class actions, that is, groups of employees or contractors who are more or less similarly situated and who band together and retain attorneys to file their complaints with the courts and to represent them during the ensuing legal proceedings. In these respects, such collective action and representation bear close resemblance to unionization and collective bargaining. The same is true for the process of decertification, which may be applied to a previously certified class for litigation and to a previously certified union for collective bargaining. These processes differ, however, with respect to the scope of employees covered by and represented in them. In wage and hour litigation, supervisory and managerial employees often constitute classes of plaintiffs. Under (private sector) unionization, only non-supervisory, non-managerial employees are legally eligible to become members of a bargaining unit whose representative(s) may then bargain collectively with management. Furthermore, in class action litigation involving workplace disputes, both former employees and current employees are represented, whereas in collective bargaining it is only current employees (and sometimes retirees) who are represented.

Another putative difference between these two processes concerns the nature of the negotiations. Litigation over wages and hours (and other matters) occurs within the adversarial system of jurisprudence in which one party presumably wins and the other party presumably loses the case at hand. Collective bargaining can feature integrative negotiations and result in mutual wins for both parties. But this difference is surely overdrawn. Most wage and hour litigation does not culminate with trial verdicts but, instead, is settled prior to or during trial. Such settlements result from negotiations between the representatives of the plaintiffs and defendants and reflect their respective assessments of the risks of winning and losing their cases. Analytically, such negotiations are not consistent with the strict win-lose, distributive, adversarial characterization of wage and hour litigation. But collective bargaining does not necessarily feature integrative or even modestly integrative negotiations, either. This is reflected not only in company efforts to drive hard bargains with unionized employees over wages and working conditions, but also in accompanying efforts to outsource work, substitute technology and capital for labor, and sometimes seek decertification of the bargaining unit. Hence, negotiations under litigation and under collective bargaining may be relatively more similar than dissimilar.

Whether workplace conflicts over misclassification can be resolved internally without resort to litigation is another question, one to which the conceptually plausible answer is "yes." Employee misclassification litigation basically involves assertions by plaintiffs that they mainly perform work that is non-exempt from the FSLA (and/or comparable state laws) and they should therefore be reclassified. Companies need not accept these assertions on their face, but they could decide to study one or more of the jobs held by such employees to make a factual determination about job content and the propriety of continuing to classify these employees as exempt — and do so before the employees become plaintiffs. Companies could also make use of such ADR methods as mediation in which a third party assists in the process of job analysis and in inter-party communications about the results and implications of the analysis. Arbitration could also be used to assist in resolving these types of disputes, consistent with its increased use in resolving other types of workplace conflict.

In order to proceed this way, however, a company has to be willing to in effect negotiate with its employees even when they are not unionized and thereby relinquish some of its sole decision-making authority. This might be acceptable to employers when the individuals claiming that they should be reclassified as non-exempt are front-line managerial employees, which is often the case.

Whether a company will be willing to attempt to resolve internally a misclassification dispute that involves independent contractors is more questionable. Contractors are by definition not employees, and the cost difference between work performed by employees and work performed by contactors may be so large as to make it highly unlikely that a company will seek to resolve such a dispute internally or through ADR. Nonetheless, in this instance, a "yes" answer to the aforementioned question is also conceptually plausible.

A "no" answer to the question is more plausible when it comes to the resolution of workplace conflict over alleged pay suppression through no-poaching agreements and alleged unreasonable, that is, excessive, executive compensation. Such disputes have increasingly become the subject of litigation, although it is more difficult to determine their actual incidence and trends than for FLSA disputes. Indeed, no poaching and executive compensation are not traditional wage and hour topics or areas of regulation, at least not regulation by labor law. Additionally, both no-poaching and executive compensation disputes typically involve employees at the highest levels of their companies, that is, CEOs and Presidents or Managing Directors. In no-poaching disputes, top executives of companies are alleged to have suppressed the pay of non-top management employees, and in executive compensation disputes top executives of companies or units thereof are alleged to have unreasonably (and illegally) inflated their own compensation. Because of this top executive involvement, it is highly unlikely that either of these types of conflicts could be settled through an internal grievance, grievance-like, ADR, or governance system. Litigation may be the only potential settlement mechanism that is feasible.

# NOTES

1. There is also a substantial research stream on employee silence as a response to workplace conflict. See, as examples, Brinsfield (2014), Gruman and Saks (2014), and Boswell and Olson-Buchanan (2004).

2. The Fair Labor Standards Act became law in 1938. Its Wage and Hour Division (WHD) is charged with enforcing the law, including by filing lawsuits on behalf of employees. However, employees or, more precisely, the attorneys who

represent them file most such lawsuits. This may occur in any one of the 94 federal district courts, which are divided into 12 regional circuits.

3. Accessed at https://www.pacer.gov, February 22, 2016.

4. The data used here are total nonfarm employment, which was 109,160,000 in December 1990 and 143,137,000 in December 2015.

5. The volume of charges filed annually with the U.S. Equal Employment Opportunity Commission (EEOC) is far larger than the volume of FLSA lawsuits shown in Fig. 1. In 2015, for example, the Commission received 89,385 charges of employment discrimination. However, most of these charges do not proceed to litigation. Instead, they are typically settled via negotiated resolution or are dismissed or withdrawn. In the same year, 2015, the Commission reported that it resolved 92,461 previously received discrimination charges (EEOC, 2016).

6. A referee of this chapter commented that most employees initiating wage and hour litigation no longer work for the companies they are filing against. However, empirical analysis of FLSA case filing data for the 1990–2015 period indicates that more than three quarters of the plaintiffs in wage and hour litigation were current employees.

7. In California, that state's law mandates that overtime pay at the rate of time and one half be paid to a (covered) employee for hours worked beyond eight in a day as well as beyond 40 in a week.

8. Cumulatively, these percentages add to more than 100 percent because FLSA lawsuits typically contain allegations of violations of more than one of the law's provisions.

9. These industry titles are from the North American Industry Classification System (NACIS).

10. USGAO (2014, p. 8).

11. *Ibid.*

12. In determining whether or not to certify a class of employee plaintiffs, Federal District Court judges apply the Federal Rule of Civil Procedure, that is Rule 23(b)(3), specifically the decision criteria specified therein, which are predominance, superiority, numerosity, commonality, typicality, and adequacy. For an example, see *Bowerman v. Field Asset Servs.* (2015). This decision was rendered on March 24, 2015 in the United States District Court for the Northern District of California.

13. USGAO, *op. cit.*, p. 5.

14. *Ibid.*

15. The private sector unionization rate in the United States declined from 12.1 percent in 1990 to 6.7 percent in 2015. The percentage of nonfarm private sector workers covered by unions in collective bargaining declined from 13.4 percent in 1990 to 7.5 percent in 2015. See "Union Membership and Coverage Database from the CPS," *Index of Tables*. Extracted on February 15, 2016 from unionstats.com

16. A referee of this chapter commented that most firms facing FLSA litigation are small firms that do not have internal conflict resolution systems. While I agree that smaller firms typically do not have such systems, the vast majority of employees (both current and former) represented in class action lawsuits alleging misclassification are (or were) employed by large companies, including those cited and/or discussed in this chapter (e.g., Allstate Insurance, Novartis, FedEx, Wal-Mart, and

Home Depot). Smaller companies are relatively more likely to be subject to lawsuits alleging violations of the minimum wage provisions of the FLSA and related state laws.

17. Also under the FLSA, an employee earning less than $455 per week (or $23,660 annually) is considered to be a non-exempt employee entitled to overtime pay for overtime hours worked. In mid-2015, the USDOL announced a proposal to increase this earnings threshold to $921 per week (or $47,892 annually) and, as well, to adjust this amount annually based on change in the cost of living. If implemented, this proposal would very substantially increase the non-exempt portion of the U.S. workforce. However, this proposal has received substantial opposition from organized employer groups and their representatives, and the Congress must approve it in order for it to become law. This almost certainly will not occur during the Presidential election year of 2016, and its prospects thereafter are uncertain as well.

18. Examples include Smart & Final, Wal-Mart, Tuesday Morning, Inc. and Home Depot.

19. *Crandall v. U-Haul* (2001).

20. In Re Novartis Wage and Hour Litigation (2010).

21. *Nettles, Czarnecki, et al. v. Allstate Insurance Company, Order* (2010). This was a bench trial, that is, a trial before a judge without a jury.

22. *Nettles, Czarnecki, et al. v. Allstate Insurance Company* (2012).

23. Retirees may also be represented in collective bargaining, but not employees who quit or were reduced in force or separated for performance or other reasons.

24. A referee of this chapter usefully points out that there are legal incentives for the parties involved in workplace discrimination claims to attempt to settle those conflicts internally. This is because the controlling legal decision (in *Faraghner et al. v. City of Boca Raton*) states that if an employee fails to engage in "reasonable" internal workplace conflict resolution options, the employer may escape liability. The FLSA and court decisions reached under this law contain no comparable incentives.

25. See USDOL (2015).

26. In Re FedEx Ground Package System, Inc. Employment Practices Litigation (2010).

27. *Slayman v. FedEx Ground Package Sys., Inc.*, 765 F.3d 1033 (9th Cir. 2014) and *Alexander v. FedEx Ground Package Sys., Inc.* (2014).

28. *In Re FedEx Ground Package System, Inc. Employment Practices Litigation. Craig, et al. v. FedEx Ground Package System, Inc.*, U.S. Court of Appeals (7th Cir. July 8, 2015, p. 4). These court decisions clearly placed strong emphasis on the criterion of control in ruling on whether FedEx delivery drivers were independent contractors or employees. But the criterion of independence may be even more compelling in this regard. To illustrate, if an independent contractor to FedEx cannot contract with another company or decide which customers to deliver to or decide which packages and other items to deliver to customers, that contractor has very little if any independence. For more on this point, including additional criteria for determining independence, see Lewin (2012).

29. See Lewin (2015) for additional detail about this process. From its inception, FedEx sought to avoid employee unionization. Thus, the GFTP and another FedEx

initiative, the Survey Feedback Action process (SFA), can be viewed as alternatives to or substitutes for unionization. FedEx's pilots became unionized in 1992, which stemmed from the company's acquisition in 1989 of Flying Tigers, whose pilots were unionized and who led the post-acquisition pilot unionization of FedEx. No other FedEx employees have become unionized since then. On types and examples of employee representation other than through unionization, see Lewin (2013) and Gollan and Lewin (2013).

30. Another difference is that the final step of the GFTP is internal Appeals Board review rather than arbitration. However, both of these final steps result in binding decisions.

31. Lewin, Dralle, and Thomson (1992). FedEx Corporation's motto is and always has been "People-Service-Profits."

32. See *Romero, et al. v. Allstate Insurance Company* (2014).

33. See, for example, *Pexa v. Farmers Insurance Company* (2012).

34. The use of arbitration to settle many types of commercial disputes has become ubiquitous. Contributing to this trend are a series of court decisions supporting deferral to arbitration in disputes involving customers of companies and employees of companies. See Lewin (2014).

35. *O'Connor v. Uber Technologies, Inc.*, No. 3:13-cv-03826-EMC (N.D. Cal. December 9, 2015).

36. *Cotter v. Lyft, Inc.*, No. 3:13-cv-04065-VC (N.D. Cal.).

37. *Curry v. Amazon.com, Inc.*, No. 2:16-cv-00007 (D. Ariz. January 5, 2016).

38. *In Re: High Tech Employee Antitrust Litigation, Consolidated Amended Complaint* (2011). The claim was not that all seven companies colluded in one overall no-poaching agreement but, rather, that dyads and triads of these companies had done so.

39. The Sherman Act of 1890 was enacted to combat cartels and their price-fixing in product markets – colloquially, to "bust the trusts." However, the first applications of the Sherman Act were to labor unions rather than to business enterprises, and for about two decades following passage of the Act courts repeatedly ruled that unions were cartels that violated its provisions. See Falcone (1962).

40. See *In Re: High Tech Employee Antitrust Litigation, Consolidated Amended Complaint*, pp. 19–20, and *United States of America v. Adobe Systems, Inc.; Apple Inc.; Google Inc.; Intel Corporation; Intuit, Inc.; and Pixar* (2011). This investigation was conducted between September 2009 and March 2011.

41. In Re High Tech Employee Antitrust Litigation, Order Granting Plaintiffs' Supplemental Motion for Class Certification (2013).

42. Analytically, it is extremely unlikely that, had they known about job vacancies at the defendant companies other than the ones at which they worked, all of the plaintiffs would have applied for those jobs and all would have been hired to fill the jobs at higher rates of pay than they were receiving at the time. But the plaintiffs' theory as well as plaintiffs' counsel's theory and plaintiffs' experts' theory was that the alleged pay suppression affected *every* member of the class.

43. These experts included faculty members from Stanford University, Cornell University, UCLA, and the London School of Economics. One of these experts argued that the no-poaching agreements constituted a labor market monopsony in Silicon Valley. Defendants' experts included faculty members from the University

of Chicago and UCLA. One of these experts argued that the Silicon Valley labor
market was highly competitive, based on analysis of company hiring and turnover
data in years prior to, during, and after the 2005–2009 class period.

44. *In re Adobe Systems, Inc., Apple, Inc., Google, Inc., and Intel Corp. v. United
States District Court for the Northern District of California. Petition for Writ of
Mandamus* (2014).

45. See U.S. Judge Approves, *Reuters*, 2015. The settlement was formally
approved in September 2015 and the process of distributing settlement amounts to
class members commenced during October 2015.

46. See, for example, Workforce.com (2015) and Fortune (2016).

47. None of the named plaintiffs were employed by any of the defendant companies when the class action lawsuit was filed in 2012. They had all worked previously
at one or another of these companies at various times during 2006–2011, typically
for about two years. See *In Re: High Tech Employee Antitrust Litigation,
Consolidated Amended Complaint*, pp. 3–4.

48. *Ibid.*

49. *Animation Workers Antitrust Litigation* (2015).

50. *Garrison v. Oracle Corporation* (2014).

51. *Seaman, et al. v. Duke University, et al.* (2015).

52. An example of each of these types of disputes is presented below. For a pri-
mer on how executive compensation should be determined, see Ellig (2014). The
extent to which executive compensation is or is not related to company financial
performance is highly debated in the research literature. See, for example, Tosi,
Werner, Katz, and Gomez-Mejia (2000).

53. Indiana Electrical Workers Pension Trust Fund, IBEW; SEIU Affiliates'
Officers and Employees Pension Plan; SEIU National Industry Pension Plan; and
Pension Plan for Employees of *SEIU v. Patricia Dunn, Carleton S. Fiorina, et al.
and Hewlett-Packard Company* (2008). More recently, in 2014, a group of Hewlett-
Packard shareholders won their lawsuit against the company and Leo Apotheker,
who served as the company's CEO for 11 months before being fired by the board of
directors in September 2011. However, that lawsuit pertained to Hewlett-Packard's
overpayment for acquiring Autonomy Corp., a British software company, during
Mr. Apotheker's tenure as CEO, rather than to his executive compensation or
severance pay. See Tan (2014).

54. Re Molycorp, Inc. (2015).

55. *Securities Investor Protection Corporation v. Bernard L. Madoff Investment
Securities LLC. Irving H.Picard, Trustee v. Peter Madoff, Estate of Marl D. Madoff,
Andrew Madoff, et al. SIPA Liquidation* (2012). Both sons are deceased, but the litiga-
tion against their estates and other named family member defendants remains in place.

56. For an example of a law firm whose top executives were charged with com-
mitting fraudulent executive compensation practices, see *Securities and Exchange
Commission (SEC) Against Steven H. Davis, Stephen Decarmine, Joel Sanders,
Francis Canellas and Thomas Mullikin, Complaint.* March 6, 2014. The defendants
were the top officers of the Dewey& LeBoeuf law firm, which declared Chapter 11
bankruptcy on May 29, 2012.

57. See, for example, *Richard Roth v. Steven Roth, Robert Roth, et al., First
Amended Complaint*, 2012.

58. *Eberl's Claim Serv., Inc. v. Commissioner* (2001, p. 6). The independent investor test is also included as one factor in the 12-factor test of the reasonableness of executive compensation discussed below.
59. See *Eberl's Claim Serv., Inc. v. Commissioner* (2001), and *B & D Foundations, Inc. v. Commissioner of I.R.S., T.C. Memo* (2001).
60. See U.S. Securities and Exchange Commission (2011).

# REFERENCES

Albrecht, S. L. (2010). Employee engagement: 10 key questions for research and practice. In S. L. Albrecht (Ed.), *Handbook of employee engagement: Perspectives, issues, research* and practice (pp. 3–19). Cheltenham: Elgar.
Alexander v. FedEx Ground Package Sys., Inc. (2014). 765 F.3d 981 (9th Cir. August).
Alper, S., Tjosvold, D., & Law, K. S. (2000). Conflict management, efficacy, and performance in organizational teams. *Personnel Psychology, 53*, 625–642.
B & D Foundations, Inc. v. Commissioner of I.R.S., T.C. Memo. 2001-262 (2001).
Bateman, T. S., & Organ, D. W. (1983). Job satisfaction and the good soldier: The relationship between affect and employee 'citizenship'. *Academy of Management Journal, 26*, 587–595.
Beth Ann Faragher, Nancy Ewanchew, et al. v. City of Boca Raton, et al. (1997). 111 F. 3rd 1530. United States Court of Appeals, Eleventh Circuit. (April 15, as Amended April 28.)
Boroff, K. E., & Lewin, D. (1997). Loyalty, voice, and intent to exit a union firm: A conceptual and empirical analysis. *Industrial and Labor Relations Review, 51*, 50–63.
Boswell, W. R., & Olson-Buchanan, J. B. (2004). Experiencing mistreatment at work: The role of grievance-filing, nature of mistreatment, and employee withdrawal. *Academy of Management Journal, 47*, 129–140.
Bowerman v. Field Asset Servs. (2015). U.S. Dist. LEXIS 37988.
Braithwaite, J. (2002). *Restorative justice and response regulation.* Oxford: Oxford University Press.
Brannick, M. T., Levine, E. L., & Morgeson, F. P. (2007). *Job and work analysis* (2nd ed.). Thousand Oaks, CA: Sage.
Brinsfield, C. T. (2014). Employee voice and silence in organizational behavior. In A. Wilkinson, J. Donaghey, T. Dundon, & R. B. Freeman (Eds.), *Handbook of Research on Employee Voice* (pp. 114–131). Cheltenham: Elgar.
Budd, J. W. (2013). *Labor relations: Striking a balance* (4th ed.). New York, NY: McGraw-Hill.
Chamberlain, N. W., & Kuhn, J. W. (1965). *Collective bargaining* (2nd ed.). New York, NY: McGraw-Hill.
Colvin, A. J. S. (2003). Institutional pressures, human resource strategies, and the rise of nonunion dispute resolution procedures. *Industrial and Labor Relations Review, 56*, 375–392.
Colvin, A. J. S. (2013). Participation versus procedures in non-union dispute resolution. *Industrial Relations, 52*, S1: 259–283.

Colvin, A. J. S., Klaas, B., & Mahoney, D. (2006). Research on alternative dispute resolution procedures. In D. Lewin (Ed.), *Contemporary issues in employment relations* (pp. 103–147). Champaign, IL: Labor and Employment Relations Association.

Cotton, J. L. (1993). *Employee involvement: Methods for improving performance and work attitudes*. Newbury Park, CA: Sage.

Crandall v. U-Haul. (2001). *Superior Court of California, County of Los Angeles, Decision and Order*, May.

Department of Labor, Wage and Hour Division (WHD). Retrieved from http://www.dol.gov. whd/overtime/fs17a_overview.htm. Accessed on February 15, 2016.

Eaton, A. E., & Keefe, J. H. (Eds.). (1999). *Employment dispute resolution and worker rights*. Champaign, IL: Industrial Relations Research Association.

Eberl's Claim Serv., Inc. v. Commissioner. *249 F.3d 994, 1 EXC 515* (2001, May 4).

Ellig, B. R. (2014). *Executive compensation* (3rd ed.). New York, NY: McGraw-Hill.

Falcone, N. S. (1962). *Labor law*. New York, NY: Wiley.

Fortune. (2016). World's most admired companies. *Fortune*. Retrieved from fortune.com/world's-most-admired-companies/. Accessed on March 5, 2016.

Garrison v. Oracle Corporation. (2014). Case No. 14-cv-004592. United States District Court, Northern District of California, San Jose Division (October 15).

Gene R. Romero, et al. v. Allstate Insurance Company, et al., Memorandum. (2014). In the United States District Court for the Eastern District of Pennsylvania. Civil Action No. 01-3894 Consolidated With No. 01-6764, No. 01-7042 (February 27).

Gollan, P. J., & Lewin, D. (2013). Employee representation in non-union firms: An overview. *Industrial Relations, 52*, S1: 173–193.

Gruman, J. A., & Saks, A. M. (2014). Being psychologically present when speaking up: Employee voice engagement. In A. Wilkinson, J. Donaghey, T. Dundon, & R. B. Freeman (Eds.), *Handbook of research on employee voice* (pp. 455–476). Cheltenham: Elgar.

Henriques, D. B. (2009). Madoff is sentenced to 150 years for Ponzi scheme. *The New York Times*, June 29.

Huselid, M. (1995). The impact of human resource management practices on turnover, productivity, and corporate financial performance. *Academy of Management Journal, 38*, 635–672.

In Re Adobe Systems, Inc., Apple Inc., Google Inc., and Intel Corp. v. United States District Court for the Northern District of California, Petition for Writ of Mandamus. (2014). United States Court of Appeals for the Ninth Circuit (September 4).

In Re Animation Workers Antitrust Litigation. Order Denying Defendants Joint Motion to Dismiss. (2015). United States District Court, Northern District of California, San Jose Division (August 20).

In Re FedEx Ground Package System, Inc. Employment Practices Litigation. MDL 1700, No. 3:05-MD-527, (2010, December 15).

In Re FedEx Ground Package System, Inc. Employment Practices Litigation. *Craig v. FedEx Ground Package System, Inc.* (2015). U.S. Court of Appeals, July 8, 2015.

In Re High Tech Employee Antitrust Litigation, Consolidated Amended Complaint. (2011). United States District Court, Northern District of California, San Jose Division (September 2).

In Re High Tech Employee Antitrust Litigation, Order Granting Plaintiffs' Supplemental Motion for Class Certification. (2013). United States District Court, Northern District of California, San Jose Division (October 24).

In Re Novartis Wage and Hour Litigation. (2010). United States Court of Appeals for the Second Circuit. August Term 2009, Decided July 6.

Indiana Electrical Workers Pension Trust Fund, IBEW; SEIU Affiliates' Officers and Employees Pension Plan; SEIU National Industry Pension Plan; and Pension Plan for Employees of SEIU, et al. v. Patricia C. Dunn, Lawrence T. Babbio, Richard A. Hackborn, George A. Keyworth, II, Robert A. Knowling, Jr., Thomas Perkins, Robert L. Ryan, Lucille Salhany, and Carleton S. Fiorina, and Hewlett-Packard Company. Order Granting Defendants' Motions to Dismiss Second Amended Complaint and Denying as Moot Defendant Directors' Motion to Strike. (2008). In the United States District Court, Northern District of California, San Jose Division (March 28).

Jehn, K., & Bendersky, C. (2003). Intragroup conflict in organizations: A contingency perspective on the conflict-outcome relationship. In R. M. Kramer & B. E. Staw (Eds.), *Research in organizational behavior* (Vol. 25, pp. 187–242). New York, NY: Elsevier.

Katz, H. C., & Keefe, J. H. (1992). Collective bargaining and industrial relations outcomes: The causes and consequences of diversity. In D. Lewin, O. S. Mitchell, & P. D. Sherer (Eds.), *Research frontiers in industrial relations and human resources* (pp. 43–75). Champaign, IL: Industrial Relations Research Association.

Kaufman, B. E., Lewin, D., & Fossum, J. (2000). Nonunion employee involvement and participation programs: The role of employee representation and the impact of the NLRA. In B. E. Kaufman & D. G. Taras (Eds.), *Nonunion employee representation: History, contemporary practice and policy* (pp. 259–286). New York, NY: Myron D. Sharpe.

Kuhn, J. W. (1961). *Bargaining in grievance settlement: The power of industrial work groups.* New York, NY: Columbia University Press.

Levine, D., & Lewin, D. (2006). The new 'managerial misclassification' challenge to old wage and hour law; or, what is managerial work? In D. Lewin (Ed.), *Contemporary issues in employment relations* (pp. 189–222). Champaign, IL: Labor and Employment Relations Association.

Lewin, D. (2008). Resolving conflict. In P. Blyton, N. Bacon, J. Fiorito, & E. Heery (Eds.), *The Sage handbook of industrial relations* (pp. 447–468). London: Sage.

Lewin, D. (2010). Mutual gains. In A. Wilkinson, P. J. Gollan, M. Marchington, & D. Lewin (Eds.), *The Oxford handbook of participation in organizations* (pp. 427–452). Oxford: Oxford University Press.

Lewin, D. (2012). Resolving Employment Disputes Through the Courts: Managerial Misclassification and Independent Contractor v. Employee Status Litigation. Presentation to the U.S. Department of Labor Centennial Symposium, Washington, DC (November).

Lewin, D. (2013). The idea and practice of contract in U.S. employment relations: Analysis and policy. *Perspectives on Work, 17,* 30–35.

Lewin, D. (2014). Individual voice: Grievance and other procedures. In A. Wilkinson, J. Donaghey, T. Dundon, & R. B. Freeman (Eds.), *Handbook of research on employee voice* (pp. 281–297).Cheltenham: Elgar.

Lewin, D. (2015). The intersection of NER and ADR: A conceptual analysis and federal express case. In P. J. Gollan, B. E. Kaufman, D. Taras, & A. Wilkinson (Eds.), *Voice and involvement at work: Experience with non-union representation* (pp. 341–365). New York, NY: Routledge.

Lewin, D., & Boroff, K. E. (1996). The role of loyalty in exit and voice: A conceptual and empirical analysis. In D. Lewin & B. E. Kaufman (Eds.), *Advances in industrial and labor relations* (Vol. 7, pp. 69–96). Greenwich, CT: JAI Press.

Lewin, D., Dralle, D., & Thomson, C. (1992). *Federal Express Inc. (A).* UCLA Anderson School of Management, 15pp.

Lewin, D., & Peterson, R. B. (1988). *The modern grievance procedure in the United States.* Westport, CT: Quorum.

Lewin, D., & Peterson, R. B. (1999). Behavioral outcomes of grievance activity. *Industrial Relations, 38,* 554–579.

Lipsky, D. B., Seeber, R. L., & Fincher, R. D. (2003). *Emerging systems for managing workplace conflict.* San Francisco, CA: Jossey-Bass.

MacDuffie, J. P. (1995). Human resource bundles and manufacturing performance: Organizational logic and flexible production systems in the world auto industry. *Industrial and Labor Relations Review, 48,* 197–221.

McGillivary, G. K., & Mechak, M. K. (n.d.). *Current trends in pursuit and defense of hybrid FLSA and state wage and hour litigation.* Washington, DC: Woodley & McGillivary.

Michael J. Pexa v. Farmers Group, Inc. *et al., Tentative Statement of Decision Post Trial, Phase I, Incorporating Prior Court Rulings on Defendants Motions for Judgment Under CCP Section 631.8(a) and B.* (2012). Superior Court of California, County of Sacramento (November 5).

Nettles, Czarnecki, et al. v. Allstate Insurance Company, Order. (2010). In the Circuit Court of Cook County Illinois, County Department, Chancery Division (July 6).

Nettles, Czarnecki, et al. v. Allstate Insurance Company. (2012). Reporter of Decision – Illinois Appellate Court (May 29).

Pfeffer, J. (1998). *The human equation: Building profits by putting people first.* Boston, MA: Harvard Business School Press.

Public Access to Court Electronic Records (PACER). (2016). Retrieved from https://www.pacer.gov

Re Molycorp, Inc. (2015). Case No. 15-11357. U.S. Bankruptcy Court, District of Delaware (Wilmington) (June 25).

Richard Roth v. Steven Roth, Robert Roth, et al., First Amended Complaint. (2012). Superior Court of the State of California, County of Los Angeles, Central Division (January 11).

Sanborn, P., & Oehler, K. (2013). *2013 trends in global employee engagement.* Chicago, IL: AonHewitt and Aon plc.

Seaman, et al. v. Duke University, et al. (2015). Case No. 1:15-cv-00462. United States District Court, Middle District of North Carolina, Durham Division (June 9).

Securities Investor Protection Corporation v. Bernard L. Madoff Investment Securities, LLC, Irving H. Picard, Trustee v. Peter Madoff, Estate of Mark D. Madoff, Andrew Madoff, et al. SIPA Liquidation. (2012). United States Bankruptcy Court, Southern District of New York (May 4).

Slayman v. FedEx Ground Package Sys., Inc. (2014). 765 F.3d 1033 (9th Cir. August).

Tan, A. (2014). HP reaches $57 million settlement in shareholder lawsuit. *Bloomberg Business,* April 1. Retrieved from www.bloomberg.com/news/articles/2014-04-01/hp-reaches-57-million-settlement-in-shareholder-lawsuit. Accessed on March 6, 2016.

Tosi, H. L., Werner, S., Katz, J. P., & Gomez-Mejia, L. R. (2000). How much does performance matter? A meta-analysis of CEO pay studies. *Journal of Management, 26,* 301–339.

United States Department of Labor (USDOL), Bureau of Labor Statistics (BLS). (2016). Employment, Hours and Earnings from the Current Employment Statistics Survey (National). *Databases, Tables and Calculators by Subject.* Retrieved from http://www.bls.gov. Accessed on February 15, 2016.

United States Department of Labor (USDOL), Wage and Hour Division (WHD). (2008). Fact
Sheet #17A: Exemption for Executives, Administrative, Professional, Computer &
Outside Sales Employees Under the Fair Labor Standards Act (FLSA), U.S.

United States Department of Labor (USDOL), Wage and Hour Division (WHD) (2015).
*Administrator's interpretation No. 2015-1* (p. 12). Washington, DC: U.S. Department of
Labor, Employment Standards Administration, Wage and Hour Division (WHD).

United States Equal Opportunity Commission (EEOC). (2016). *All Statutes Statistics, FY
1997 – FY 2015.* Retrieved from http:www1.eeoc.gov//eeoc/statistics/enforcement/all.
cfm?/renderforprint. Accessed on February 17, 2016.

United States Government Accountability Office (USGAO). (2013). *Fair Labor Standards Act:
Department of Labor needs a more systematic approach to developing its guidance.*
Report to the Chairman, Subcommittee on Workforce Protections, Committee on
Education and the Workforce, House of Representatives.Washington, DC: USGAO
(January, 32pp.).

United States Government Accountability Office (USGAO). (2014). *Fair Labor Standards Act:
Department of Labor needs a more systematic approach to developing its guidance.*
Statement of Andrew Sherrill, Director, Education, Workforce, and Income Security.
Testimony Before the Subcommittee on Workforce Protections, Committee on
Education and the Workforce, U.S. House of Representatives (July 23, 14pp.).

United States of America v. Adobe Systems, Inc.; Apple, Inc.; Google, Inc.; Intel Corporation;
Intuit Corporation; and Pixar. *Final Judgment.* (2011). United States District Court for
the District of Columbia (March 17).

United States Securities and Exchange Commission (SEC). (2011). *U.S. Adopts rules for say-
on-pay and golden parachute compensation as required under Dodd-Frank Act.* January
25. Retrieved from https://www.sec.gov/news/press/2011/2011-25.htm. Accessed on
February 29, 2016.

U.S. Judge approves $415 mln settlement in tech worker lawsuit. (2015). *Reuters*, September 3.
Retrieved from http://www.reuters.com/article/2015/09/03/apple-google%20ruling-
idUSL1N11908520150903.

Walton, R. E., & McKersie, R. B. (1965). *A behavioral theory of labor negotiations.* New York,
NY: McGraw-Hill.

Workforce.com. (2015). 2015 Workforce 100: Ranking the world's top companies for HR.
*Workforce*, May 22. Retrieved from www.workforce.com/articles/21293-2015-Work
force-100-List. Accessed on March 3, 2016.

# REMEDY-SEEKING RESPONSES TO DISCRIMINATION: DOES MANAGEMENT-EMPLOYEE SIMILARITY MATTER?

Cynthia L. Gramm and John F. Schnell

## ABSTRACT

Purpose — *We investigate the effects of management-employee similarity on mistreated employees' propensities to engage in legal and organizational claiming, to quit, and to not seek a remedy in ongoing employment relationships.*

Methodology/approach — *We test hypotheses generated by the similarity-attraction and similarity-betrayal paradigms using Tobit regression and data from vignette-based employee surveys.*

Findings — *Mistreated employees with same-sex supervisors are more likely to initiate legal claims and to quit than those with opposite-sex supervisors, but less likely to initiate legal claims and to quit when they have a same-race supervisor than when they have a different-race supervisor. The effects of management-employee similarity on mistreated employees' remedy-seeking responses exhibit asymmetries by gender and*

Managing and Resolving Workplace Conflict
Advances in Industrial and Labor Relations, Volume 22, 69–103
Copyright © 2016 by Emerald Group Publishing Limited
All rights of reproduction in any form reserved
ISSN: 0742-6186/doi:10.1108/S0742-618620160000022004

*by race. The presence of same-race supervisors or other managers appears to diminish the greater reluctance of nonwhite employees, compared to white employees, to use organizational claiming mechanisms.*

*Originality/value — We know of no prior published research that has investigated the determinants of employees' propensities to engage in multiple forms of remedy seeking, as well as the propensity to not seek a remedy, in response to plausibly illegal mistreatment not involving dismissal.*

**Keywords:** Mistreated employees; management-employment similarity; attraction or betrayal; claiming; remedy-seeking; vignette-based studies

Employees who experience workplace mistreatment may seek remediation from their employer. This chapter's purpose is to advance our understanding of the determinants of employee remedy-seeking responses to workplace mistreatment that it would be reasonable to perceive as illegal and that occurs in an ongoing employment relationship. In such cases, employee remedy seeking may involve a legal claim. To avoid the high costs of employee legal claims, employers often encourage mistreated employees to rely on organizational mechanisms, ranging from informal complaints to a manager to the use of formal alternative dispute resolution (ADR) procedures. Quitting also remedies the situation by ending the employee's exposure to the mistreatment. Thus, mistreated employees in ongoing employment relationships have four remedy-seeking options available: (1) complaining to a manager, (2) filing a formal grievance, (3) legal claiming, and (4) quitting. Absent contractual constraints, they can pursue multiple remedy-seeking options, either simultaneously or consecutively or, alternatively, can opt to not seek a remedy. Henceforth, references to *mistreatment* will mean mistreatment that it is plausible to regard as illegal.

Prior empirical research on the determinants of employee remedy seeking for mistreatment focuses on legal claiming (i.e., Bies & Tyler, 1993; Goldman, 2001; Groth, Goldman, Gilliland, & Bies, 2002; Lind, Greenberg, Scott, & Welchans, 2000; Wanberg, Bunce, & Gavin, 1999). We are aware of only one study investigating the determinants of both legal and organizational remedy seeking by mistreated employees, as well as their propensity to not seek a remedy (Gramm, Schnell, & Weatherly, 2006). Most studies investigate remedy-seeking responses to *dismissal* (Goldman, 2001; Gramm et al., 2006; Lind, Allen, Greenberg, Scott, & Welchans, 2000; Wanberg et al., 1999). To our knowledge, no prior published research has investigated the determinants of employees' propensities to engage in multiple forms of remedy seeking and the propensity to *not* seek a remedy, in response to plausibly illegal mistreatment that does not involve dismissal. This chapter addresses that gap in the literature.

Our theoretical focus is on developing and testing hypotheses regarding the effects of management's similarity to the mistreated employee on dependent variables measuring the employee's propensities to engage in each of the aforementioned remedy-seeking actions. We measure management-employee similarity on three dimensions — gender, race, and "deep-level" (i.e., beliefs, interests, and values) similarity — at two levels for each dimension: (1) the supervisor's similarity to the employee and (2) the management team's similarity to the employee. Following Gramm et al. (2006), we use two alternative paradigms — the similarity-attraction paradigm and the similarity-betrayal paradigm — to generate hypotheses. We predict that the hypothesized effects of management-employee similarity on some remedy-seeking options differ, however, depending on whether the employment relationship is ongoing (the context of our study) or has been severed (the context of the Gramm et al., 2006 study).

Our hypotheses apply broadly to employees who have experienced plausibly illegal workplace mistreatment in an ongoing employment relationship. We test them with data on employees' intended responses to two hypothetical vignettes involving different forms of sex discrimination. This allows us to explore whether employees' remedy-seeking responses differ with the type of mistreatment.

## CONCEPTUAL FRAMEWORK

The following discussion closely follows that of Gramm et al. (2006, p. 270). Relational demographic research has drawn on theories of similarity-attraction (Byrne, 1971), social categorization (Turner, 1985), and social identity (Tajfel & Turner, 1986). Applied to relationships between employees and managers, these theories generate predictions that employee-management similarity will have a positive effect on (1) an employee's trust in management, (2) an employee's expectation of favorable treatment from management, (3) the extent to which an employee is comfortable communicating with managers, (4) an employee's desire to please managers, and (5) employee behaviors that benefit the employing organization; and will have a negative effect on (6) employee behaviors that harm the employing organization (e.g., Gramm et al., 2006; Gramm & Schnell, 1997; Tsui & O'Reilly, 1989). The effects of management-employee similarity on employee attitudes and behavior can extend to non-interactive relationships (e.g., higher level managers) as well as interactive relationships (e.g., supervisors) (Tsui, Egan, & O'Reilly, 1992). Following Gramm et al. (2006), we refer to this set of predictions as the similarity-attraction (S-A) paradigm.

Drawing on research on trust and betrayal by Bies and Tripp (1996), Currall and Judge (1995), and Koehler and Gershoff (2003), Gramm et al. (2006) propose an alternate set of predictions, labeled the similarity-betrayal (S-B) paradigm, which may apply if experiencing workplace mistreatment alters the way that management-employee similarity influences employees. The S-B paradigm predicts that when an individual experiences mistreatment due to the action or inaction of a party who was entrusted to prevent such mistreatment, the mistreated individual will feel betrayed. Betrayals diminish trust in the responsible party and may motivate attempts to seek revenge. Because managers collectively share responsibility for providing a work environment in which treatment of employees is fair and legal, employees are likely to hold management responsible for failing to protect them from workplace mistreatment and to feel betrayed by management when they experience such mistreatment. Therefore, Gramm et al. (2006) predicted that although management-employee similarity initially enhances employees' trust in management, subsequent to the experience of workplace mistreatment, such similarity will elicit greater feelings of betrayal from a mistreated employee than would occur under management-employee dissimilarity. The greater sense of betrayal that mistreated employees feel when management is similar, in turn, will negatively influence (1) mistreated employees' trust in management, (2) their expectations of favorable treatment from management, (3) the extent to which they feel comfortable communicating with management, (4) their desire to please management, and (5) their propensity to engage in behaviors that benefit the employing organization; and (6) will positively influence the mistreated employees' propensity to engage in behaviors that harm the employing organization.

In essence, the S-B paradigm asserts that experiencing workplace mistreatment negates and reverses the attraction employees would otherwise have to managers who are similar. Thus, under the S-B paradigm the predicted effects that management-employee similarity has on employees' attitudes and behavior following mistreatment are the opposite of the effects predicted by the S-A paradigm. We next use these two paradigms to develop hypotheses linking management-employee similarity to employee's propensities to engage in each of the four aforementioned remedy-seeking options *in the context of an ongoing employment relationship.*

## Propensity to Engage in Legal Claiming

For employers, the high costs of employee legal claims are likely to outweigh their sole benefit — being alerted to, and thereby given the opportunity to prevent recurrence of, illegal actions by their agents — especially since organizational claiming can produce the same benefit at a lesser cost. If similarity breeds attraction, management-employee similarity diminishes the likelihood that a mistreated employee will seek to impose such costs on the employer via legal claiming. Conversely, under the S-B paradigm, such similarity will increase the employee's desire to harm the employer by taking legal action; this is consistent with Goldman's (2003) observation that legal claims by mistreated employees frequently are motivated by the employee's desire for revenge. Thus, the S-A and S-B paradigms generate two competing hypotheses: (1) Management-employee similarity will have a *negative* effect on a mistreated employee's propensity to initiate a legal claim against the employer ($H1^{S-A}$); and (2) Management-employee similarity will have a *positive* effect on a mistreated employee's propensity to initiate a legal claim against the employer ($H1^{S-B}$).

## Propensity to Engage in Organizational Claiming

Organizations encourage the use of organizational claiming to remedy employee mistreatment because it alerts management to the mistreatment, giving the organization a chance to "nip it in the bud" by preventing its recurrence, as well as minimizing other costly outcomes, such as quits (Olson-Buchanan & Boswell, 2008). Thus, when mistreated employees opt to seek a remedy through organizational claiming, the firm benefits because the likelihood of current and future legal claims, as well as quits, is decreased. Organizational claiming may take the form of informal complaints to a manager or filing a formal grievance. Although both forms of organizational claiming may benefit the firm by deterring legal claims and quits, these processes differ in their costs to the firm. These differences have implications for hypothesis generation. It is beyond the scope of this study to review the literature on organizational claiming and grievance initiation, most of which does not focus on remedy seeking for mistreatment that is plausibly illegal. See Olson-Buchanan and Boswell (2008) for a recent review and theoretical treatment.

*Complain to a Manager*
Informal complaints avoid public allegations of organizational wrong-doing; facilitate private, cooperative efforts to remedy perceived mistreatment (Colvin, Klaas, & Mahoney, 2006; Lewin, 1999); and require low managerial time investments and minimal financial costs. Even organizations with formal grievance procedures encourage employees to discuss their concerns informally with their supervisors as a *first resort* (Lewin, 1999). For these reasons, *when the employment relationship is ongoing*, we assume that mistreated employees will view informal complaints to a manager as the remedy-seeking action that is least harmful to the employer. Additionally, employees will be more likely to approach a manager with their complaint when they are comfortable communicating with managers and when they trust managers to respond fairly (Gramm et al., 2006). The foregoing discussion suggests two competing hypotheses under the S-A and S-B paradigms, respectively: management-employee similarity will have (1) a *positive* effect on a mistreated employee's propensity to complain to a manager (H2$^{\text{S-A}}$) and (2) a *negative* effect on a mistreated employee's propensity to complain to a manager (H2$^{\text{S-B}}$).

*File a Grievance*
Like informal complaints, managerial decision-makers typically will be involved in hearing claims pursued via a formal grievance or ADR procedure, at least during the initial steps of the procedure (Lewin, 1999). A recent literature review suggests that employees who file grievances may risk subsequent retaliation from management in the form of lower performance ratings, less desirable job assignments, and fewer rewards for performance (Colvin et al., 2006). Consequently, employee willingness to file formal grievances will be higher when an employee trusts management.

Although formal grievances may enable employers to avoid litigation costs, they do so at a higher cost to the organization than informal complaints to a manager. In contrast to informal complaints, a formal grievance makes the complaint visible to other workers and managers in the organization, which can adversely affect organizational morale and result in a more distributive process (Colvin et al., 2006; Lewin, 1999). Compared to informal complaints, formal grievances require greater managerial time investments and, if mediation or arbitration is involved, impose higher direct costs on the employer. It is not clear, therefore, whether the benefits to the employer of this form of remedy seeking outweigh the costs. Consequently, neither the S-A nor the S-B paradigm yields an unambiguous prediction regarding whether the net effect of management's similarity to an employee on the employee's propensity to file a grievance will be positive or negative. We therefore propose a two-tailed hypothesis: Management-employee similarity will have an effect on a mistreated employee's propensity to file a grievance (H3).

### *Propensity to Quit*

The S-A paradigm suggests that management-employee similarity will have a positive influence on the employee's attachment to management and, in turn, to the employing organization. In contrast, the S-B paradigm suggests that in the wake of mistreatment, management's similarity to an employee will have a negative effect on the employee's attachment to the employing organization. Moreover, when a mistreated employee quits, the employer loses its investment in recruiting, selecting, and training the employee and incurs the costs of recruiting, selecting, and training a replacement. In addition, quits do not alert the employer that potentially illegal mistreatment occurred and that steps may need to be taken to prevent similar mistreatment of other employees. If, as the S-A paradigm predicts, management-employee similarity discourages employee behaviors that are harmful to the firm, such similarity should discourage quits; the S-B paradigm predicts an opposing effect. We propose, therefore, two competing hypotheses: (1) Management's similarity to a mistreated employee will have a *negative* effect on the employee's propensity to quit ($H4^{S-A}$); and (2) Management's similarity to a mistreated employee will have a *positive* effect on the employee's propensity to quit ($H4^{S-B}$).

### *Propensity to Not Seek a Remedy*

When a mistreated employee chooses neither to quit nor to initiate any form of organizational or legal remedy seeking, the employer benefits by avoiding the costs of those actions. A mistreated employee's failure to seek a remedy also imposes costs on the employer, however. Such costs stem from unresolved negative feelings that can lead an employee to be less productive on the job and absent more frequently (e.g., Klaas, 1989; Olson-Buchanan, 1996). Because it is unclear whether the net effect of a mistreated employee's decision to not seek a remedy is harmful or beneficial to the employer, neither the S-A nor the S-B paradigm yields a clear prediction regarding whether the net effect of management-employee similarity on the employee's propensity to not seek a remedy will be positive or negative. We therefore propose a two-tailed hypothesis: Management's similarity to a mistreated employee will have an effect on the employee's propensity to not seek a remedy (H5).

*Context Implications*

Table 1 summarizes the hypothesized effects under each paradigm of management-employee similarity on the employee's propensities to engage in each remedy-seeking option in the context of an ongoing employment relationship and contrasts these hypotheses to those relevant to terminated employees. Note that the hypotheses differ by context for two of the dependent variables, *not seek remedy* and *complain to manager*. This is true because the net benefit to the firm associated with the option of complaining to management is higher when the mistreated employee remains in its employ and because an employee's decision to forego remedy seeking is more costly to the employer when there is an ongoing employment relationship than when the mistreated employee has been dismissed.

## METHODS

Our empirical analyses use a convenience sample of 241 employed U.S. citizens. Data were collected by surveying students in undergraduate and graduate business and engineering courses at an urban state university that caters to employed adult students. The survey was administered to all students in the classes. Students who did not wish to participate were instructed to return their surveys blank. The response rate exceeded 95 percent. Dropping respondents who were not employed and those who were not U.S. citizens from the sample and list-wise deletion of missing values

**Table 1.** Dependent Variable Descriptive Statistics and Hypothesized Effects of Management-Employee Similarity by Paradigm and Context.

| Dependent Variable: | Descriptive Statistics by Vignette | | | | t-Statistic for Difference of Means by Vignette | Hypothesized Effect of Management-Employee Similarity Derived from: | | | |
|---|---|---|---|---|---|---|---|---|---|
| | Sex-based pay discrimination vignette | | Sexual harassment vignette | | | S-A Paradigm | | S-B Paradigm | |
| | Mean | S.D. | Mean | S.D. | | Context: Ongoing relationship | Context: Employee was dismissed | Context: Ongoing relationship | Context: Employee was dismissed |
| *Propensity to:* | | | | | | | | | |
| Not seek remedy | 26.00 | (34.01) | 12.79 | (26.94) | 5.32 | +/- | + | +/- | - |
| Complain to manager | 58.67 | (37.20) | 67.70 | (36.11) | 3.32 | + | +/- | - | +/- |
| File grievance | 35.94 | (37.36) | 56.31 | (39.66) | 6.59 | +/- | +/- | +/- | + |
| File regulatory complaint | 16.79 | (27.13) | 27.73 | (33.60) | 5.28 | - | - | + | + |
| Consult a lawyer | 12.76 | (23.70) | 25.97 | (33.24) | 6.42 | - | Not applicable | + | Not applicable |
| Quit | 15.73 | (26.32) | 11.74 | (22.01) | 1.81 | | | | |

*Note:* The sample size for *file grievance* is 172; for all other variables, the sample size is 241. Hypothesized effects for the context in which the employee was dismissed are taken from Gramm et al. (2006).

resulted in the sample of 241 employed U.S. citizens used in our analyses. The majority (53 percent) of respondents in the sample were employed full-time, one-third in managerial positions. Their ages ranged from 19 to 53, with a mean of 27; about one-quarter of the respondents were age 30 or over. Slightly less than half (47 percent) of the sample were female; 26 percent were nonwhite.

## Dependent Variables

Our dependent variables measure the employee's behavioral intentions to engage in alternative remedy-seeking options in response to two hypothetical vignettes involving sex-based pay discrimination and sexual harassment, respectively. We constructed vignettes that both males and females might experience and plausibly regard as illegal. In follow-up interviews with employees who participated in the pilot test of the questionnaire, all participants indicated that the vignettes could credibly occur at their workplaces. The versions of the vignettes given to females follow; the versions for males were modified to refer to a female coworker in the sex-based pay-discrimination vignette and a female manager in the sexual-harassment vignette.

*Sex-Based Pay-Discrimination Vignette:*
Your employer has recently hired a male employee who has the same job title as you. You have been responsible for training him on the job. When his training is completed, he will have the same job responsibilities as you. Although the new employee is about your age and has a similar amount of education to you, in other respects, his qualifications are not as good as yours: he has both less work experience and less seniority with the company. Moreover, his education, training and work experience are less relevant to the job. You have just learned that, despite his lower qualifications, his rate of pay is higher than yours.

*Sexual harassment vignette:*
A married male manager at your workplace asked you to go out for a drink after work. You said no. He subsequently asked you out for a drink several additional times. He continues to ignore your refusals. In addition to regularly asking you out, he has been sending you romantic cards, phoning you at home, and driving by your house. At work, he makes frequent comments about how sexy he thinks you are and how attracted to you he is. Whenever possible he sits or stands next to you

and either tries to put his arm around you or strokes your hair. You have repeatedly refused to go out with him, have told him that you think it is inappropriate for him to ask you out, and have told him that his remarks and attention at work are unwanted. Yesterday, he came up behind you at work and kissed the back of your neck.

Respondents were asked to imagine that each vignette happened to them *in their current job* and then to indicate the probability, on a scale from 0 to 100 percent, that they would take each of six remedy-seeking options in response to the situation described in the vignette. These responses were used to construct six dependent variables for each vignette, each measured as a percentage: (1) *not seek remedy*, (2) *complain to manager*, (3) *file grievance*, (4) *file regulatory complaint*, (5) *consult lawyer*, and (6) *quit*.

## Management-Employee Similarity Measures and Control Variables

To capture the supervisor's gender and racial similarity to the employee, we use two indicator variables (yes = 1; otherwise = 0), *same-sex supervisor* (mean = 0.64, s.d. = 0.48) and *same-race supervisor* (mean = 0.71, s.d. = 0.45), respectively. The management team's gender similarity to the employee is measured by the variable *management's gender similarity* (mean = 57.50, s.d. = 32.16), defined as the percent of the employing organization's management team who are the same gender as the employee. The management team's racial similarity to the employee is measured by the variable *management's racial similarity* (mean = 69.97, s.d. = 36.62), defined as the percent of the employing organization's management team who are members of the same racial group as the employee. Deep-level similarity between the employee and managers is measured by the variables *supervisor's deep-level similarity* (mean = 4.37, s.d. = 1.25) and *management's deep-level similarity* (mean = 4.17, s.d. = 1.08); each of these variables is the mean of the employee's responses to four items asking the extent to which the employee agreed with the statements indicating that the employee's supervisor and the management team, respectively, are similar to the employee in terms of: (1) religious beliefs; (2) political beliefs; (3) interests outside of work; and (4) outlook, perspective, and values. Response options to each item ranged from strongly disagree (1) to strongly agree (7). The coefficient alpha reliability was 0.79 for *supervisor's deep-level similarity* and 0.82 for *management's deep-level similarity*. The "management team" is defined as all managers in the organization that the employee knows through personal contact or by reputation.

We also investigated the effect of employer ADR practices, which are measured by the variables *grievance procedure, doesn't know if has grievance procedure; mandatory arbitration* and *doesn't know if mandatory arbitration.* The former two variables are based on responses to the question, "Some employers have procedures for addressing their employees' work-related concerns or complaints. Does (did) your employer have a formal grievance procedure or complaint resolution procedure available for addressing employee complaints or grievances?" Our goal was to frame the question broadly enough to capture access to any type of ADR procedure offered by the employer. The variables *mandatory arbitration* and *doesn't know if mandatory arbitration* are based on responses to the question, "Some employers require their employees to sign an agreement to submit any work-related grievances or complaints to arbitration and to give up the right to sue the employer over such complaints. Did you sign an agreement to submit any work-related grievances to arbitration and to give up the right to sue your employer over such grievances?" We were somewhat surprised that 10 percent of our respondents did not know if their employers offered a grievance procedure and 20 percent did not know if they had signed mandatory arbitration agreements. We decided to retain these observations in the sample to avoid the loss of observations and, as well, to explore whether employees who do "not know" what their employer's policies are have different behavioral tendencies than workers who know what their employer's policies are.

Our models also include controls for a variety of respondent traits (i.e., *female; nonwhite; age; married, spouse employed; married, spouse not employed; children; tenure; graduate student; job satisfaction; expected probability of winning*), and job characteristics (i.e., *full-time; manager*). Table 2 provides definitions and descriptive statistics of all control variables. A (lengthy) table of bivariate-correlations among all of the variables included in our models is available from the authors upon request.

## Models and Estimator

For each vignette, we estimate three models for each dependent variable. We estimate all models using a two-limit Tobit estimator because our dependent variables are truncated on the left and on the right of their distributions; as a result, they violate the assumptions of ordinary least

*Table 2.* Control Variable Definitions and Descriptive Statistics.

| Variable | Definition | Mean | S.D. |
|---|---|---|---|
| Female | Equals 1 if female, otherwise = 0. | 0.47 | 0.50 |
| Nonwhite | Equals 1 if nonwhite, otherwise = 0. | 0.26 | 0.44 |
| Age | Age in years. | 26.64 | 7.72 |
| Married, spouse employed | Equals 1 if married with an employed spouse, otherwise = 0. | 0.29 | 0.46 |
| Married, spouse not employed | Equals 1 if employee is married and spouse is not employed, otherwise = 0. | 0.08 | 0.28 |
| Children | Equals 1 if employee has dependent children, otherwise = 0. | 0.22 | 0.42 |
| Graduate student | Equals 1 if employee is a graduate student; otherwise = 0. | 0.30 | 0.46 |
| Full-time | Equals 1 if job is full-time (i.e., ≥35 hours/week), otherwise = 0. | 0.53 | 0.50 |
| Manager | Equals 1 if employee is a manager or supervisor, otherwise = 0. | 0.33 | 0.47 |
| Job satisfaction | Mean of six items rating employee's satisfaction with their pay, supervisor, advancement opportunities, co-workers, work (tasks and responsibilities), and job, in general, respectively. Item responses range from strongly dissatisfied (1) to strongly satisfied (7). | 5.01 | 1.12 |
| Tenure | The number of years the employee has worked for the employer. | 3.29 | 4.98 |
| Expected probability of winning | Employee's estimate of the probability (ranging from 0% to 100%) of obtaining a favorable decision if the employee complained to a court or government agency about the mistreatment described in this vignette. **Pay discrimination vignette:** / **Sexual harassment vignette:** | 44.76 / 71.51 | 30.87 / 29.65 |
| Grievance procedure | Equals 1 if employee's employer has a formal grievance procedure or complaint resolution procedure available for addressing employee's work-related complaints or grievances, otherwise = 0. | 0.56 | 0.50 |
| Doesn't know if has grievance procedure | Equals 1 if employee does not know if employer has formal grievance or complaint resolution procedure, otherwise = 0. | 0.15 | 0.36 |
| Mandatory arbitration | Equals 1 if the employee had signed an agreement with his/her employer to submit any work-related grievances to arbitration and to give up the right to sue over such grievances, otherwise = 0. | 0.10 | 0.31 |
| Doesn't know if mandatory arbitration | Equals 1 if employee had signed an agreement with employer to submit any work-related grievances to arbitration and to give up the right to sue over such grievances, otherwise = 0. | 0.20 | 0.40 |

squares (OLS) regression. Tobit coefficients and standard errors can be interpreted similarly to those generated by OLS.

Model 1 estimates the main effects of our measures of management's gender and racial similarity to the employee. Model 2 investigates whether there are asymmetries by gender in reactions to the supervisor's gender similarity to the employee and asymmetries by race in reactions to the supervisor's racial similarity. To accomplish this, we replace the variables, *same-sex supervisor* and *female*, with three interaction variables (coded 1, 0): *female with male supervisor, male with female supervisor*, and *female with female supervisor* (the reference category is a male with a male supervisor); we also replace the variables, *same-race supervisor* and *nonwhite*, with three interaction variables (coded 1, 0): *nonwhite with same-race supervisor, white with different-race supervisor*, and *nonwhite with different-race supervisor* (the reference category is a white employee with a white supervisor). In Model 3, we examine whether gender moderates the relationship between *management's gender similarity* and each of our dependent variables and whether race moderates the relationship between *management's racial similarity* and each of our dependent variables. To do so, we add the variables, *female\*management's gender similarity* and *nonwhite\*management's racial similarity*, to the set of variables included in Model 1.

## Limitations

The following limitations should be considered in interpreting the results reported below. First, we use a convenience sample of employed students at a single university. As a result, our sample may not be broadly representative of the population of U.S. employed adults. In particular, our sample is drawn from a narrow geographic area, skews younger than the U.S. employed population as a whole (U.S. Bureau of Labor Statistics, n.d.-a), and is likely to be more educated than the population of employed adults. We note, however, that in regard to gender and race, our sample is similar to the broader population of employed: Our sample is 47 percent female and 74 percent white, figures that are similar to those of the U.S. employed population (47 percent female and 79 percent white).[1] Although a review of research related to justice and fairness concluded that patterns of choices in studies using student samples are similar to those in studies using non-student samples (Konow, 2003), we caution that our use of a convenience sample of employed students may limit the generalizability of our results.

In addition, the small size of our sample made it impractical to examine some important empirical questions. First, the small size of our nonwhite subsample prevents us from exploring the effects of finer ethnic distinctions on remedy-seeking behaviors. Similarly, the small number of respondents represented by unions and collinearity between union representation and other variables preclude estimation of the effect of union membership on remedy seeking and make it impossible to test whether the impact of access to a grievance procedure differs depending on whether or not the employee is represented by a union. These limitations suggest important avenues for future research.

A third potential drawback is that our dependent variables are measured as behavioral intentions in response to mistreatment vignettes. Alternate approaches to the study of employee remedy seeking include field studies and laboratory experiments. We regard these approaches as complementary. A brief comparison of the advantages and disadvantages of each is worth considering. The key advantage of field studies is the ability to examine remedy-seeking behaviors in their natural setting; the major disadvantages are the high cost of obtaining a large enough field sample of employees who have experienced mistreatment severe enough to motivate remedy seeking as well as the difficulty of controlling for the nature and severity of the precipitating mistreatment event. Both vignette studies and laboratory experiments have the advantage of making it possible to ensure that all subjects experience a similar (actual or hypothetical) precipitating mistreatment event; moreover, the contextual richness of vignettes can aid reasoning and avoid misunderstandings by subjects (Konow, 2003). A disadvantage of vignette studies and laboratory experiments, however, is that employees may not respond to hypothetical or simulated mistreatment in the same manner that they would respond to actual mistreatment.

# RESULTS

Descriptive statistics for the dependent variables and difference-of-means tests for each dependent variable across vignettes are reported in Table 1. For both vignettes, the remedy with the highest probability is complaining to a manager. Consulting a lawyer is the least probable response to sex-based pay discrimination, whereas quitting is the least probable response to sexual harassment. For both forms of sex discrimination, employees report being more likely to engage in organizational claiming than in legal claiming. Both *not seek remedy* and *quit* are significantly higher in response to sex-based pay discrimination than in response to sexual harassment. Conversely, (1) *complain to manager*, (2) *file grievance*, (3) *file regulatory complaint*, and (4) *consult lawyer* are all significantly lower in response to sex-based pay discrimination than in response to sexual harassment. Note that we drop observations in which the respondent reported that the employer did not have a grievance procedure when *file grievance* is the dependent variable. This results in a smaller sample size ($N = 172$) for estimating descriptive statistics and regression models using that dependent variable; in the *file grievance* specifications, the reference category for the variable *grievance procedure* is that the respondent doesn't know if the employer has a grievance procedure.

*Results for Measures of Management-Employee Similarity*

To conserve space, our discussion of results will focus on estimated effects that are statistically significant.

*Model 1*

Results for Model 1 are reported in Table 3. Our findings for the variable *same-sex supervisor* provide support for the S-B paradigm. Compared to employees with opposite-sex supervisors, employees with same-sex supervisors are more likely to consult a lawyer in response to both vignettes (H1[S-B]), are more likely to file a regulatory complaint in response to sexual harassment (H1[S-B]), and are more likely to quit in response to sex-based pay discrimination (H4[S-B]). Conversely, our findings for the variable *same-race supervisor* provide support for the S-A paradigm. Specifically, compared to employees with a different-race supervisor, employees with a same-race supervisor are significantly less likely to file a regulatory complaint in response to sexual harassment (H1[S-A]) and are less likely to consult a lawyer (H1[S-A]) and to quit (H4[S-A]) in response to both vignettes.

Also consistent with the S-A paradigm, we find that, in response to sexual harassment, *management's gender similarity* is positively related to *complain to manager* (H2[S-A]) and *management's racial similarity* is negatively related to *consult lawyer* (H1[S-A]). We also find that *management's gender similarity* is positively related to *file a grievance* in response to sex-based pay discrimination. Neither the *supervisor's deep-level similarity*

*Table 3.* Model 1 Tobit Results.

| Explanatory Variables | Sex-Based Pay Discrimination Vignette | | | | | | Sexual Harassment Vignette | | | | | |
|---|---|---|---|---|---|---|---|---|---|---|---|---|
| | Dependent variables | | | | | | Dependent variables | | | | | |
| | Not seek remedy | Complain to manager | File grievance | File regulatory complaint | Consult lawyer | Quit | Not seek remedy | Complain to manager | File grievance | File regulatory complaint | Consult lawyer | Quit |
| Same-sex supervisor | -2.47 (8.17) | 8.26 (7.76) | -2.52 (10.53) | 10.76 (7.94) | 20.83*** (7.99) | 24.03*** (8.95) | 14.65 (12.77) | -6.27 (9.37) | 14.94 (11.65) | 14.42* (8.75) | 14.82* (8.68) | 8.74 (8.14) |
| Same-race supervisor | 7.49 (12.30) | -17.29 (11.78) | 8.19 (14.97) | -13.88 (11.48) | -25.95** (11.54) | -35.63*** (13.10) | 10.92 (19.09) | -6.65 (13.99) | 13.71 (16.34) | -22.46* (12.67) | -33.78*** (12.45) | -26.26** (11.91) |
| Supervisor's deep-level similarity | 1.07 (3.92) | 3.33 (3.70) | -1.81 (4.69) | -0.33 (3.66) | -1.23 (3.68) | -1.35 (4.12) | -1.63 (6.36) | 3.74 (4.48) | 2.03 (5.33) | 1.94 (4.08) | 3.00 (4.06) | 1.87 (3.84) |
| Managements' gender similarity | -0.11 (0.15) | 0.09 (0.14) | 0.34* (0.19) | -0.04 (0.14) | -0.09 (0.15) | -0.15 (0.15) | -0.20 (0.23) | 0.37** (0.17) | 0.21 (0.21) | -0.01 (0.15) | -0.09 (0.15) | -0.01 (0.14) |
| Managements' racial similarity | -0.13 (0.15) | -0.13 (0.14) | 0.19 (0.18) | -0.10 (0.14) | -0.14 (0.14) | 0.13 (0.16) | -0.07 (0.24) | -0.26 (0.17) | -0.16 (0.20) | -0.19 (0.16) | -0.26* (0.15) | -0.05 (0.15) |
| Managements' deep-level similarity | 6.50 (4.56) | -2.43 (4.35) | -6.59 (5.64) | -4.62 (4.28) | 0.06 (4.23) | -2.80 (4.68) | 2.50 (7.15) | -2.60 (5.19) | 2.66 (6.31) | 2.37 (4.81) | 1.42 (4.72) | 3.97 (4.51) |
| Female | -16.04* (8.91) | 6.86 (8.40) | 17.75 (11.63) | 12.11 (8.30) | 7.61 (8.28) | -1.88 (9.17) | -53.63*** (13.96) | 47.03*** (10.32) | 68.68*** (13.89) | 49.06*** (9.51) | 21.47*** (9.13) | 28.29*** (8.79) |
| Nonwhite | -6.60 (14.73) | -40.17*** (13.94) | 17.31 (18.08) | -8.16 (13.19) | -23.85* (13.19) | 34.12** (14.80) | -11.53 (23.05) | -36.90** (16.40) | -21.99 (20.30) | -17.57 (14.65) | -28.33** (14.26) | -33.72** (14.36) |
| Age | 1.87** (0.79) | -2.03*** (0.77) | -3.08*** (1.14) | 0.08 (0.82) | 0.06 (0.83) | -1.97** (0.96) | -1.53 (1.14) | 0.08 (0.94) | -0.01 (1.11) | 0.57 (0.89) | 0.26 (0.88) | -0.84 (0.94) |
| Married, spouse employed | -16.21* (8.98) | -1.25 (8.53) | 0.19 (11.28) | -7.83 (8.83) | -20.96** (9.00) | 1.14 (9.21) | -3.64 (13.72) | 1.04 (10.39) | -5.36 (12.88) | 1.71 (9.70) | -3.49 (9.56) | -4.80 (9.00) |
| Married, spouse not employed | -21.02 (15.89) | 6.23 (15.52) | -1.67 (20.90) | 10.65 (15.79) | -3.69 (15.46) | 25.06 (16.20) | 41.38* (22.40) | 3.08 (18.51) | -43.00* (23.20) | -6.01 (18.39) | -31.25* (18.77) | 4.89 (17.11) |
| Children | -11.71 (10.95) | 8.08 (10.48) | 29.65** (13.50) | 5.93 (10.85) | 21.30** (10.85) | 8.82 (11.90) | -5.00 (17.55) | -5.41 (12.73) | 35.29** (14.82) | 5.27 (11.93) | 3.55 (11.66) | -4.72 (11.80) |
| Full-time | 18.18** (8.42) | -8.41 (8.00) | -4.56 (10.68) | -2.66 (8.07) | -2.69 (7.87) | -3.12 (8.75) | 11.29 (12.27) | -6.17 (9.55) | 15.34 (12.21) | -14.30 (9.09) | -22.32*** (8.89) | -3.41 (8.48) |
| Tenure | -1.54* (0.94) | 0.90 (0.92) | 0.82 (1.21) | 0.06 (0.98) | 0.33 (0.97) | 1.15 (1.08) | -1.47 (1.58) | 0.92 (1.13) | -1.10 (1.24) | 0.18 (1.03) | 1.43 (1.01) | 1.63 (1.03) |
| Manager | -16.30** (7.90) | 15.76** (7.52) | 18.90* (10.40) | 2.63 (7.46) | 0.71 (7.50) | 13.30* (8.02) | -7.34 (11.98) | -3.97 (9.06) | 3.48 (11.71) | 0.26 (8.35) | 2.51 (8.22) | -6.26 (7.98) |
| Grievance procedure | -14.78* (8.42) | 6.52 (8.04) | -1.52 (10.69) | 11.48 (7.94) | 1.19 (7.97) | -9.69 (8.71) | -14.11 (12.18) | 16.49** (9.61) | -3.03 (11.98) | -3.22 (9.05) | 0.99 (8.89) | -16.63** (8.50) |

# Table 3. (Continued)

| Explanatory Variables | Sex-Based Pay Discrimination Vignette | | | | | | Sexual Harassment Vignette | | | | | |
|---|---|---|---|---|---|---|---|---|---|---|---|---|
| | Dependent variables | | | | | | Dependent variables | | | | | |
| | Not seek remedy | Complain to manager | File grievance | File regulatory complaint | Consult lawyer | Quit | Not seek remedy | Complain to manager | File grievance | File regulatory complaint | Consult lawyer | Quit |
| Doesn't know if has grievance procedure | 4.82 | −0.30 | — | 6.91 | 8.75 | −9.69 | −26.59 | 25.30* | — | 0.39 | 10.13 | 4.27 |
| | (10.78) | (10.64) | | (10.83) | (10.67) | (11.65) | (17.01) | (13.02) | | (11.89) | (11.66) | (10.48) |
| Mandatory arbitration | 25.15** | −3.81 | −14.56 | 2.06 | −0.40 | 9.46 | 27.32* | −27.41** | −15.90 | −0.05 | 9.63 | 24.23** |
| | (11.42) | (11.09) | (13.17) | (10.80) | (11.06) | (11.91) | (16.29) | (13.06) | (14.80) | (12.16) | (11.97) | (11.14) |
| Doesn't know if mandatory arbitration | 6.22 | −2.25 | −10.23 | −0.03 | 3.60 | 11.43 | 13.75 | −15.97 | −23.45** | −8.52 | −4.16 | 7.74 |
| | (8.76) | (8.40) | (9.96) | (8.42) | (8.32) | (8.98) | (12.95) | (10.14) | (11.02) | (9.54) | (9.34) | (8.77) |
| Graduate student | 12.95 | 17.83* | −8.70 | −7.35 | −9.26 | 5.22 | −4.62 | 13.94 | −8.34 | 7.37 | 4.53 | 6.95 |
| | (10.20) | (9.98) | (13.32) | (10.27) | (10.55) | (11.31) | (14.59) | (11.82) | (14.24) | (11.22) | (10.98) | (11.06) |
| Job satisfaction | 5.37 | −4.11 | 7.44 | −3.62 | 0.28 | −8.45** | 1.73 | 1.94 | −4.91 | −0.63 | 0.81 | −5.24 |
| | (3.42) | (3.27) | (4.66) | (3.30) | (3.28) | (3.57) | (5.09) | (3.85) | (5.15) | (3.65) | (3.58) | (3.40) |
| Expected probability of winning | −0.38*** | 0.51*** | 0.38** | 0.34*** | 0.33*** | 0.06 | −0.68*** | 0.26* | 0.32* | 0.25* | 0.43*** | 0.13 |
| | (0.12) | (0.12) | (0.16) | (0.12) | (0.12) | (0.13) | (0.17) | (0.14) | (0.17) | (0.14) | (0.14) | (0.13) |
| Constant | −49.57 | 114.98*** | 38.07 | 24.85 | 2.21 | 112.74*** | 75.60* | 29.63 | 2.92 | −26.36 | −8.24 | 15.27 |
| | (30.48) | (29.01) | (40.93) | (29.06) | (29.09) | (32.89) | (44.38) | (35.45) | (45.81) | (33.79) | (33.09) | (33.28) |
| *F-Statistic, Difference-of-Coefficients Tests* | | | | | | | | | | | | |
| $\beta_{Married, \text{ spouse employed}} = \beta_{Married, \text{ spouse not employed}}$ | 0.11 | 0.28 | 0.01 | 1.68 | 1.48 | 2.62 | 5.06** | 0.01 | 3.38* | 0.22 | 2.73* | 0.39 |
| LR-$\chi^2$ | 67.49*** | 45.19*** | 52.33*** | 40.63*** | 41.49*** | 36.82** | 78.94*** | 51.27*** | 60.58*** | 61.80*** | 63.01*** | 37.00** |

*Note*: N equals 241, except for *file grievance* specification, in which it is 172. Tobit coefficients are non-standardized with standard errors in parentheses. The LR-$\chi^2$ is the test statistic for the significance of the model as a whole; this test is analogous to the use of the *F*-statistic in OLS regression to test whether the model explains a significant portion of the variation in the dependent variable.

*Significant at the .10 level; ** at the .05 level; *** at the .01 level.

nor *management's deep-level similarity* has a statistically significant influence on any remedy-seeking option.

*Model 2*
Table 4 reports our Model 2 results. First, we investigate whether gender moderates the effect of having a same-sex supervisor on each of our dependent variables by testing the null hypothesis that $\beta_{\text{male with female supervisor}} = \beta_{\text{female with male supervisor}} - \beta_{\text{female with female supervisor}}$ (Jaccard & Turrisi, 2003). We are unable to reject this null hypothesis for any of our dependent variables.

Next, we investigate the effect of the supervisor's gender similarity conditioned on being male and female, respectively. For men, this conditional effect is captured by the coefficient on *male with female supervisor*, which is significant in two specifications. In response to sex-based pay discrimination, men are both more likely to consult a lawyer ($H1^{\text{S-B}}$) and more likely to quit ($H4^{\text{S-B}}$) when they have a same-sex supervisor than when they have an opposite-sex supervisor. For women, we investigate this conditional effect by testing the null hypothesis, $\beta_{\text{Female with Female Supervisor}} = \beta_{\text{Female with Male Supervisor}}$. We reject this null hypothesis in three specifications, concluding that women with women supervisors are: (1) more likely than women with male supervisors to consult a lawyer in response to sex-based pay discrimination and sexual harassment ($H1^{\text{S-B}}$) and (2) more likely than women with male supervisors to quit in response to sex-based pay discrimination ($H4^{\text{S-B}}$).

We also investigate whether race moderates the effects of having a same-race supervisor by testing the null hypothesis: $\beta_{\text{White with Different-Race Supervisor}} = \beta_{\text{Nonwhite with Different-Race Supervisor}} - \beta_{\text{Nonwhite with Same-Race Supervisor}}$. We find a significant moderator effect only in one specification, concluding that among white employees, the propensity to complain to a manager about sex-based pay discrimination is *lower* with a same-race supervisor than with a different-race supervisor, which supports $H2^{\text{S-B}}$; in contrast, for nonwhites, the propensity to complain to a manager about sex-based pay discrimination is *higher* with a same-race supervisor than with a different-race supervisor, which supports $H2^{\text{S-A}}$.

Finally, we investigate the effect of the supervisor's racial similarity conditioned on being white and nonwhite, respectively. For whites, the *white-with-different-race-supervisor* coefficient tests this conditional effect. Consistent with $H2^{\text{S-B}}$, whites with a same-race supervisor are less likely to complain to a manager than whites with a different-race supervisor in response to both vignettes. However, consistent with $H1^{\text{S-A}}$, whites with a

*Table 4.* Model 2 Tobit Results.

| Explanatory variables | Sex-Based Pay Discrimination Vignette | | | | | | Sexual Harassment Vignette | | | | | |
|---|---|---|---|---|---|---|---|---|---|---|---|---|
| | Dependent variables | | | | | | Dependent variables | | | | | |
| | Not seek remedy | Complain to manager | File grievance | File regulatory complaint | Consult lawyer | Quit | Not seek remedy | Complain to manager | File grievance | File regulatory complaint | Consult lawyer | Quit |
| Female with female supervisor | -25.20** (10.77) | 4.03 (10.05) | 20.86 (13.01) | 9.81 (9.89) | 5.97 (9.63) | -6.91 (10.76) | -63.02*** (16.82) | 48.13*** (12.27) | 75.10*** (15.64) | 48.15*** (11.19) | 23.45** (10.72) | 26.20*** (10.09) |
| Female with male supervisor | -12.02 (11.25) | -2.05 (10.78) | 19.31 (15.16) | 1.54 (11.02) | -13.15 (11.00) | -25.11** (12.17) | -62.46*** (18.50) | 52.44*** (13.28) | 51.22*** (17.11) | 34.49*** (12.05) | 5.90 (11.93) | 18.78* (11.05) |
| Male with female supervisor | -10.56 (11.92) | -13.50 (11.44) | 9.74 (16.63) | -14.69 (12.22) | -24.10* (12.66) | -32.96** (13.61) | -25.68 (16.73) | 7.06 (13.50) | -3.78 (17.48) | -16.23 (14.04) | -11.50 (13.41) | -14.10 (13.49) |
| Nonwhite with same-race supervisor | -12.39 (23.80) | -13.32 (21.57) | 13.28 (30.03) | -7.94 (21.16) | -21.03 (21.96) | -27.31 (26.05) | -20.04 (40.22) | -10.38 (25.43) | -14.79 (33.70) | -14.18 (22.99) | -18.16 (22.40) | -13.63 (22.53) |
| Nonwhite with different-race supervisor | -13.99 (12.78) | -23.88** (11.95) | 9.11 (14.87) | 5.75 (11.66) | 2.08 (11.64) | 1.44 (13.24) | -22.21 (20.05) | -31.37** (14.11) | -36.14** (16.71) | 4.79 (13.12) | 5.09 (12.61) | -8.35 (13.07) |
| White with different-race supervisor | -8.20 (14.63) | 30.63** (14.31) | -10.31 (18.31) | 14.10 (13.89) | 27.34** (13.59) | 38.41*** (14.61) | -63.02*** (16.82) | 48.13*** (12.27) | 75.10*** (15.64) | 48.15*** (11.19) | 23.45** (10.72) | 26.20*** (10.09) |

F-Statistic, Difference-of-Coefficients Tests

| Null hypotheses | Not seek remedy | Complain to manager | File grievance | File regulatory complaint | Consult lawyer | Quit | Not seek remedy | Complain to manager | File grievance | File regulatory complaint | Consult lawyer | Quit |
|---|---|---|---|---|---|---|---|---|---|---|---|---|
| $\beta_{\text{Female with female supervisor}}$ = $\beta_{\text{Female with male supervisor}}$ | 1.52 | 0.37 | 0.01 | 0.70 | 3.85* | 2.71* | 0.00 | 0.10 | 2.47 | 1.65 | 2.72* | 0.58 |
| $\beta_{\text{Male with female supervisor}}$ = $\beta_{\text{Female with female supervisor}}$ | 0.01 | 0.86 | 0.26 | 1.62 | 0.68 | 0.30 | 3.29* | 8.96*** | 6.94*** | 12.13*** | 1.53 | 5.47** |
| $\beta_{\text{Male with female supervisor}}$ = $\beta_{\text{Female with male supervisor}}$ | 1.24 | 2.04 | 0.39 | 3.77** | 5.33** | 3.33* | 3.47* | 7.66*** | 15.30*** | 19.21*** | 6.23*** | 8.21*** |
| $\beta_{\text{Male with female supervisor}}$ = $(\beta_{\text{Female with male supervisor}} - \beta_{\text{Female with female supervisor}})$ | 2.34 | 0.25 | 0.30 | 0.18 | 0.11 | 0.78 | 1.19 | 0.03 | 0.78 | 0.02 | 0.14 | 0.17 |

| Null hypotheses | Not seek remedy | Complain to manager | File grievance | File regulatory complaint | Consult lawyer | Quit | Not seek remedy | Complain to manager | File grievance | File regulatory complaint | Consult lawyer | Quit |
|---|---|---|---|---|---|---|---|---|---|---|---|---|
| $\beta_{\text{Nonwhite with same-race supervisor}}$ = $\beta_{\text{Nonwhite with different-race supervisor}}$ | 0.00 | 0.26 | 0.02 | 0.45 | 1.18 | 1.20 | 0.00 | 0.72 | 0.44 | 0.73 | 1.14 | 0.06 |
| $\beta_{\text{Nonwhite with same-race supervisor}}$ = $\beta_{\text{White with different-race supervisor}}$ | 0.03 | 3.25* | 0.52 | 0.88 | 4.00** | 5.28** | 0.03 | 1.07 | 0.01 | 2.23 | 5.00** | 3.81** |
| $\beta_{\text{White with different-race supervisor}}$ = $\beta_{\text{Nonwhite with different-race supervisor}}$ | 0.12 | 10.88*** | 0.83 | 0.29 | 2.79* | 4.92** | 0.12 | 6.75*** | 1.12 | 1.27 | 3.85** | 6.93*** |
| $\beta_{\text{White with different-race supervisor}}$ = $\beta_{\text{Nonwhite with same-race supervisor}}$ $(\beta_{\text{Nonwhite with different-race supervisor}} - \beta_{\text{Nonwhite with same-race supervisor}})$ | 0.06 | 2.67* | 0.04 | 0.00 | 0.03 | 0.11 | 0.06 | 1.83 | 0.35 | 0.04 | 0.32 | 1.31 |
| LR-$\chi^2$ | 69.93** | 47.99*** | 48.94*** | 40.81** | 41.62** | 37.66*** | 80.20*** | 53.20*** | 88.32*** | 61.85*** | 63.50*** | 38.42** |

*Note:* $N$ equals 241, except for *file grievance* specification, in which it is 172. Tobit coefficients are non-standardized with standard errors in parentheses. The LR-$\chi^2$ is the test statistic for the significance of the model as a whole; this test is analogous to the use of the $F$-statistic in OLS regression to test whether the model explains a significant portion of the variation in the dependent variable in Model 1, Table 3, except for the variables, *female* and *nonwhite*. Each estimating equation includes the same control variables as reported in Model 1, Table 3, except for the variables, *female* and *nonwhite*. Results for control variables are not reported in this table due to space limitations, but are available from the authors upon request.
*Significant at the .10 level; ** at the .05 level; *** at the .01 level.

same-race supervisor have lower propensities to consult a lawyer in response to both vignettes and to file a regulatory complaint in response to sexual harassment. In response to both vignettes, whites with a same-race supervisor have lower propensities to quit than whites with a different-race supervisor, which supports H4$^{\text{S-A}}$. For nonwhites, we investigate this conditional effect by testing the null hypothesis, $\beta_{\text{Nonwhite with Same-Race Supervisor}} = \beta_{\text{Nonwhite with Different-Race Supervisor}}$; we fail to reject this hypothesis in all of our specifications.

*Model 3*

Results for Model 3 are reported in Table 5. In this model, a significant coefficient on the product term *female\*management's gender similarity* indicates that gender moderates the relationship between the management team's gender similarity to the employee and the dependent variable (Jaccard & Turrisi, 2003). This coefficient is significant only in the *quit* specification in response to sex-based pay discrimination.

Fig. 1 illustrates the asymmetries implied by this moderator effect: Consistent with H4$^{\text{S-A}}$, *management's gender similarity* is negatively related to female employees' propensity to quit; conversely and consistent with H4$^{\text{S-B}}$, it is positively related to male employees' propensity to quit.

A significant coefficient on *nonwhite\*management's racial similarity* indicates that race moderates the relationship between the management team's racial similarity to the employee and the dependent variable. The *nonwhite\*management's racial similarity* coefficient is negative and significant in both specifications for *file grievance* and for *file regulatory complaint* and in the *quit* specification in response to sexual harassment. The asymmetries implied by these moderator effects are illustrated in Figs. 2–4, respectively. Fig. 2 suggests that the relationship between *management's racial similarity* to an employee and *file grievance* is negative for nonwhites, but positive for whites.

Figs. 3 and 4 portray a similar pattern of asymmetric responses by race to *management's racial similarity* to the employee. For whites, consistent with the S-B paradigm, *management's racial similarity* is positively related to the propensity to *file regulatory complaint* in response to both vignettes (Fig. 3) and to *quit* in response to the sexual harassment vignette (Fig. 4). Conversely and consistent with the S-A paradigm, for nonwhites, *management's racial similarity* is negatively related to *file regulatory complaint* (Fig. 3) in response to both vignettes and to *quit* in response to the sexual harassment vignette (Fig. 4).

## Table 5. Model 3 Tobit Results.

**a. Results for Sex-Based Pay Discrimination Vignette** — Dependent Variable

| Explanatory variables | Not seek remedy | Complain to manager | File grievance | File regulatory complaint | Consult lawyer | Quit |
|---|---|---|---|---|---|---|
| Female | -13.60 (18.38) | 8.31 (17.93) | -18.99 (26.31) | 7.42 (18.26) | 9.81 (18.20) | 39.72** (19.84) |
| Management's gender similarity | -0.09 (0.23) | 0.10 (0.23) | -0.01 (0.34) | -0.07 (0.24) | -0.04 (0.23) | 0.33 (0.25) |
| Female*Management's gender similarity | -0.04 (0.28) | -0.03 (0.27) | 0.61 (0.38) | 0.09 (0.27) | -0.03 (0.27) | -0.69** (0.29) |
| Nonwhite | -13.06 (20.38) | -49.44*** (19.77) | 61.30*** (24.49) | 12.61 (18.06) | -4.08 (17.85) | -35.38* (19.91) |
| Management's racial similarity | -0.20 (0.21) | -0.23 (0.20) | 0.60** (0.24) | 0.11 (0.19) | 0.06 (0.19) | 0.10 (0.21) |
| Nonwhite * Management's racial similarity | 0.13 (0.29) | 0.18 (0.27) | -0.88** (0.35) | -0.44* (0.269) | -0.44 (0.27) | -0.05 (0.28) |

**b. Results for Sexual Harassment Vignette** — Dependent Variable

| Explanatory variables | Not seek remedy | Complain to manager | File grievance | File regulatory complaint | Consult lawyer | Quit |
|---|---|---|---|---|---|---|
| Female | -51.75** (26.20) | 52.01** (21.15) | 61.64** (29.58) | 37.51* (20.20) | 22.08 (19.69) | 30.36 (19.01) |
| Management's gender similarity | -0.20 (0.32) | 0.44 (0.27) | 0.19 (0.37) | -0.11 (0.26) | -0.06 (0.25) | 0.05 (0.24) |
| Female*Management's gender similarity | -0.04 (0.41) | -0.08 (0.32) | 0.14 (0.43) | 0.19 (0.30) | -0.01 (0.29) | -0.04 (0.28) |
| Nonwhite | -31.28 (30.27) | -24.60 (23.01) | 12.32 (27.53) | 13.72 (20.40) | -10.16 (19.67) | -1.09 (20.18) |
| Management's racial similarity | -0.25 (0.30) | -0.15 (0.23) | 0.17 (0.27) | 0.12 (0.21) | -0.09 (0.20) | 0.26 (0.21) |
| Nonwhite * Management's racial similarity | 0.43 (0.45) | -0.25 (0.32) | -0.70* (0.39) | -0.63** (0.30) | -0.38 (0.29) | -0.74** (0.33) |

*Note:* N equals 241, except for *file grievance* specification, in which it is 172. Tobit coefficients are non-standardized with standard errors in parentheses. Each estimating equation includes the same control variables as reported in Model 1, Table 3. Results for control variables are not reported in this table due to space limitations, but are available from the authors upon request.

*Significant at the .10 level; ** at the .05 level; *** at the .01 level.

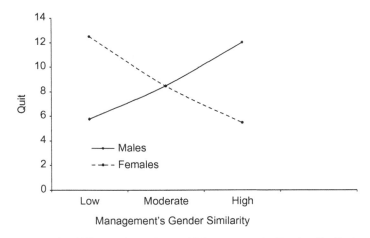

*Fig. 1.* Interacting Effects of Gender and Management's Gender Similarity on the Propensity to Quit in Response to Sex-Based Pay Discrimination.

*Note*: We use results from the *Quit* in response to sex-based pay discrimination specification in Table 5 to generate predicted values of *quit* at low, moderate, and high levels of *Management's Gender Similarity* holding all other variables constant. The moderate, low, and high levels of the *Management's Gender Similarity* are the sample mean, one standard deviation below, and one standard deviation above the mean, respectively. Other variables are held constant at their most frequent value in the sample, 1 or 0, for indicator variables and at the sample mean for other variables.

## Results for Gender and Race

### Gender

Our results for Model 1 suggest that women are less likely than men to not seek a remedy in response to both vignettes and that, in response to sexual harassment, women are more likely than men to *engage in* each remedy-seeking option. Model 2 permits investigation of the relationship between gender and each dependent variable, conditioned on supervisor gender or employee-supervisor gender similarity. We find the following significant conditional effects:

- Among employees with same-sex supervisors, women are less likely than men not to seek a remedy in response to both vignettes; and in response to sexual harassment, women are more likely than men to avail themselves of each remedy-seeking option, including quitting ($H_0$: $\beta_{\text{female with female supervisor}} = 0$).

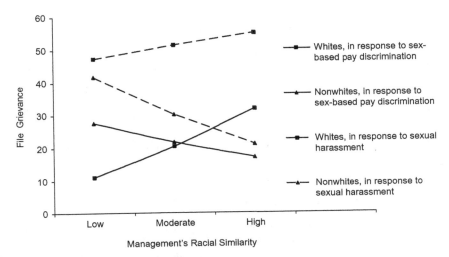

*Fig. 2.* Interacting Effects of Race and the Management's Racial Similarity on the Propensity to File a Grievance.

*Note*: We use results from the *File Grievance specifications* in Table 5 to generate predicted values of *File Grievance* at low, moderate, and high levels of *Management's Racial Similarity* holding all other variables constant. The moderate, low, and high levels of *Management's Racial Similarity* are the sample mean, one standard deviation below the mean, and 100 (slightly less than one standard deviation above the mean), respectively. Other variables are held constant at their most frequent value in the sample, 1 or 0, for indicator variables and at the sample mean for other variables.

- Among those with opposite-sex supervisors, compared to men, women again are less likely to not seek a remedy; and more likely to complain to a manager, file a grievance, file a regulatory complaint, and quit in response to sexual harassment ($H_0$: $\beta_{\text{female with male supervisor}} = \beta_{\text{male with female supervisor}}$).
- Among those with male supervisors, women are less likely than men to not seek a remedy, but more likely than men to complain to a manager, file a grievance, and file a regulatory complaint in response to sexual harassment. Interestingly, among those with male supervisors, women are more likely than men to quit in response to sexual harassment but less likely than men to quit in response to sex-based pay discrimination ($H_0$: $\beta_{\text{female with male supervisor}} = 0$).
- Among those with female supervisors, compared to men, women are more likely to file a regulatory complaint and consult a lawyer in

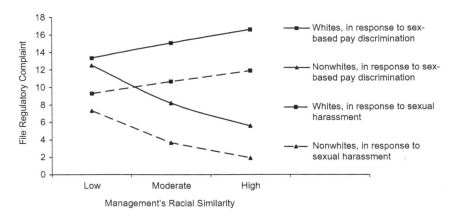

*Fig. 3.* Interacting Effects of Race and the Management's Racial Similarity on the Propensity to File a Regulatory Complaint.

*Note*: We use results from the *File Regulatory Complaint specifications* in Table 5 to generate predicted values of *File Regulatory Complaint* at low, moderate, and high levels of *Management's Racial Similarity* holding all other variables constant. The moderate, low, and high levels of the *Management's Racial Similarity* are the sample mean, one standard deviation below the mean, and 100 (slightly less than one standard deviation above the mean), respectively. Other variables are held constant at their most frequent value in the sample, 1 or 0, for indicator variables and at the sample mean for other variables.

response to both vignettes; are less likely than men to quit in response to sex-based pay discrimination and, in response to sexual harassment, are less likely to not seek a remedy but more likely to complain to a manager, file a grievance, and quit ($H_0$: $\beta_{\text{female with female supervisor}} = \beta_{\text{male with female supervisor}}$).

## Race

In Model 1, we find that nonwhites are less likely than whites to complain to a manager, consult a lawyer, and quit in response to both vignettes. Model 2 permits investigation of the relationship between race and each dependent variable, conditioned on supervisor race or supervisor-employee racial similarity. We find the following significant conditional effects:

• Among those with different-race supervisors, nonwhites are less likely than whites to complain to a manager, consult a lawyer, and quit in response to both vignettes ($H_0$: $\beta_{\text{nonwhite with different-race supervisor}} = \beta_{\text{white with different-race supervisor}}$).

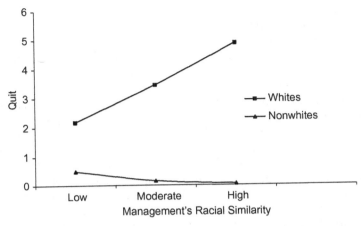

*Fig. 4.* Interacting Effects of Race and Management's Racial Similarity on the Propensity to Quit in Response to Sexual Harassment.

*Note:* We use results from *Quit* in response to sexual harassment specification in Table 5 to generate predicted values of *quit* at low, moderate, and high levels of *Management's Racial Similarity* holding all other variables constant. The moderate, low, and high levels of the *Management's Racial Similarity* are the sample mean, one standard deviation below the mean, and 100 (slightly less than one standard deviation above the mean), respectively. Other variables are held constant at their most frequent value in the sample, 1 or 0, for indicator variables and at the sample mean for other variables.

- Among those with white supervisors, nonwhites are less likely than whites to complain to a manager in response to both vignettes and to file a grievance in response to sexual harassment ($H_0$: $\beta_{\text{nonwhite with different-race supervisor}} = 0$).
- Among those with nonwhite supervisors, nonwhites are less likely than whites to complain to a manager in response to sex-based pay discrimination and to consult a lawyer and quit in response to both vignettes ($H_0$: $\beta_{\text{nonwhite with same-race supervisor}} = \beta_{\text{white with different-race supervisor}}$).

### Results for Control Variables

To conserve space, we will only discuss results for the remaining variables as reported in Model 1 specifications (Table 3). Models 2 and 3 produce similar results for these variables, which are available from the authors on request.

*Measures of Employer's ADR Practices*
Compared to employees who lack access to a formal organizational grievance procedure, employees with access to such a procedure are significantly more likely to complain to a manager in response to sexual harassment, significantly less likely to quit in response to sexual harassment, and significantly less likely to not seek a remedy in response to sex-based pay discrimination. Difference-of-coefficients tests indicate that, compared to employees who are unsure if they have a grievance procedure, employees with access to a grievance procedure are significantly less likely to do nothing in response to sex-based pay discrimination and to quit in response to sexual harassment ($F_{1, 219} = 4.01$, significance level = 0.047).

Employees who signed mandatory arbitration contracts have significantly higher propensities to not seek a remedy in response to both vignettes. Employees who signed mandatory arbitration contracts have significantly lower propensities to complain to a manager in response to sexual harassment; the *mandatory arbitration* coefficient is also negative, but not significant in the complaint-to-a-manager specification in response to sex-based pay discrimination. Finally, employees who signed mandatory arbitration contracts have significantly higher quit propensities in response to sexual harassment than employees who did not sign such contracts; again, the *mandatory arbitration* coefficient has the same sign in the quit specification in response to sex-based pay discrimination, but is not significant.

*Other Control Variables*
The propensity to *not seek a remedy* in response to sex-based pay discrimination increases with age. In contrast, age has a negative effect on the propensities to *complain to manager, file grievance,* and *quit* in response to sex-based pay discrimination. The *age* coefficients are not significant in any specifications for remedy-seeking behaviors in response to sexual harassment.

The propensity not to seek a remedy in response to sex-based pay discrimination increases with *tenure*. Graduate students are more likely than undergraduates to complain to a manager in response to sex-based pay discrimination. Having *children* is positively related to *file grievance* in response to both vignettes and negatively related to *consult lawyer* in response to sex-based pay discrimination. In response to sex-based pay discrimination, married employees with employed spouses are less likely than unmarried employees to not seek a remedy and to consult a lawyer. In response to sexual harassment, married employees with spouses who are not employed are more likely to not seek a remedy, but less likely to file a grievance and to consult a lawyer than both unmarried employees and married employees with employed spouses. *Job satisfaction* is negatively related to *quit* in response to sex-based pay discrimination. The *expected probability of winning* is negatively related to *not seek remedy* but positively related to *complain to manager, file grievance, file regulatory complaint,* and *consult lawyer* in response to both vignettes. Compared to part-time employees, full-time employees are more likely to not seek a remedy in response to sex-based pay discrimination and less likely to consult a lawyer in response to sexual harassment. Compared to nonmanagerial employees, managers are less likely not to seek a remedy but more likely to complain to a manager, file a grievance, and quit in response to sex-based pay discrimination.

## Robustness Check

We did not control for union representation because unions represented only 13 members of our sample. Failure to control for union representation may bias results, however, for some other right-hand-side variables. To explore the sensitivity of our findings to this omission, we estimated each model on only the subsample that results after dropping the 13 respondents represented by unions. The estimated effects of measures of management-employee similarity in the subsample are similar to those in the full sample, with the following exceptions: In Model 1, the coefficient on *management's racial similarity* remains negative and becomes significant in the specification for *complain to manager* in response to sexual harassment; the coefficient on *management's racial similarity* remains negative but is no longer significant in the specification for *consult a lawyer* in response to sexual harassment; the coefficient for *same-race supervisor* remains negative but is no longer significant in the specification for *file regulatory complaint* in response to sexual harassment. In Model 2, women with same-sex supervisors are no more likely to *consult a lawyer* in response to sexual harassment than women with opposite-sex supervisors; in the specification for *file grievance* in response to sexual harassment, the coefficient for *female with female supervisor* is significantly greater than the coefficient for *female with male supervisor*, suggesting that women with same-sex supervisors are more likely to feel comfortable using organizational grievance procedures in nonunion settings; however, the coefficient for *nonwhite with same-race supervisor* is no longer significantly different from the *nonwhite with different-race supervisor* coefficient.

The results for most of the other right-hand-side variables are consistent with results reported in the chapter for the full sample, although there are some slight changes in significance levels. Most notably, the coefficient for *has grievance procedure* remains negative, but is no longer significant in the specification for *not seek remedy* in response to sex-based pay discrimination; the grievance procedure coefficient remains positive, but is no longer significant in the specification for *complain to manager* in response to sexual harassment. Complete results for models estimated using the nonunion subsample are available from the authors upon request.

## CONCLUSIONS AND RECOMMENDATIONS FOR FUTURE RESEARCH

To our knowledge, this chapter is the first (1) to investigate the effects of management-employee similarity on a mistreated employee's propensities to quit, engage in organizational and legal remedy-seeking, and to *not* seek a remedy, in the context of an ongoing employment relationship; and (2) to apply the similarity-attraction and similarity-betrayal paradigms to remedy seeking in the context of an ongoing employment relationship. Our results do not clearly support one paradigm over the other.

Consistent with the S-A paradigm, the management team's racial similarity to a sexually harassed employee negatively influences the propensity to consult a lawyer in response to sexual harassment; this result is consistent with a similar study by Gramm et al. (2006) of remedy seeking in response to wrongful dismissal. Also consistent with the S-A paradigm, we found that the management team's gender similarity to a sexually harassed employee positively influences the propensity to complain to a manager and that having a same-race supervisor decreases propensities to initiate legal claims and to quit. In contrast, having a same-sex supervisor increases propensities to initiate legal claims and to quit, which is consistent with the S-B paradigm. We are unaware of any prior studies providing evidence of these relationships.

Our results also reveal interesting asymmetries by gender and racial category in the effects of management-employee similarity on remedy-seeking responses to mistreatment. Where we observe significant relationships between measures of management-employee gender similarity and men's remedy-seeking responses, our results support S-B paradigm hypotheses; our results for women do not consistently support either paradigm.

For nonwhites, where we observe significant relationships between measures of management-employee racial similarity and employee remedy-seeking responses, our results support S-A paradigm hypotheses; for whites, our findings do not consistently support either paradigm. These asymmetries are consistent with those found in the Gramm et al. (2006) study of remedy seeking in response to wrongful dismissal.

Compared to whites, our findings that mistreated nonwhites are less likely to initiate legal claims in an ongoing employment relationship are consistent with results in prior studies of remedy seeking in response to dismissal (e.g., Goldman, 2003; Gramm et al., 2006). Nonwhites also are less likely to engage in organizational claiming and to quit in response to workplace mistreatment in an ongoing relationship; to our knowledge, this is the first study to investigate these relationships. We also find that women are less likely than men to not seek a remedy and, in response to sexual harassment, are more likely than men to quit. We find that women are also more likely than men to file grievances and initiate legal claims. The latter result is consistent with findings in one prior study of legal claiming in response to dismissal (Gramm et al., 2006); in other such studies, the effect of gender on legal claiming is not significant (e.g., Goldman, 2003; Lind et al., 2000). Differences among demographic groups in remedy-seeking propensities may be attributable, in part, to differences across these groups in other unobserved factors, such as attachment to the labor force and the financial, social, and psychological consequences of claiming and quitting. Additional research is needed to isolate demographic effects on remedy seeking from the effects of these other factors. Moreover, future research using larger samples would facilitate examining the effects of race and gender interactions (e.g., differences among white males, white females, nonwhite males, and nonwhite females), as well as the effects of finer ethnic distinctions on remedy-seeking behaviors.

Our results provide some evidence that access to a grievance procedure may deter quits and encourage the use of informal complaints to managers. However, this result is sensitive to the type of mistreatment. Additional research is needed to investigate whether this result can be replicated in larger and more diverse samples. Note, in addition, that our grievance procedure measure is broad and general. In practice, there is considerable diversity in the types of ADR practices being used by employers; in addition to traditional rights arbitration and mediation, employers are using practices such as factfinding, peer review, conflict coaching, and early neutral evaluation, as well as systems of practices that may offer employees multiple options for accessing the system and for dispute resolution (e.g.,

Lipsky, Seeber, & Fincher, 2003). Our single grievance procedure measure does not capture the variety or complexity of ADR techniques being used in contemporary workplaces. We think that it is plausible that different types of ADR procedures and systems are likely to induce different levels of trust from employees and, consequently, that the type of ADR procedure or system of procedures available will influence the relative attractiveness of different remedy-seeking options. Exploring the effects of different types of ADR procedures on employees' propensity to use different remedy-seeking options is an interesting avenue for future research. Addressing it, however, will be methodologically challenging. Scholars will need to give careful thought to which aspects of an ADR procedure to capture; this will be especially complex when seeking to measure systems of procedures. Additionally, if, as our findings suggest, many employees don't know if they have a grievance procedure, we suspect that employees also will commonly lack information about the details of how their employer's ADR procedure works. As a result, it may be necessary to adopt research designs that can elicit information both from employees about their preferred remedy-seeking options and from their employers regarding the available ADR practices.

Colvin (forthcoming) observes that mandatory arbitration adopted unilaterally by employers is a process that tends to favor employers over employees, citing evidence that employee win rates and damages awarded are lower under mandatory arbitration than under litigation. Our findings suggest that mandatory arbitration agreements are associated with higher employee propensities to not seek a remedy in response to both of our mistreatment vignettes. In the case of the sexual harassment mistreatment vignette, we find that requiring employees to sign mandatory arbitration agreements appears to discourage informal complaints to managers. Discouraging informal complaining can backfire if the result is that management remains unaware of festering employee concerns. We also find that mandatory arbitration agreements are associated with higher quit propensities, which can cause firms to lose their training investments and incur costs associated with recruiting, selecting, and replacing the employees who quit. In summary, our findings suggest that mandatory arbitration may influence employee remedy seeking in ways that have costly unintended consequences for employers. Future research is needed to better quantify these costs. On a practical level, employers considering the adoption of mandatory arbitration agreements with employees may be wise to consider whether the expected benefits from avoiding litigation are outweighed by the expected costs associated with higher quit rates and reduced employee willingness to use informal complaints to managers to express concerns.

Finally, the incidence of each remedy-seeking option and the effects of some explanatory variables on a given remedy-seeking option differ across vignettes. This underscores the need for future research investigating how the nature of workplace mistreatment influences employees' remedy-seeking behaviors; for example, are there systematic differences in how employees respond to mistreatment with adverse financial repercussions compared to mistreatment that aversely impacts the quality of the work environment?

# NOTE

1. We calculated the percentages of the U.S. employed population who are female and white, respectively, using 2015 data from the U.S. Bureau of Labor Statistics (n.d.-b).

# REFERENCES

Bies, R. J., & Tripp, T. M. (1996). Beyond distrust: "Getting even" and the need for revenge. In R. M. Kramer & T. R. Tyler (Eds.), *Trust in organizations: Frontiers of theory and research*. Thousand Oaks, CA: Sage.

Bies, R. J., & Tyler, T. R. (1993). The "litigation mentality" in organizations: A test of alternative psychological explanations. *Organization Science, 4*, 352–366.

Byrne, D. (1971). *The attraction paradigm*. New York, NY: Academic Press.

Colvin, A. J. S. (forthcoming). Conflict and employment relations in the individual rights era. In D. Lipsky, A. Avgar, & J. R. Lamare (Eds.), *Advances in industrial and labor relations: Managing and resolving workplace conflict*.

Colvin, A. J. S., Klaas, B., & Mahoney, D. (2006). Research on alternative dispute resolution procedures. In *Contemporary issues in employment relations* (pp. 103–147). Champaign, IL: David Lewin Labor and Employment Relations Association.

Currall, S. C., & Judge, T. A. (1995). Measuring trust between organizational boundary role persons. *Organizational Behavior and Human Decision Processes, 64*, 151–170.

Goldman, B. M. (2001). Toward an understanding of employment discrimination claiming: An integration of organizational justice and social information processing theories. *Personnel Psychology, 54*, 361–386.

Goldman, B. M. (2003). The application of referent cognitions theory to legal-claiming by terminated workers: The role of organizational justice and anger. *Journal of Management, 29*, 705–728.

Gramm, C. L., & Schnell, J. F. (1997). Following the deader: Race and player behavior in the 1987 NFL strike. In W. E. Hendricks (Ed.), *Advances in the economics of sports* (Vol. 2, pp. 115–143). Greenwich, CT: JAI Press.

Gramm, C. L., Schnell, J. F., & Weatherly, E. W. (2006). Remedy-seeking responses to wrongful dismissal: Comparing the similarity-attraction and similarity-betrayal paradigms. *International Journal of Conflict Management, 47*, 266–290.

Groth, M., Goldman, B. M., Gilliland, S. W., & Bies, R. J. (2002). Commitment to legal claiming: Influences of attributions, social guidance, and organizational tenure. *Journal of Applied Psychology, 87*, 781–788.

Jaccard, J., & Turrisi, R. (2003). *Interaction effects in multiple regression*. Thousand Oaks, CA: Sage.

Klaas, B. S. (1989). Determinants of grievance activity and the grievance system's impact on employee behavior: An integrative perspective. *Academy of Management Review, 14*, 445–458.

Koehler, J. J., & Gershoff, A. D. (2003). Betrayal aversion: When agents of protection become agents of harm. *Organizational Behavior and Human Decision Processes, 90*, 244–261.

Konow, J. (2003). Which is the fairest one of all? A positive analysis of justice theories. *Journal of Economic Literature, XLI*, 1188–1239.

Lewin, D. (1999). Theoretical and empirical research on the grievance procedure and arbitration: A critical review. In Adrienne. In E. Eaton & J. H. Keefe (Eds.), *Employment dispute resolution and worker rights* (pp.137–186). Champaign, IL: Industrial Relations Research Association.

Lind, E., Allen, J., Greenberg, K. S., Scott, K., & Welchans, T. D. (2000). The winding road from employee to complainant: Situational and psychological determinants of wrongful-termination claims. *Administrative Science Quarterly, 42*, 557–590.

Lipsky, D. B., Seeber, R. L., & Fincher, R. D. (2003). *Emerging systems for managing workplace conflict: Lessons from American corporations for managers and dispute resolution professionals*. San Francisco, CA: Jossey-Bass.

Olson-Buchanan, J. B. (1996). Voicing discontent: What happens to the grievance filer after the grievance? *Journal of Applied Psychology, 81*, 52–63.

Olson-Buchanan, J. B., & Boswell, W. R. (2008). An integrative model of experiencing and responding to mistreatment at work. *Academy of Management Review, 31*, 76–96.

Tajfel, H., & Turner, J. C. (1986). The social identity theory of intergroup behavior. In S. Worschel & W. G. Austin (Eds.), *Psychology of intergroup relations* (2nd ed., pp. 7–24). Chicago, IL: Nelson-Hall.

Tsui, A. S., Egan, T. D., & O'Reilly, C. A. (1992). Being different: Relational demography and organizational attachment. *Administrative Science Quarterly, 37*, 549–579.

Tsui, A. S., & O'Reilly, C. A. (1989). Beyond simple demographic effects: The importance of relational demography in superior-subordinate dyads. *Academy of Management Journal, 32*, 402–423.

Turner, J. C. (1985). Social categorization and the self-concept: A social cognitive theory of group behavior. In E. J. Lawler (Ed.), *Advances in group processes: Theory and research* (Vol. 2, pp. 77–121). Greenwich, CT: JAI Press.

U.S. Bureau of Labor Statistics. (n.d.-a). Labor force statistics from the current population survey. Annual table: Employed persons by detailed occupation and age, including median age. Retrieved from http://www.bls.gov/cps/cpsaat11b.pdf. Accessed on February 16, 2016.

U.S. Bureau of Labor Statistics. (n.d.-b). Labor force statistics from the current population survey. Household Data Annual Averages. 5. Employment status of the civilian noninstitutional population by sex, age, and race. Retrieved from http://www.bls.gov/cps/cpsaat05.htm. Accessed on February 16, 2016.

Wanberg, C. R., Bunce, L. W., & Gavin, M. B. (1999). Perceived fairness of layoffs among individuals who have been laid off: A longitudinal study. *Personnel Psychology*, *52*, 59–84.

# EMPLOYMENT LAWYERS AND MANDATORY ARBITRATION: FACILITATING OR FORESTALLING ACCESS TO JUSTICE?

Mark D. Gough

## ABSTRACT

Purpose — *This chapter investigates attributes of an unexplored actor in the contemporary industrial relations system — plaintiff-side employment attorneys — and the premise that pre-dispute mandatory employment arbitration expands employee access to justice.*

Methodology/approach — *It presents data from a novel survey of 1,256 employment plaintiff attorneys and the universe of employment disputes administered by the five largest arbitration providers in the United States.*

Findings — *I report multiple measures indicating employment lawyers hold negative views of arbitration and that arbitration acts as a barrier to employee access to justice: A majority of attorneys say employment*

Managing and Resolving Workplace Conflict
Advances in Industrial and Labor Relations, Volume 22, 105–134
Copyright © 2016 by Emerald Group Publishing Limited
All rights of reproduction in any form reserved
ISSN: 0742-6186/doi:10.1108/S0742-618620160000022005

*arbitration clauses have a positive impact on their willingness to reject a case for representation and a negative impact on their willingness to accept a client under a contingency-fee arrangement, and report negative perceptions of the fairness of outcomes and the adequacy of due process protections in arbitration relative to litigation. Furthermore, attorneys report accepting potential clients covered by arbitration agreements at half the rate of potential clients able to sue in court. Finally, arbitration and litigation filing statistics reveal no evidence that low-income or low-value claimants or claims are accessing the arbitration forum.*

Originality/value — *Novel data compiled here illuminate the institutional characteristics of plaintiff-side employment lawyers and the arbitration forum. They question the assertion that arbitration is an accessible dispute resolution forum for employment disputes relative to civil litigation.*

**Keywords:** Arbitration; alternative dispute resolution; employment law; access to justice

Before the law sits a gatekeeper. To this gatekeeper comes a man from the country who asks to gain entry into the law. But the gatekeeper says that he cannot grant him entry at the moment. The man thinks about it and then asks if he will be allowed to come in later on. "It is possible," says the gatekeeper, "but not now."

— Franz Kafka "Before the Law"

Statutory employment laws are crucial to the determination of the rights, protections, and workplace conditions of contemporary workers (Colvin, 2012, 2014; Piore & Safford, 2006). The Fair Labor Standards Act (FLSA) was an early employment law landmark as was the Civil Rights Act of 1964, specifically Title VII, which prohibits discrimination on the basis of race, color, religion, sex, or national origin. In recent years, The Employee Retirement Income Security Act (ERISA), Age Discrimination in Employment Act (ADEA), Pregnancy Discrimination Act (PDA), Americans with Disabilities Act (ADA), Family Medical Leave Act (FMLA), and legislation passed at the state and local level have created a vast constellation of statutory protections for workers. Though such legislation extends uniform, public rights to broad groups of workers, their enforcement relies on employees privately submitting — and funding — individual claims. In stark contrast to the collective rights defining the New Deal era, the direct protections afforded by these wide-reaching statutes are only as deep — or shallow — as the ability of individual employees to file claims and have them effectively redressed.

The civil litigation system, comprising state and federal courts, is the traditional venue for statutory and contractual employment rights enforcement, but, in recent decades, it has shared this imperative with private arbitration forums. As a general dispute resolution technique, arbitration is characterized as an efficient and accessible alternative to strikes, traditional litigation, and other manifestations of conflict. Indeed, the Supreme Court has explicitly endorsed arbitration's potential to offer streamlined, tailored, and effective access to justice throughout several decades: in the commercial setting since the 1920s, in the unionized setting since the 1960s, for consumer disputes since the 1980s, and in the nonunion employment arena since the 1990s (Resnick, 2015; Stone, 1996).

One particularly provocative instantiation of arbitration practiced today is mandatory employment arbitration, also known as pre-dispute mandatory employment arbitration (referred to hereafter as "employment arbitration" or simply "arbitration"). Employment arbitration clauses bar nonunion employees from pursuing claims in court, even those involving statutory rights.[1] Employers require current or prospective employees to waive their rights to resolve claims in court and to agree to have all future disputes submitted to a private arbitration forum. Employers can present such contracts on a take-it-or-leave-it basis, requiring employees to agree to arbitration as a condition of employment (Stone, 1996). In arbitration, a private third-party neutral, not a judge or jury, adjudicates all disputes emanating from the employment relationship. Arbitrators' decisions are final and binding; only under extraordinary circumstances will an arbitrator's decision be overturned in court. In this way, employment arbitration is similar to grievance arbitration as practiced in unionized settings, but it operates in a distinct institutional environment.

Given the sensitive contractual, statutory, and even constitutional rights at stake, scholars criticize mandatory employment arbitration as coercive, stymieing legal development, providing inadequate due process, and harboring the potential for arbitrator bias and repeat-player effects (Bingham, 1997; Colvin, 2011; Colvin & Gough, 2015; Stone, 1996). Studies have also shown that employee win rates and award amounts in arbitration are substantially lower than outcomes in litigation (Colvin, 2011; Gough, 2014).

Despite such criticisms, the legality of mandatory employment arbitration is firmly entrenched. Many proponents, including the U.S. Supreme

Court, concede employment arbitration has its drawbacks, but assert that it is more effective and accessible than the alternative (i.e., civil litigation) (Eisenberg & Hill, 2003; Estreicher, 2001; Howard, 1995; Sherwyn, Tracey, & Eigen, 1999; St. Antoine, 2008). This nuanced support rests on the premise that the majority of workers with meritorious but low-value claims never see the inside of a court room. It is argued that attorneys will not take such low-value cases on contingency fees and most workers' wages and finances are insufficient to pay for substantial representation costs out of pocket. As recounted by Estreicher (2001, p. 563):

> The unspoken (yet undeniable) truth is that most claims filed by employees do not attract the attention of private lawyers because the stakes are too small and outcomes too uncertain to warrant the investment of lawyer time and resources .... The people who benefit under a litigation-based system are those whose salaries are high enough to warrant the costs and risks of a lawsuit undertaken by competent counsel. ... Very few claimants, however, are able to obtain a position in this "litigation lottery."

Predicating support for employment arbitration on its accessibility resonates because it moves beyond formal arguments as to why arbitration *is* legal and creates a positive normative vision of why it *should be* legal.

The supposition that arbitration expands access to justice, however, has received little scholarly attention and even less empirical scrutiny (notable exceptions include Colvin, 2011; Sternlight, 2015). To date, most research on arbitration is limited to investigating employee win rates and award amounts (Clermont & Schwab, 2004, 2009; Colvin, 2011; Colvin & Gough, 2015; Eisenberg & Hill, 2003; Lamare & Lipsky, 2014). Such scholarship is essential and relevant, but distributive outcomes is just one of several metrics needed to evaluate dispute resolution procedures (Budd & Colvin, 2012). Furthermore, focusing exclusively on outcomes in arbitration ignores the role of principle actors in this industrial relations system — employment attorneys (Dunlop, 1958). Inferior distributive outcomes and due process protections in arbitration are valid areas of concern, but whether arbitration affects the volume or feasibility of filing individual claims deserves attention as well.

Here, I take a new approach to assessing the suitability of employment arbitration by examining whether arbitration is more accessible relative to litigation and how it interacts with the institutional characteristics of employment lawyers. In the first stage of analysis, I use 1,256 survey responses from members of the country's largest organization of plaintiff-side employment lawyers to explore their professional attributes and how arbitration affects the ability of employees to obtain legal representation.

In the second stage of analysis I supplement this survey data with the universe of employment disputes administered by the largest U.S. arbitration providers and in federal court to further investigate whether arbitration provides employees increased access to justice relative to the civil litigation system. Specifically, I use claimant salaries, size of monetary claims, and the volume of filings in litigation and arbitration to assess the accessibility of arbitration. This study contributes to extant literature by compiling novel data illuminating members of a crucial, unexplored stakeholder at the center of the accessibility debate — plaintiff-side employment attorneys — and exploring the premise that (1) attorneys are more willing to take cases in arbitration and (2) arbitration is a more accessible forum than litigation.

## MOTIVATION FOR STUDY

Scholars have long acknowledged that access to lawyers and access to the law are nearly synonymous (Curran, 1977; Felstiner, Abel, & Sarat, 1980; Galanter, 1976). This is especially true for employment statutes, given their reliance on individual employees for enforcement, unlike predecessor labor laws that adopted a bureaucracy-centered enforcement regime (Weil, 1997). Even where government bureaucracies are granted enforcement authority, such as in the case of the Equal Employment Opportunity Commission (EEOC) and antidiscrimination statutes or the Department of Labor (DOL) and FLSA, enforcement is anemic. The EEOC filed suit in just 167 of 88,778 total discrimination charges received in 2014 — nearly a 20 percent increase from 2013 when it filed suit in just 142 out of 93,727 (EEOC, 2015). The DOL's Wage and Hour Division reports a similar record (Weil, 1997).

In the absence of government enforcement, navigating complex employment law and the equally complex rules of legal institutions requires attorney assistance (Sandefur, 2015). Employees proceeding without attorney representation, known as *pro se*, are associated with lower win rates, awards, and rates of settlement and higher rates of dismissal in both litigation (Clermont & Schwab, 2004, 2009; Nelson, Nielsen & Lancaster, 2010) and arbitration (Colvin, 2011; Colvin & Gough, 2015). Given the apparent disadvantages experienced by *pro se* litigants, the rights available to workers may rest not only in contractual or statutory language, but also in their ability to attract private attorney counsel.

But what determines whether an attorney is willing to take on a case when an employee comes to him or her seeking representation? Despite the gatekeeping role they play in the industrial relations and legal system, little is known about the calculus of employment plaintiff attorney case selection. Blasi and Doherty (2011) report that obtaining representation will require an employee to have provable damages between $50,000 and $150,000, but they base this number on conversations with nine plaintiff-side lawyers in California. An oft-cited figure that employment lawyers accept approximately 5 percent of potential clients and require at least $60,000 in provable damages is based on 300 responses to a 1991 survey of National Employment Law Association members (Howard, 1995). This figure would exceed $100,000 in 2015 inflation-adjusted dollars and predates the proliferation of employment arbitration and the passage of the Civil Rights Act of 1991, substantially limiting its applicability to the current legal environment.

It is commonly accepted that the majority of employment attorneys operate under contingency-fee arrangements, where clients are not charged hourly fees but pay a percentage of any amount recovered through award or settlement. Operating on contingency fees, employment lawyers are best off, monetarily, selecting cases where risk and costs are minimized and the size and probability of payoffs are maximized (Kritzer, 1997, 2004; Selmi, 1997; Sherwyn et al., 1999). Nearly all previous findings on the case selection practices of contingency-fee attorneys find preferred cases have a high probability of success, minimal costs, and high prospective rewards (Farhang, 2009; Kritzer, 1997, 2004; Mongoven, 2004). This has led some to question whether lawyers value their own monetary gain over justice under the law (Sandefur, 2015). With respect to employment lawyers specifically, both Selmi (1997) and Sherwyn et al. (1999) present models of attorney case selection based on rational choice theory that balance the expected rewards and costs of pursuing a claim. This is consistent with the broader literature on contingency-fee lawyers, but these specific models are prescriptive and untested.

Supporting the contention that contingency-fee lawyers, and specifically employment lawyers, are economically motivated actors, as suggested by the literature, when Congress increased the damages and attorney fee awards in the Civil Rights Act of 1991 one primary goal was to induce private attorneys to increase the number of claims brought under the act (Farhang, 2009; Selmi, 1997). And, indeed, in the decade following its passage, employment civil rights filings in federal court increased over 300 percent (Clermont & Schwab, 2004). Despite the explosion of civil rights litigation in the federal docket in the 1990s, though, filings have waned in recent years (Clermont & Schwab, 2009). And there is evidence that legal needs in the employment arena continue to be underserved (Nielsen & Nelson, 2005).

It is within this environment that arbitration proponents advance the view that arbitration improves upon the civil litigation enforcement regime. In *Circuit City v. Adams* (2001) the Supreme Court upheld the legality of mandatory employment arbitration stating, "[a]rbitration agreements allow parties to avoid the costs of litigation, a benefit that may be of particular importance in employment litigation, which often involves smaller sums of money than disputes concerning commercial contracts." Notably, Estreicher (2001) argues that only high-income individuals or those with high-value claims can attract an attorney and mobilize their employment rights in the civil litigation system. The typical claimant with a low-stakes, complicated, or risky case cannot secure representation on contingency fees and, therefore, is locked out of court. The litigation system, he argues, provides "Cadillacs" for the lucky few who gain access to civil courts but "rickshaws" for the many who are excluded. In his view, arbitration's efficiency and low costs provide a "Saturn," making representation of these low-value cases economical and providing justice to the masses.

The intuition that arbitration affects attorney case selection decisions is consistent with theories of contingency-fee lawyer behavior. However, concluding that arbitration has a *positive* effect on attorney case selection and claiming arbitration facilitates employee access to justice is unjustified. As previously established, the literature suggests that employment lawyers work on contingency fees and, consequently, that arbitration should affect their willingness to accept prospective clients. Specifically, arbitration should affect attorney assessment of the likelihood of establishing liability (i.e., winning), the expected size of their monetary recovery (i.e., award amounts), and the costs of pursuing the claim (i.e., time, negotiating costs, and so forth).

Whether the net effect of this calculation is positive, negative, or neutral is not known, but current empirical scholarship is illuminating. Colvin (2011) reports an employee win rate of 21.4 percent, median and mean award amounts of $43,879 and $132,066, respectively, for 1,213 AAA employment arbitrations decided between 2003 and 2007. He also finds the mean time spent between filing and disposition for tried arbitration cases is 362 days. Using an expanded dataset, Colvin and Gough (2015) report similar findings: employees win roughly 20 percent of cases adjudicated in arbitration with a mean award slightly below $113,000. In comparison, however, in employee civil rights cases in federal court, Clermont and Schwab (2004) report an employee win rate of 36 percent and mean and median damages of approximately $1 million and $90,000 in inflation-adjusted dollars, respectively. Eisenberg and Hill (2003) show employees won 36.4 percent of 1,430 discrimination cases filed in federal court, received mean and median damages of approximately $190,000 and $450,000, respectively, and spent 709 days on the docket if their case proceeded to trial. At the state level, Eisenberg and Hill (2003) find a 57 percent employee win rate, average award amount above $600,000, and a mean docket time of 723 days in 145 employment non-civil rights cases disposed in state court. Finally, using a sample of 389 employment disputes decided in California state court between 1998 and 1999, Oppenheimer (2003) reports an employee win rate of 53 percent, and a median verdict of over $355,000 in inflation-adjusted 2015 dollars.

Clear trends emerge from these studies: employee awards, win rates, and docket times are lower in arbitration than in either state or federal court. Interpreting these raw findings requires caution, however, because differences in the types of cases resolved in the forums are not accounted for. Nor are potential differences in attorney case-selection standards. If claims by Estreicher (2001) and similar arbitration proponents are accurate and attorneys are bringing lower value or less-meritorious claims to arbitration, this would be consistent with the observed low win rates, award amounts, and faster resolution times. Contrary to selection effect concerns, though, recent studies by Colvin and Pike (2014) and Gough (2014) find that the characteristics of the population of cases disposed in arbitration and litigation are similar. This suggests that inferior employee outcomes reflect embedded inequities in employment arbitration.

Indeed, if, as the literature implies, contingency fees are ubiquitous among plaintiff-side employment lawyers, lower average awards and success rates should have a negative effect on employment attorney willingness to accept arbitration cases relative to litigated claims, all else held constant. However, faster resolution times, all else held constant, should have a positive effect on attorney willingness to accept arbitration cases. The net effect of arbitration on attorney case selection behavior is not clear. If, as proponents contend, arbitration has a net positive effect on attorney representation decisions, leading attorneys to accept cases they would otherwise reject in the litigation context, support for arbitration may be warranted even in an environment of relatively low award amounts and employee win rates.

Alternatively, a net negative effect on attorney case selection decisions would suggest that arbitration forestalls employee access to justice, compounding the injustice of inferior distributive outcomes.

The existing literature provides very little guidance on this issue. A dearth of publically available data on arbitration makes even indirect assessments of its accessibility difficult. For example, estimates of the coverage rate of arbitration are few and inconsistent (see Colvin, 2004; Lipsky, Seeber, & Fincher, 2003; Stipanowich & Lamare, 2014). Furthermore, there is no consensus on even the most fundamental attributes of the arbitral forum, such as the total number of employment arbitration claims filed throughout the United States every year. How do the institutional characteristics of employment lawyers interact with the institutional characteristics of arbitration? Are potential clients headed for arbitration more appealing than those headed to litigation? Do case characteristics in arbitration provide evidence of increased accessibility for low-value claims or low-income claimants? I discuss the data used to analyze these key questions below.

## DATA

I examine data from three comprehensive sources covering characteristics of employment lawyers, employment disputes in arbitration, and employment disputes in civil litigation. Employment attorney characteristics and case selection criteria are at the center of the accessibility debate. Therefore, the first and primary data I analyze are from a survey of attorney members of the National Employment Lawyers Association (NELA) and its largest state affiliate, the California Employment Lawyers Association (CELA). Founded in 1985, NELA is the largest organization of practicing plaintiff-side employment attorneys in the country, with 69 affiliates at the circuit, state, and local level (NELA, 2016). Full membership requires that a majority of an attorney's legal practice involve employment-related matters on the side of employees.

The survey frame consisted of 1,890 NELA and 828 CELA members. NELA and CELA generously provided contact information for their membership and sent an introductory email on behalf of the research team in early 2014. We later emailed attorneys with a link to a Qualtrics survey and subsequently mailed physical copies of the survey instrument to nonrespondents. Of the 2,718 employment attorneys surveyed, we collected

1,256 completed instruments, representing a response rate of over 46 percent. Of these, 69 percent responded to the web-based survey instrument and 31 percent responded via the mailed survey instrument.[2]

The survey covers attorney case selection requirements, attitudes towards arbitration, and experiences in arbitration and litigation. The respondents provided the following information about their practices and case-selection criteria: the type and size of their law practice, the composition of their caseloads, their minimum case-selection criteria, the rate at which they accept clients, their estimate of the coverage rate of employment arbitration, and the effect of arbitration on procedural and distributive justice.

In addition they provided information about their most recent employment discrimination cases taken to verdict in arbitration and litigation. In total, respondents described 525 employment discrimination cases reaching verdict in state or federal courts and 277 employment discrimination cases adjudicated pursuant to mandatory arbitration clauses.[3]

Our sampling only NELA and CELA members means that respondent characteristics, perceptions, and experiences may not be representative of the general population of plaintiff-side employment lawyers. Furthermore, the survey results alone cannot demonstrate as empirical fact whether mandatory employment arbitration expands or restricts employee access to justice. This is especially noteworthy because NELA has played a prominent role in legislative efforts to restrict the use of mandatory employment arbitration agreements (NELA, 2016). Still, this survey provides insight into the attributes and perceptions of plaintiff-side employment attorneys. Furthermore, these data afford a sample of claims across multiple states, forums, and arbitration providers beyond what the limited public disclosure statements analyzed in previous research have provided (Colvin, 2011; Colvin & Gough, 2015; Lamare & Lipsky, 2014).

To complement the survey data and further explore the assertion that arbitration facilitates access to justice, we evaluated a second dataset; it comprises the universe of employment arbitration cases administered nationally between January 1, 2009, and December 31, 2013, by the five largest providers of employment arbitrations: the American Arbitration Association (AAA), Judicial Arbitration and Mediation Services, Inc. (JAMS), ADR Services, Inc. (ADR), Judicate West, and Alternative Resolution Centers (ARC).[4] Data are restricted to this period to reflect the contemporary arbitration environment and maintain consistency with the NELA survey. These providers publish limited information on all case dispositions derived from pre-dispute mandatory employment arbitration clauses pursuant to several state disclosure laws, including damages claimed, filing and disposition dates, method of disposition, prevailing party, and award amount, if any.

These five agencies are responsible for more than four-fifths of all employment arbitrations proceeding under mandatory agreements administered by private providers nationwide (Colvin & Gough, 2015). The five agencies administered a combined 8,815 employment disputes during the period analyzed. Of these, 6,982 were disposed by the AAA, making it the largest arbitration provider in the sample; 1,042 were disposed by JAMS, 610 by ADR, 290 by Judicate West, and 45 by ARC. Here again, compiling disclosure reports of five arbitration providers constitutes the most representative dataset of its kind and extends existing studies that rely on more-limited samples, providing a more robust picture of employment dispute resolution in the arbitral forum across several providers (Colvin, 2011; Colvin & Gough, 2015; Lamare & Lipsky, 2014).

Finally, The Administrative Office of the U.S. Courts (AO) collects data on every individual civil case filing and disposition to provide an official record of the business of the federal district courts. The federal AO database contains filing and termination dates, the jurisdictional basis of the case, the type and amount of damages claimed, the procedural method of disposition, and the type and amount of damages awarded along with the prevailing party, if relevant. The AO database used in this analysis contains 169,405 civil employment-related cases filed in federal district court between January 1, 2009, and December 31, 2013.[5]

The ambition of this research is not to provide a comprehensive account of employment dispute resolution in arbitration and federal court. Rather, I assemble the data described above to assess institutional attributes of arbitration and explore a neglected stakeholder at the center of the accessibility debates — employment plaintiff attorneys. A dominant perspective supporting a public policy in favor of employment arbitration is that the traditional civil litigation system is inaccessible, because attorneys accept only high-value cases, and arbitration provides an accessible alternative for aspiring claimants. Recounted by St. Antoine (2008):

> The vast majority of ordinary, lower- and middle-income employees ... cannot get access to the courts to vindicate their contractual and statutory rights. Most lawyers will not find their cases worth the time and expense. Their only practical hope is the generally cheaper, faster, and more informal process of arbitration. If that is so-called mandatory arbitration, so be it. There is no viable alternative.

Providing a forum where such low-value claims can attract attorney representation and enforce employees' statutory rights is an appealing narrative. But is this promise being realized? How do the institutional characteristics of plaintiff attorneys interact with arbitration? Do we find evidence of expanded access for lower- and middle-income employees? To begin to answer these questions, I present key characteristics of employment plaintiff attorneys and their assessments of employment arbitration next.


## EMPLOYMENT ATTORNEY SURVEY RESULTS

The 1,256, NELA and CELA survey responses came from 49 states and the District of Columbia.[6] The details of the responses, shown in Table 1, indicate that respondents are experienced employment law specialists who have practiced an average of 20 years. For these attorneys, 83 percent of their practice is dedicated to employment law matters, and 91 percent of their employment-related caseload involves matters representing employees, on average, as opposed to defense-side work for employers.

Table 1 also shows that responding attorneys practice largely in solo or small firms. Only one percent and 3 percent work for government agencies or non-profits, respectively, and one percent of respondents indicate they typically work pro bono. Table 1 further demonstrates the dominance of contingent-fee arrangements among attorney respondents: a combined 92 percent of attorneys primarily accept clients under a pure contingency-fee arrangement, typically 35 percent of any damages, or a hybrid arrangement where attorneys still typically require a 35 percent contingency in addition to a retainer in the range of $2,500−5,000. Only 5 percent of the sample recorded that they typically operate under hourly fees.

This is in line with the predominance of small practices and low rates of non-profit and government employment found in the general population of lawyers (Carson, 2012). The high proportion of contingency-fee arrangements, coupled with the small proportion of pro bono, non-profit, and government attorneys reflects the American legal system's reliance on private enforcement of statutory and contractual rights (Carson, 2012; Glover, 2012). These results further validate concerns about employee access to legal representation; if those with employment disputes cannot attract a private attorney to take a case on contingency, their prospects for alternative representation are bleak. This is explored further in Table 2.

**Table 1.**   Respondent Attorney Characteristics.

| Firm Type | Distribution (%) |
|---|---|
| Solo | 32 |
| Law firm – single location | 52 |
| Law firm – multiple locations | 11 |
| Government | 1 |
| Non-profit or advocacy group | 3 |

| Attorneys at Firm | Distribution (%) |
|---|---|
| 0–5 | 69 |
| 6–10 | 16 |
| 11–20 | 8 |
| 21–50 | 5 |
| 51–100 | 1 |
| More than 100 | 1 |

| Title or Position | Distribution (%) |
|---|---|
| Associate | 14 |
| Of counsel | 2 |
| Other | 13 |
| Partner | 71 |

| Specialization | Mean (Median) |
|---|---|
| % Practice dedicated to employment law | 83 (94) |
| % Practice dedicated to employee representation | 91 (98) |
| Years of experience | 20 (20) |

| Fee Arrangement | Distribution (%) |
|---|---|
| Contingent | 68 |
| Contingent hybrid | 24 |
| Hourly | 5 |
| Pro bono | 1 |
| Other | 3 |

What damages must be present to obtain representation under the typical contingency fee? And what does the alternative (i.e., paying hourly fees) cost? Table 2[7] presents the minimal size of matter attorneys require to accept a client for representation[8] and attorneys' typical hourly fee.[9] The average hourly fee charged by all employment attorneys in the sample is $395, but there is substantial variation at the state level. California attorneys have the highest hourly rates, charging an average of $442 per hour. Attorneys in Alabama report the lowest fees, charging an average of

*Table 2.* Attorney Fees and Damage Requirements.

| State | Minimal Size of Matter for Representation | | | | Hourly Fee | |
|---|---|---|---|---|---|---|
| | Mean ($) | Median ($) | 75th Percentile ($) | 25th Percentile ($) | Mean ($) | Median ($) |
| National | 55,839 | 35,000 | 75,000 | 20,000 | 395 | 375 |
| CA | 76,417 | 50,000 | 100,000 | 25,000 | 442 | 425 |
| NY | 58,403 | 35,000 | 67,500 | 15,000 | 418 | 375 |
| DC | 51,563 | 50,000 | 62,500 | 22,500 | 399 | 450 |
| TX | 60,703 | 40,000 | 75,000 | 25,000 | 383 | 363 |
| PA | 40,321 | 25,000 | 50,000 | 12,500 | 330 | 323 |
| IL | 53,400 | 50,000 | 65,000 | 12,500 | 366 | 363 |
| MO | 41,500 | 50,000 | 50,000 | 20,000 | 329 | 300 |
| FL | 47,136 | 25,000 | 60,000 | 10,000 | 345 | 363 |
| GA | 41,250 | 22,500 | 55,000 | 10,000 | 304 | 300 |
| CO | 32,000 | 25,000 | 50,000 | 15,000 | 305 | 295 |

$281 per hour. Even the lowest average hourly fees are likely out of range of the typical employment dispute claimants, especially given the strong likelihood of having lost their jobs. This reinforces the key role contingency-fee arrangements play in the legal regime and brings the legal system's inaccessibility into sharp relief.

In Table 2, there is also substantial variation both between and within states in the minimal case value required by attorneys to accept a case for representation. The minimal size of matter represents the lowest case value, based on expected settlement or total damages including attorney fees, that attorneys are likely to accept for representation. Throughout the United States this average value is approximately $56,000. The median requirement, however, is $35,000. Attorneys practicing in California, New York, Florida, Illinois, Pennsylvania, and Georgia are also characterized by particularly high variation between the 75th and 25th percentiles.

Employment rights and access to justice are indeed areas of national concern, but as seen in Table 2, unique state-level environments must be taken into account. Nationwide averages hide the variation found within the employment plaintiff's bar. At least a quarter of all attorneys require a minimum of only $20,000 or less in total damages to accept a case for representation. In Florida and Georgia, cases involving as little as $10,000 may attract the attention of a quarter of the attorney population.

## Factors Affecting Attorney Case Selection Decisions

The basic attributes and economic parameters described above are informative and essential to understanding which cases are accepted and which are denied representation. Employment lawyers overwhelmingly rely on contingency fees, presumably selecting cases where the expected benefits are high and their own costs are low, and require approximately $56,000 in expected total damages to accept a case. The dominance of contingency-fee arrangements and high damage requirements reinforces the plausibility of a simple expected value-based explanation for attorney selection decisions. However, these attributes alone do not reveal the effect of mandatory employment arbitration on attorney selection decisions or employee access to justice.

One measure of accessibility is the percentage of representation requests employment attorneys accept from prospective clients covered under arbitration agreements and those free to pursue disputes in civil litigation. If employment lawyers found arbitration conducive to their interests, this should be reflected in higher acceptance rates for clients covered under arbitration agreements than for those who are not, all else held constant. Indeed, this is the fulcrum upon which proponents, including the Supreme Court, rest their support for arbitration: arbitration appeals to attorneys and claimants because it demands fewer resources (both monetarily and time) and, therefore, expands access to justice for employees.

On the surface, the observed client acceptance rates between forums do not support this narrative. Attorneys report accepting 11 percent of clients who contact them with claims covered under mandatory arbitration agreements, on average, but 19 percent of clients unencumbered by arbitration clauses.[10] Median acceptance rates reveal the same trend: 5 percent for clients covered under mandatory arbitration agreements and 10 percent for those who are not. These represent practically and statistically significant ($p < .01$) differences in client acceptance rates.

Single or low double-digit acceptance rates legitimize concerns over employee access to justice. Acceptance rates at such low absolute levels suggest the extant enforcement regime is, by and large, inaccessible to employees seeking legal redress. Moreover, the fact that attorney acceptance rates for arbitration clients are half the acceptance rates for litigation clients implies that arbitration may be exacerbating the very pathologies proponents claim it is designed to address.

It should be noted that stronger conclusions could be drawn if characteristics of both populations of aspiring claimants could be observed. Studies comparing employee outcomes between arbitration and litigation have been plagued with similar limitations: the outputs of arbitration are observable — be it client acceptance rates or employee win rates — but adequate controls to isolate the independent effect of arbitration are not (Colvin, 2011; Eisenberg & Hill, 2003). The types of employees or claims covered under arbitration clauses may systematically vary from the types of employees or claims where arbitration clauses are absent. Therefore, this single measure is revealing in context but cannot determine whether or to what degree differences in acceptance rates are caused by the arbitral forum itself or result from systematic variation among clients seeking representation.

Attorney responses assessing the independent effect of arbitration directly, however, ameliorate the above concerns. The likelihood that employment arbitration agreements and six other factors would lead attorneys to reject a prospective client on a scale of 1 (very unlikely to reject for this reason) to 7 (very likely to reject for this reason) are reported in Table 3.[11,12]

The trends apparent in Table 3 are in accord with the prevailing theoretical and empirical scholarship emphasizing the economic calculations of contingency-fee lawyers. An untrustworthy client, a claim that lacks legal viability, inadequate damages, and cases outside attorney expertise are all

*Table 3.* How Likely Are You to Reject a Prospective Client for the Following Reasons?

|  | Very Unlikely (%) | Unlikely (%) | Somewhat Unlikely (%) | Undecided (%) | Somewhat Likely (%) | Likely (%) | Very Likely (%) |
|---|---|---|---|---|---|---|---|
| No legal basis for claim | 0 | 0 | 0 | 0 | 1 | 5 | 93 |
| Mandatory arbitration clause | 5 | 12 | 12 | 18 | 26 | 15 | 13 |
| Inadequate damages | 2 | 4 | 6 | 6 | 21 | 33 | 28 |
| Outside area of expertise | 2 | 3 | 3 | 4 | 11 | 25 | 53 |
| Attorney fees not recoverable | 5 | 12 | 15 | 15 | 23 | 17 | 13 |
| Client not reliable/ trustworthy | 3 | 1 | 1 | 1 | 5 | 18 | 72 |

likely to negatively affect the expected value of cases and, therefore, the willingness of contingency-fee attorneys to accept them. The emphasis given to economic considerations is further apparent from attorney qualitative responses. For example, when asked why particular cases are accepted and others rejected, a 2008 law school graduate in the Midwest responded: "Money. It came down to money, that's pretty much it." A West Coast employment lawyer with over 25 years of experience describes his case selection concerns as follows: "All we care about is if there is money in it. Does the plaintiff have a case? And does the defendant has [sic] money, so that we can recover damages?" Finally, a 1998 graduate of Cornell Law School succinctly quipped, "I will not take a case if there is not money in it."

Regarding arbitration, attorneys report they are more likely than not to reject a prospective client covered under a mandatory arbitration clause. A majority of attorneys report that the presence of an arbitration agreement would make them between "Somewhat" and "Very Likely" to reject a potential client, whereas 30 percent indicate an arbitration agreement is "Very" to "Somewhat Unlikely" to lead to a client rejection, and 18 percent are undecided. And though reactions are generally negative, the arbitration clause item received the most responses between the "Undecided" and "Very Unlikely" range, suggesting it may be the least rebarbative factor within the six items presented.

However, where a full 54 percent of attorneys respond they are at least "Somewhat Likely" to reject a prospective client because of the presence of a mandatory arbitration clause, suggestions that attorneys are embracing the forum are not supported. One California attorney explains a "Very Unlikely" response to the mandatory arbitration item in this way:

> I would not turn away a case because of an arbitration clause. I turn away all cases that do not have merit. Typically, I consider the exposure on a case (damages) and I assess the plaintiff (Is he truthful? Credible? Likeable? Trustworthy?) The presence of an arbitration clause affects the damages. So, an arbitration clause is a factor when I assess the value of a case.

Several attorneys who responded in the unlikely range to the arbitration item provided similar comments, suggesting arbitration may have an even more severe impact on employees' abilities to gain representation if one acknowledges its indirect effects.

While Table 3 shows that arbitration agreements increase the likelihood attorneys report rejecting prospective clients seeking representation, Table 4 indicates several potential explanations as to *why* this is so.

*Table 4.* What Is the Impact of Mandatory Arbitration on Each of the Following Factors?[13]

| | Very Negative (%) | Negative (%) | Somewhat Negative (%) | Undecided (%) | Somewhat Positive (%) | Positive (%) | Very Positive (%) |
|---|---|---|---|---|---|---|---|
| Your willingness to represent a prospective client | 18 | 22 | 37 | 20 | 2 | 1 | 1 |
| Your willingness to represent a prospective client on a contingency-fee basis | 19 | 22 | 28 | 26 | 2 | 2 | 1 |
| Your willingness to invest time and resources in a case | 16 | 22 | 29 | 28 | 2 | 2 | 1 |
| Fairness of outcomes | 30 | 28 | 24 | 12 | 3 | 1 | 1 |
| Fairness of proceeding | 29 | 27 | 26 | 13 | 2 | 2 | 1 |
| Adequacy of discovery | 27 | 31 | 25 | 13 | 2 | 2 | 0 |
| Expediency of proceeding | 11 | 14 | 15 | 25 | 25 | 8 | 2 |
| Your willingness to settle a case | 3 | 5 | 10 | 42 | 20 | 13 | 7 |
| Employer willingness to settle a case | 18 | 26 | 22 | 20 | 8 | 3 | 2 |

The table presents responses to the question: "With respect to employment-related claims, what effect does a pre-dispute mandatory arbitration clause have on each of the following factors?"

Table 4 continues to show negative attorney perceptions of mandatory arbitration and factors relevant to representation decisions. Nearly three quarters of all respondents said arbitration had between a "Somewhat Negative" and "Very Negative" impact on their willingness to represent a prospective client, their willingness to invest time and resources in a case, and their willingness to represent a prospective client on a contingency-fee basis. Approximately a quarter report they are undecided about arbitration's effect for each individual item. Illustrating a majority sentiment, a female employment lawyer with 23 years of experience described arbitration in the following terms: "The awards are a fraction of what a jury would award. The attorneys' fees awards are a fraction of what a court would award. It is not quicker. It is not more efficient. It's just unfair."

Approximately 5 percent of respondents report mandatory arbitration clauses have a positive effect of some level on their willingness to represent clients or invest resources in a case. A partner at a small Illinois employment firm expressed this minority viewpoint: "I have not had to turn down a case due to an arbitration clause. Instead, I have found the existence of the clause to be more useful in getting cases resolved quickly and helping my clients move on with their lives."

Suggesting several explanations for their aversion to accepting arbitration cases, attorneys hold negative perceptions of arbitration's effect on the fairness of outcomes, the fairness of proceedings, and the adequacy of discovery, with relatively few reporting as undecided. Again, only approximately 5 percent of respondents indicate mandatory arbitration has a positive effect at any level on any of these items. This is consistent with previous findings and continues to expose attorneys' negative perceptions of arbitration, which is seen as a potential impediment to employee access to justice.

Despite the widely held perception that arbitration is quicker and more efficient than traditional litigation, attorneys are ambivalent about the effects arbitration clauses have on the expediency of proceedings. This item produced the greatest variation, splitting attorney responses nearly in thirds. Concerning expediency, 40 percent of attorneys view arbitration as having a *negative* effect, a quarter are undecided, and 35 percent view arbitration as having a positive effect. Respondents who indicate a negative effect on employer willingness to settle are significantly more likely to report a negative effect on expediency, suggesting a possible explanation.

Furthermore, several respondents indicate that they are unaware of the existence of arbitration clauses until after they file a claim in civil court when defendants file a motion to compel arbitration. While the arbitration hearing itself may be faster than litigation, attorneys learning about such clauses late in the process can ultimately have a negative impact on the expediency of the entire process, suggesting another possible explanation. One attorney who perceived arbitration as having a "Very Negative" effect on expediency provides an illustrative example:

> where the client did not remember signing the arbitration agreement and I did not recognize the employer previously as using them. It puts a real damper on the proceedings when we discover the agreement and makes it hard to proceed with the negotiation, litigation, ADR, or even with client relations.

This confusion may also be related to the large number of "Undecided" responses (42 percent) to the item indicating arbitration's effect on their own willingness to settle.

Existing scholarship merely establishes a correlation between arbitration and inferior win rates and award amounts, low rates of settlement, and violations of due process (Clermont & Schwab, 2004; Colvin, 2011; Eisenberg & Hill, 2003; Gough, 2014). Yet respondents clearly report that arbitration has an independent negative effect on their willingness to accept clients and view arbitration clauses as discouraging employer willingness to settle, diminishing certain aspects of procedural and distributive justice, and, for some, creating a longer, less-efficient process. Where arbitration frustrates employee attempts to attain legal counsel, as implied in multiple measures above, the forum acts to restrict, rather than expand, access to justice. Indeed, if these results are representative of the general population of plaintiff-side employment attorneys, and not an artifact of sampling bias, pervasive claims of arbitration's accessibility are untenable.

Having described attorney characteristics and their perceptions of arbitration, I proceed to analyze attributes of the general population of employment disputes in arbitration and litigation to supplement the findings above and further investigate whether arbitration better accommodates the needs of low-income and low-value claimants.

## Arbitration Claimant and Claim Characteristics

This section uses the data from the NELA survey in conjunction with the five arbitration providers (Provider Reports) and the federal docket (AO) data to evaluate the degree to which employment arbitration provides an accessible forum to low-income and low-value claimants. Accessibility can be evaluated using multiple measures and along multiple dimensions. I specifically report employee claimant salaries, monetary claim amounts, and the volume of cases filed in arbitration and litigation to explore whether arbitration ameliorates limitations of the litigation system or whether it is equally or even more limited in its accessibility.

As in previous studies of arbitration case characteristics, the data presented below do not allow a comparison of systematically matched cases between the forums. Basic descriptive statistics, however, illuminate the general contours of the arbitration and litigation forums and provide another basis from which to assess the themes developed above. Furthermore, the data analyzed here provide a more comprehensive and contemporary analysis of employment disputes than has been available previously.

The greatest promise of arbitration rests in its potential to provide a cheaper, faster, and more informal forum for employment disputes. It has been well documented that those with low salaries and low-value claims are not granted access to traditional courts (Estreicher, 2001; Nelson, Nielsen & Lancaster, 2010; Sandefur, 2015). If arbitration is a more accessible forum for low-value claims and claimants with low salaries, we would expect to see evidence of this in the attributes of arbitration claims filings. I begin by examining the salary range of employees in arbitration, using both the provider database and arbitration data described in the NELA survey, and litigation, using only the litigated cases described in the NELA survey. Regrettably, the AO does not report or collect data on the salary level of claimants involved in employment disputes. Results are presented in Table 5.

Within employment arbitration cases in the five arbitration provider disclosures covering 2009 through 2013, only JAMS and AAA report claimant salary level. Furthermore, of the 7,865 JAMS and AAA claims, salary data is present in only 2,784 observations. It is missing for the remaining 5,081

*Table 5.* Distribution of Employee Salaries, by Forum and Data Source.

| Salary Range | Provider Reports | NELA Survey | |
| --- | --- | --- | --- |
| | Arbitration (%) | Arbitration (%) | Litigation (%) |
| >$100,000 | 79 | 69 | 84 |
| $100,000–250,000 | 14 | 31 | 16 |
| <$250,000 | 7 | | |

cases, or 64.6 percent of the data. Of the 35.4 percent observations included, 79 percent of employees earned salaries of $100,000 or less, 14 percent earned between $100,000 and $250,000, and 7 percent earned more than $250,000 a year. The fact that a large majority of employee claimants earned less than $100,000 a year suggests accessibility. However, those with high incomes (salaries over $100,000) appeared in arbitration at nearly three times the rate found in the distribution of incomes nationwide (IRS, 2015). Without having the equivalent population data of employee salary in federal courts, it is difficult to assess arbitration's accessibility relative to the courts using the provider reports.

The 277 and 543 arbitrated and litigated cases from the NELA survey suggest, however, that it actually is litigation that is the more accessible forum for low-salaried plaintiffs. Attorneys were asked to report whether, in their most recently arbitrated and litigated cases taken to verdict, their employee client's salary was "less than $100,000" or "$100,000 or more." In arbitration, 191, or 69 percent, of employee claimants had salaries of less than $100,000 while 86, or 31 percent, had incomes of $100,000 or more. In the 543 litigated cases described by NELA members, 84 percent earned less than $100,000 a year while 16 percent earned $100,000 or more. This difference is statistically ($p < .01$) and practically significant.

Low-income plaintiffs make up a *smaller* proportion of cases taken to verdict in arbitration by NELA members. Although, as noted above, the data presented cannot control for the potential for systematic differences between arbitrated and litigated case filings, the observed relationship is consistent with attorney responses indicating arbitration is not conducive to low-value claims and represents a gap that should be explained.

Like employee salaries, if arbitration is conducive to low-value claims and low-income claimants, we would expect to see this reflected in claiming statistics. Table 6 offers comparisons of claim amounts registered in

***Table 6.*** Claim Amounts (2,015$).

|  | Provider Reports (Arbitration) 2009–2013 | AO Data (Federal Docket) 2009–2013 | NELA Survey | |
| --- | --- | --- | --- | --- |
|  |  |  | Arbitration | Litigation |
| Mean ($) | 841,396 | 534,000 | 1,860,059 | 923,820 |
| Median ($) | 250,000 | 113,000 | 300,000 | 250,000 |
| 25th ($) | 95,719 | 63,000 | 132,500 | 100,000 |

employment disputes found in the Provider Reports, the NELA survey data, separated into arbitrated and litigated samples, and the AO data.

With respect to the universe of employment claims administered by the five largest arbitration providers, the mean dollar amount claimed was $841,396, the median value claimed was $250,000, and the 25th percentile value was $95,719. Only 12 percent of cases in the database consisted of a claim for less than $50,000. Of all the cases disposed on the federal docket between 2009 and 2013, the mean amount claimed was $534,000, the median amount claimed was $113,000, and the 25th percentile value was $63,000. Of cases filed in federal court between 2009 and 2013, 20 percent involved claims of less than $50,000. Turning to the cases described by NELA members, the same distinct pattern is observed: at the mean, median, and 25th percentile, claims made in arbitration are larger than claims in litigation. If we use claims below $50,000 as an additional indicator of accessibility, such claims represent just 3.5 percent of claims tried by NELA members in arbitration but 10 percent of claims tried in litigation.

Here again, this relationship — that arbitration claim amounts are higher at all levels than claims made in court — is not what one would expect if arbitration was fulfilling its potential to provide an accessible forum. If arbitration is more accessible than litigation to low-value claims, what is causing this gap? There may be systematic differences between the population of employees filing in the two forums, perhaps with respect to industry, occupation, geography, or employer policies, which may explain all or part of the observed difference in claim amounts. However, in an absolute sense, the small percentage of cases claiming less than $50,000 found in the universe of employment cases filed with the five largest arbitration providers indicates arbitration is not available or not being used for low-value claims.

Finally, Table 7 presents a final measure of accessibility of a dispute resolution forum, the volume of claims filed.

Table 7 shows that nearly 18 times more cases are filed in federal court than in arbitration. Between 2009 and 2013, 156,973 employment claims were filed in federal court; that is an average of 31,395 per year. Employment arbitration cases administered by the five largest providers

***Table 7.*** Volume of Filings, by Forum.

| Provider Reports (Arbitration) 2009–2013 | AO Data (Federal Docket) 2009–2013 |
|---|---|
| 8,815 | 156,973 |

(AAA, JAMS, ADR, ARC, Judicate West) over this same period totaled 8,815, or an average of 1,763 per year. It is important to reiterate that the five providers cover approximately 83 percent of privately administered employment arbitrations nationwide, producing a slight underestimation of the volume of mandatory arbitration filings nationwide (Colvin & Gough, 2014).

Notwithstanding continued concerns over selection effects, the volume of cases filed in arbitration has little meaning without knowing the coverage rate of arbitration and putting it in context. Determining the coverage rate of mandatory arbitration is difficult, however. To date, Colvin (2004) has produced the best estimates from his study of the telecommunications industry. He reports that 14 percent of telecommunications firms studied indicated they used mandatory arbitration procedures. When adjustments were made for the size of the workforce, almost 23 percent of the nonunion workforce was covered. The NELA and CELA survey data provide another estimate of the coverage rate of mandatory arbitration agreements: based on 1,130 attorney responses, the average estimate of the coverage rate of arbitration is 20 percent.[14]

While approximately 20 percent of employees are covered by arbitration agreements, only a disproportionate few end up pursuing arbitration. Indeed, these calculations can be refined, most notably by factoring in the number of cases filed in state courts or by making adjustments based on public sector employment or unionization rates. However, given the magnitude of the difference between the estimated coverage rate and the percentage of claims being filed in arbitration, adjustments to this equation are unlikely to change the substantive interpretation of the relationship.

## CONCLUSION

The purpose of this research was to gain insight into the attributes of employment attorneys and investigate the claim that employment arbitration is an accessible, albeit imperfect, forum. The evidence examined here suggests such claims are aspirational. In light of the data presented on the institutional characteristics of members of the largest employment plaintiff attorney organization in the country, their perceptions of arbitration, and the full caseloads of recent employment disputes resolved in several arbitral and litigation forums, the picture that emerges is one in which obtaining legal representation is harder for those covered under arbitration clauses while low-value claims and low-income claimants fail to materialize.

In a regime centered on individual enforcement of statutory and contractual employment rights, competent attorney representation is essential. Plaintiff attorneys are vested with "the keys to the courthouse," and effectively decide who gains access to justice. In this respect, the data on attorney characteristics are in line with the narrative presented by arbitration proponents. Attorneys reject between 80 and 90 percent of prospective employees that come to them seeking representation. Hourly fee arrangements are rarely offered and outside the means of most workers. Pro bono or government assistance is likewise exceedingly rare. Therefore, where employees cannot attract legal counsel under contingency fees, the principle avenue to legal remedies is cut off.

The average minimal case value attorneys will accept on contingency is $56,000, surprisingly similar to the unadjusted $60,000 minimum damage requirement provided by Howard (1995) 20 years ago, but nearly half Howard's estimate if adjusted for inflation. Where awards are based primarily on back pay and lost wages, this requirement prevents the majority of employees with low incomes from access to representation. This is particularly true in arbitration given the infrequency of attorneys' fee awards and relatively modest award amounts and win rates (Colvin, 2011; Colvin & Gough, 2015; Colvin & Pike, 2014). However, relying on the nationwide mean ignores state-level variance and the range of requirements within states. A quarter of attorneys report minimum damage requirements at or below $20,000, and a larger proportion of attorneys in several states are amenable to even lower value claims. Through this lens, the current enforcement regime may not be nearly as exclusionary as popularly envisaged.

Overall, these results validate arbitration proponents' description of the civil litigation system's flaws. The courts, proponents, and opponents agree that employees experience difficulties accessing justice. However, rather than facilitating employee access, the data consistently suggest arbitration forestalls employee access to justice. Attorneys consistently report negative perceptions of arbitration: a majority says it has a positive impact on their willingness to reject a case for representation and a negative impact on their willingness to accept a client under a contingency fee arrangement. They report negative perceptions of the fairness of outcomes and the adequacy of due process protections, and the creation of a longer, less-efficient process for some employees. Furthermore, the acceptance rates for employees covered by arbitration agreements are half that for employees able to sue in court. Multiple measures demonstrate employment lawyers hold negative views of arbitration and are less willing to represent employees covered under such clauses.

The analysis of the population of employment cases filed with the five largest mandatory employment arbitration providers in the nation and federal court, while far from definitive, reveals relationships that are consistent with the attorney survey results. The data reveal a relatively low volume of filings and a lower proportion of low-income claims and low-value claimants in arbitration than in litigation. This is consistent with attorney reports of more stringent acceptance standards imposed on arbitration claimants, but could also be explained by systematic differences between cases filed in the two forums.

It should be reiterated that NELA and CELA member responses may not be representative of the general population of plaintiff-side employment lawyers. While certain attributes of sampled attorneys, such as the size and type of firm they work at, overlap with population statistics of all lawyers nationwide (Carson, 2012), because they self-select into NELA or CELA membership, these attorneys' views and experiences with arbitration may not be generalizable. Still, this study provides valuable insight into the two largest plaintiff-side employment attorney organizations in the country.

I caution against interpreting these findings as a wholesale endorsement of the civil litigation system. Certainly, as the court and supporters of arbitration suggest, with or without arbitration, the doors of the courtroom remain securely shut to many, if not the majority, of employees with work-related grievances. Employees must still traverse their insecurities about publically classifying themselves as a victim (Bumiller, 1987), public agencies are out of reach or ineffectual (Glover, 2012), many cannot afford to pay for attorney representation out of pocket (Nelson, Nielsen & Lancaster 2011), and apparent hostility to employment claims — especially those alleging discrimination — from judges themselves (Clermont & Schwab, 2004, 2009). Even when employee plaintiffs are granted access to their day in court, proceed through trial, and receive a ruling in their favor, as Berrey, Hoffman, and Nielsen (2012) report, employees lament "the institutional barriers they faced in securing competent legal assistance, the devastating toll of litigation on their financial and emotional well-being, and the lack of a clear resolution to their original workplace grievance."

Likewise, these findings do not invalidate the *potential* for arbitration to provide an accessible forum. As with any dispute resolution forum, the characteristics of employment arbitration may differ in the procedural rules of the proceeding and in whether outcomes are binding, the process is mandatory or voluntary, and class actions are allowed to advance, and in what provider administers the proceeding. The analysis presented here focuses on binding, pre-dispute mandatory employment arbitration, but alternative arbitration regimes exist in theory and practice. So while the relationships identified in this analysis suggest arbitration is not serving the needs of low-income claimants or their attorneys and may have an undeserved reputation for accessibility, it is possible that other types of arbitration realize these potentials.

## NOTES

1. After the Supreme Court's decision in *14 Penn Plaza LLC v. Pyett*, 556 U.S. 247 (2009), mandatory arbitration clauses are also enforceable when clearly enunciated in collective bargaining agreements. These so-called *Pyett* cases are outside the scope of this analysis given the vast differences between their institutional context and that of nonunion employment arbitration.

2. An investigation did not reveal significant differences between online and mailed responses in the data reported herein.

3. The number of cases described is not equal to the number of responses received because a large minority of attorneys had not taken a claim to verdict in either forum within the last five years. In both arbitration and litigation, the majority of cases are disposed prior to a trial verdict (Clermont & Schwab, 2004; Colvin & Gough, 2015). Furthermore, only mandatory pre-dispute arbitration cases are analyzed; arbitrations proceeding under voluntary/individually negotiated, post-dispute, and non-binding clauses are excluded from this analysis.

4. While the FMCS and FINRA provide arbitration services, neither fits the given definition of employment arbitration. The FMCS almost exclusively provides arbitration services in labor disputes, and employment discrimination claims are currently excluded from the mandatory arbitration requirement under FINRA rules (Lamare & Lipsky, 2014).

5. Employment-related cases are defined as claims under the FLSA, Title VII of the Civil Rights Act (CRA) of 1964, the ADA, the ADEA, the FMLA, the Equal Pay Act (EPA) of 1963, §1983 of the Civil Rights Act of 1871, and §1981 of the Civil Rights Act of 1866, The Occupational Safety and Health Act (OSHA), and ERISA.

6. Montana is the only state from which we did not receive a response. This may reflect the unique employment regulation regime in Montana, the only state in the United States to have broadly amended the employment-at-will doctrine.

7. Non-profit, government, and lawyers specializing in class actions were excluded from this analysis.

8. The precise question presented read: "With regard to employment-related claims, with the exception of pro bono cases, what is the approximate minimal size

of matter (based on potential settlement value or total damages including attorney fees) that you are likely to accept for representation?"

9. The precise question presented read: "What is your usual hourly rate?"

10. The precise questions read: "Of potential clients who contact you with employment-related claims covered under a mandatory pre-dispute arbitration clause, approximately what percentage do you accept for representation? (If you have no experience with mandatory arbitration clauses, please leave blank)" and "Of potential clients who contact you with employment-related claims to be heard in civil court or a government agency, approximately what percentage do you accept for representation?"

11. A second version of this question (along with an inverted scale) was randomly interchanged with the one presented here and read, "How likely are you to accept a prospective client despite the following?" There were no differences between the distributions or interpretations of results between these two versions.

12. Non-profit, government, and lawyers specializing in class actions were excluded from this analysis.

13. See Note 12.

14. The precise question is as follows: "Of potential clients who contact you with employment-related claims, approximately what percentage is covered under mandatory pre-dispute arbitration clauses?"

# REFERENCES

Berrey, E., Hoffman, S., & Nielsen, L. B. (2012). Situated justice: Plaintiffs' and defendants' perceptions of fairness in employment civil rights cases. *Law and Society Review, 46*, 1–36.

Bingham, L. B. (1997). Employment arbitration: The repeat player effect. *Employee Rights and Employment Policy Journal, 1*, 189.

Blasi, G., & Doherty, J. W. (2011). California employment discrimination law and its enforcement: The fair employment and housing act at 50. *UCLA-Rand Center for Law & Public Policy, 11*, 1–64.

Budd, J., & Colvin, A. J. S. (2012). Improved metrics for workplace dispute resolution procedures: Efficiency, equity, and voice. *Industrial Relations: A Journal of Economy and Society, 47*(3), 460–479.

Bumiller, K. (1987). Victims in the shadow of the law: A critique of the model of legal protection. *Signs, 12*(3), 421–439.

Carson, C. N. (2012). The lawyer statistical report: The U.S. legal profession in 2005. Report by American Bar Foundation.

Clermont, K. J., & Schwab, S. J. (2004). How employment discrimination plaintiffs fare in federal court. *Journal of Empirical Legal Studies, 1*, 429.

Clermont, K. J., & Schwab, S. J. (2009). Employment discrimination plaintiffs in federal courts: From bad to worse? *Harvard Law and Policy Review, 2*, 08–022.

Colvin, A. J. (2014). Mandatory arbitration and inequality of justice in employment. *Berkeley Journal of Employment and Labor Law, 35*, 71.

Colvin, A. J., & Gough, M. (2014). *Comparing mandatory arbitration and litigation: Access, process, and outcomes.* Research report to National Employment Lawyers Association.

Colvin, A. J., & Gough, M. D. (2015). Individual employment rights arbitration in the United States actors and outcomes. *ILR Review, 68*(5), 1019–1042.

Colvin, A. J. S. (2004). Adoption and use of dispute resolution procedures in the nonunion workplace. Advances in industrial and labor relations, *13*, 71–97.

Colvin, A. J. S. (2011). An empirical study of employment arbitration: Case outcomes and processes. *Journal of Empirical Legal Studies, 8*(1), 1–23.

Colvin, A. J. S. (2012). American workplace dispute resolution in the individual rights era. *International Journal of Human Resource Management, 23*(3), 459–475.

Colvin, A. J. S., & Pike, K. (2014). Saturns and rickshaws revisited: What kind of employment arbitration system has developed? *Ohio State Journal on Dispute Resolution, 29*, 59.

Curran, B. A. (1977). *The legal needs of the public: The final report of a national survey* (pp. 152–156). Chicago, IL: American Bar Foundation.

Dunlop, J. (1958). *Industrial relations systems.* Cambridge, MA: Harvard University Press.

Eisenberg, T. (1988). Litigation models and trial outcomes in civil rights and prisoner cases. *Georgetown Law Journal, 77*, 1567.

Eisenberg, T., & Hill, E. (2003). Arbitration and litigation of employment claims: An empirical comparison. *Dispute Resolution Journal, 58*(4), 44–54.

Estreicher, S. (2001). Saturns for rickshaws: The stakes in the debate over predispute employment arbitration decisions. *Ohio State Journal on Dispute Resolution, 16*, 559.

Equal Employment Opportunity Commission (EEOC). (2016). *EEOC litigation statistics.* Retrieved from https://www.eeoc.gov/eeoc/statistics/enforcement/litigation.cfm. Accessed on June 23, 2016.

Farhang, S. (2009). The political development of job discrimination litigation, 1963–1976. *Studies in American Political Development, 23*, 24.

Felstiner, W. L. F., Abel, R. L., & Sarat, A. (1980). The emergence and transformation of disputes: Naming, blaming, claiming …. *Law & Society Review, 15*, 631–654.

Galanter, M. (1974). Why the "Haves" come out ahead: Speculations on the limits of legal change. *Law and Society Review, 9*(1), 95–160.

Galanter, M. (1976). Delivering legality: Some proposals for the direction of research. *Law and Society Review, 11*, 225–246.

Glover, M. J. (2012). The structural role of private enforcement mechanisms in public law. *William & Mary Law Review, 53*, 1137.

Gough, M. (2014). The high costs of an inexpensive forum: An empirical analysis of employment discrimination claims heard in arbitration and civil litigation. *Berkeley Journal of Employment and Labor Law, 35*(2), 91–112.

Howard, W. M. (1995). Arbitrating claims of employment discrimination: What really does happen? What really should happen? *Dispute Resolution Journal, 50*(4), 40–50.

Internal Revenue Service (IRS). (2015). *Individual statistical tables by size of adjusted gross income.* Retrieved from https://www.irs.gov/uac/soi-tax-stats-individual-statistical-tables-by-size-of-adjusted-gross-income. Accessed on June 23, 2016.

Kritzer, H. M. (1997, July–August). Contingency fee lawyers as gatekeepers in the American civil justice system. *Judicature, 81*, 22.

Kritzer, H. M. (2004). *Risks, reputations, and rewards: Contingency fee legal practice in the United States.* Stanford, CA: Stanford University Press.

Lamare, R., & Lipsky, D. (2014). Employment arbitration in the securities industry: Lessons drawn from recent empirical research. *Berkeley Journal of Employment and Labor Law, 35*(2), 113–133.

Lipsky, D., Seeber, R., & Fincher, R. (2003). Emerging systems for managing workplace conflict: Lessons from American corporation for managers and dispute resolution professionals.

Mongoven, K. M. (2004). Impact of contingency fee agreements on reasonable attorney fees awarded pursuant to Wisconsin fee-shifting statutes. *Marquette Law Review, 88*, 1013.

National Employment Lawyers Association (NELA). (2016). *Who we are*. Retrieved from https://www.nela.org. Accessed on June 23, 2016.

Nelson, R. L., Nielsen, L. B., & Lancaster, R. (2010). Individual justice or collective legal mobilization? Employment discrimination litigation in post-civil rights United States. *Journal of Empirical Legal Studies, 7*, 175–201.

Nielsen, L. B., & Nelson, R. L. (2005). Scaling the pyramid: A sociolegal model of employment discrimination litigation. In *Handbook of employment discrimination research* (pp. 3–34). Netherlands: Springer.

Oppenheimer, D. B. (2003). Verdicts matter: An empirical study of California employment discrimination and wrongful discharge jury verdicts reveals low success rates for women and minorities. *UC Davis Law Review, 37*, 535–549.

Piore, M., & Safford, S. (2006). Changing regimes of workplace governance, shifting axes of social mobilization and the challenge to industrial relations theory. *Industrial Relations, 45*(3), 299–325.

Resnick, J. (2015). Diffusing disputes: The public in the private of arbitration, the private in courts, and the erasure of rights. *Yale Law Journal, 124*, 2804.

Sandefur, R. (2008). Access to civil justice and race, class, and gender inequality. *Annual Review of Sociology, 34*, 339–358.

Sandefur, R. (2015). Elements of professional expertise: Understanding relational and substantive expertise through lawyers' impact. *American Sociological Review, 80*, 909–933.

Selmi, M. (1997). Public vs. private enforcement of civil rights: The case of housing and employment. *UCLA Law Review, 45*, 1401.

Sherwyn, D., Tracey, J. B., & Eigen, Z. J. (1999). In defense of mandatory arbitration of employment disputes: Saving the baby, tossing out the bath water and constructing a new sink in the process. *University of Pennsylvania Journal of Labor and Employment Law, 2*, 73.

St. Antoine, T. J. (2008). Mandatory arbitration: Why it's better than it looks. *University of Michigan Journal of Law Reform, 41*(4), 783–812.

Sternlight, J. (2015). Disarming employees: How American employers are using mandatory arbitration to deprive workers of legal protection. *Brooklyn Law Review, 80*, 1309.

Stipanowich, T. J., & Lamare, J. R. (2014). Living with ADR: Evolving perceptions and use of mediation, arbitration, and conflict management in fortune 1000 corporations. *Harvard Negotiation Law Journal, 1*, 152–194.

Stone, K. V. W. (1996). Mandatory arbitration of individual employment rights: The yellow dog contract of the 1990s. *Denver University Law Review, 73*, 1017.

Weil, D. (1997). Implementing employment regulation: Insights on the determinants of regulatory performance. In B. E. Kaufman (Ed.), *Government regulation of the employment relationship* (pp. 429–474). Champaign, IL: Industrial Relations Research Association.

# FURTHER READINGS

Mitsubishi Motors v. Soler Chrysler-Plymouth, Inc., 473 U.S. 614 (1985).
Gilmer v. Interstate/Johnson Lane Corp., 500 U.S. 20 (1991).
Circuit City Stores, Inc. v. Adams, 532 U.S. 105 (2001).
14 Penn Plaza LLC v. Pyett, 556 U.S. 247 (2009).

# BEYOND REPEAT PLAYERS: EXPERIENCE AND EMPLOYMENT ARBITRATION OUTCOMES IN THE SECURITIES INDUSTRY

J. Ryan Lamare

## ABSTRACT

Purpose — *This chapter analyzes the extent to which more experienced employers, arbitrators, and attorneys fare better in securities industry arbitration. Although studies into experience have identified a so-called repeat-player effect on outcomes, I argue that more nuanced considerations of experience are required.*

Methodology/approach — *I empirically analyze all employment arbitration awards from the securities system's inception through 2008. I separate experience into two categories (between- and within-group effects) and run hybrid random- and fixed-effects regressions modeling increasing employer, attorney, and arbitrator experience on arbitration outcomes.*

Findings — *I find that between-group experience affects awards but that within-group experience is nonsignificant, except in civil rights cases. This implies that so-called repeat players gain an advantage over*

Managing and Resolving Workplace Conflict
Advances in Industrial and Labor Relations, Volume 22, 135—160
ISSN: 0742-6186/doi:10.1108/S0742-618620160000022006

*inexperienced players due to their entity-specific characteristics, not necessarily by learning to use the system to their advantage. I conclude that, although the securities arbitration system suffers from power imbalances, there is little evidence of systemic exploitation by firms.*

Originality/value — *Prior studies into employment arbitration are limited both by their definitions of experience and by their methodological approaches. I overcome these issues by employing a novel methodological approach to measure between- and within-entity experience, which adds a more multifaceted and nuanced framework to the literature than the common repeat-player versus single-player dichotomy.*

**Keywords:** Employment arbitration; repeat player effects; securities industry; hybrid-effects model; FINRA

Research assessing the adequacy of employment arbitration in resolving employment disputes has raised the possibility that parties who engage in arbitration the most enjoy inherent advantages over parties who use the system only once. Although a number of attempts to measure the effects of experience on employment arbitration outcomes have been made, several gaps remain. Studies into the subject face methodological concerns in that they use truncated samples, relying on limited models of repetition and awards, and omit factors that might confound the findings. In particular, research has failed thus far to adequately control for employer characteristics that might correlate with both experience and outcomes, assuming instead that correlations between employer repetition and arbitrator awards are sufficiently determinative of a so-called repeat-player effect. Theoretical concerns emerge as well, in that the literature tends to view private workplace dispute systems monolithically, rarely considering the likelihood that heterogeneity within and across systems may also affect outcomes.

This chapter aims to fill several of these theoretical and methodological gaps. I analyze a longitudinal panel of all employment arbitration decisions rendered within the securities industry by the Financial Industry Regulatory Authority (FINRA) over the period 1989–2008, reflecting claims made between 1986 and 2007.[1] I model experience using a hybrid approach that distinguishes between aggregate experience and individual case-by-case deviations from the aggregate. In doing so, I am able to isolate the effects of both within-entity and between-entity variations in experience, which allows for a more nuanced account of how so-called repeat players should be appropriately defined. I consider not only employer and arbitrator experience but also the experience levels of employee and employer attorneys. Finally, I model the extent to which experience effects are subject to heterogeneity depending on the type of dispute at hand (i.e., allegations of civil rights violations vs. allegations of contractual violations). The results have implications not only for the academic community, but also potentially for policy interpretation: judges have raised concerns, for instance, that securities industry employer repetition creates a biased and imbalanced situation and have drawn on these concerns when issuing awards (see, for instance, *Wells Fargo Advisors, LLC, v. Watts*, 5:11cv48).

## THEORIES OF REPETITION

The most useful framework under which experience is assigned value in arbitration comes from research into so-called repeat-player effects, which was first formally conceptualized by Galanter (1974). Galanter argued that in any legal system, repeat players garner advantages over single-shot players for several reasons: repeat players are more knowledgeable about the forum in which they operate, having been there before; they have access to specialists on the issue; they are able to develop informal institutional relationships; they are viewed as more committed to certain bargaining positions; they are able to take more risks; they can use their influence to lobby for favorable rules; and they are more likely to invest greater resources in order to affect the rules. On the other hand, one-shot players have more to lose; may employ risk-averse strategies; have no interest in long-term gains or relationships; are unconcerned with precedent and future rule changes; have no institutional relationship; have no knowledge-experience base from which to draw; and have lesser access to advocates who are experts on the issue (Bingham, 1997, citing Galanter, 1974). This, according to Galanter, contributes to a legal system in which the "haves" (typically, large, well-resourced firms) enjoy significant advantages over the "have nots" (typically, aggrieved individuals).

Galanter's repeat-player theory was first applied to the employment arbitration sphere by Bingham (1997, 1998b), who determined that employers involved in multiple arbitration cases fared better than those engaging in only a single case. In explaining this finding, Bingham suggested several reasons related to arbitration policy distinctions between single-shot players and repeat players, including the possibility that experienced repeat players could more easily identify and settle unwinnable cases. Bingham also suggested that pro-employer bias might exist within employment arbitration, where arbitrators would favor firms in order to gain future business. These results have been methodologically challenged on grounds related to sample size and sample truncation, however, in addition to concerns that the findings of arbitrator bias may be conflated with many other factors, including employer size, experience, and institutional memory (Colvin, 2011; Hill, 2003; Sherwyn, Estreicher, & Heise, 2005).

More recent work on the issue (Colvin, 2011; Colvin & Gough, 2015) overcomes many of these problems. These studies employ larger samples, broader time frames, and more nuanced analyses of possible employer-arbitrator biases. Although correlations between experience and awards emerge within these studies, consideration is given to the likelihood that experience effects might be serving to proxy for employer size, echoing a portion of Galanter's theory on repetition. Larger employers are more likely to repeat. These firms may also enjoy certain advantages (resource availability, legal expertise, and knowledge of the arbitral forum), may adopt HR practices that ensure fairer employment decisions, and may be more likely to settle meritorious cases using internal grievance systems. Therefore, any between-firm experience correlations might occur as a result of firm characteristics, not systemic biases.

These studies also find a smaller, but still significant, repeat employer-arbitrator effect (where employers selecting the same arbitrator multiple times tend to receive favorable outcomes). These results are claimed to indicate arbitrator bias, attributable to both arbitrators' hope for future business by employers, and also to repeat firms' greater expertise in selecting pro-employer arbitrators. Normatively, the possibility that experienced employers select the same arbitrator repeatedly in order to receive better outcomes raises significant concerns and calls into question the equity aspects of employment arbitration systems.

Even in light of recent empirical research into the subject, several issues surrounding the effects of experience on arbitration outcomes remain unresolved. First, all repeat-player studies have faced problems of sample truncation. Without being able to study an arbitration system from its inception, the data used to analyze repetition effects cannot ensure that parties identified as single-shot players did not participate in cases within the system prior to the time frame chosen for analysis. Second, many studies on repetition have treated the key independent variable in only a dichotomized manner. All repeat players are treated equally when measured against those who do not repeat. Thus, an employer entering into arbitration twice over some time period is given equivalence to a firm appearing, say, 50 times within the same forum. Third, problems persist with operationalizing the dependent variable. Most empirical research (for exceptions see Colvin, 2011; Colvin & Gough, 2015) has measured only the total monetary amounts awarded and dichotomized "win-loss" outcomes, where any value over zero counts as a victory for employees. As Colvin (2011) notes, this is an extremely narrow definition of what might constitute a win for one side and a loss for another, with little justification for this method of modeling arbitrator behavior.

Fourth, a major concern with the literature is one of omitted variables. Many confounding factors that might affect both repetition and outcomes remain unaccounted for within previous studies. For instance, although scholars suggest that access to expert lawyers may explain the repeat-player results, the literature has rarely accounted for attorney effects. Crucially, all studies on the subject suffer from an inability to model the influence of such individual employer characteristics as the company's size and culture, which, as noted, have been argued to proxy for repetition effects. Many of these omitted variable concerns arise from methodological tendencies either to rely on cross-sectional data or to take less than full advantage of longitudinal data.

This study overcomes many of these issues and, in doing so, provides the most thorough analysis to date of experience effects on employment arbitration.[2] For one, I have a non-truncated universe constituting all decisions rendered within the FINRA employment arbitration system since its inception. For another, I am able to consider degrees of experience; I treat experience continuously according to the date of the case. This allows me to account for the effects of increasing units of experience on arbitration outcomes. I account for the effects of attorney experience on awards, which allows me to test whether employees can counterbalance employer experience by hiring experienced attorneys. I include in the model what I believe is the most comprehensive array of factors that might also affect outcomes to date, including claim size, party gender, location, year, case complexity, allegations, and indirect measures of case strength.

Finally, my methodological approach incorporates both fixed and random effects for employers, arbitrators, and attorneys, which allows me to isolate within-group experience effects uniquely from between-group experience effects. This distinguishes the study from prior work in that I am able to isolate mean entity-by-entity experience results, which are likely instruments for time-invariant characteristics (such as a company's size and institutional culture or an attorney's educational attainment or tenure). I measure these between-entity results distinctly from a single entity's deviation from its mean experience in any given case (the within-entity effect). The deviation from the mean can be thought of as the firm's (or attorney's, or arbitrator's) degree of learning within the system as the entity gains experience after conditioning on all time-variant and time-invariant effects listed previously. Operationalizing experience as a function of both characteristics and learning in this way provides a richer understanding of the extent to which repeat players are successful either because they learn to use the arbitration system to their advantage or because of system-exogenous factors like resources.

## MOTIVATION FOR STUDYING THE FINRA SYSTEM

Although it shares many commonalities with other conflict management systems, FINRA's approach to resolving securities industry disputes differs in key respects, and these differences make it worthy of study in its own right as a unique platform for resolving conflict. This is particularly true when one compares FINRA with the American Arbitration Association (AAA), the other major arbitration system to receive empirical scholarly attention in employment arbitration research thus far. System heterogeneity helps to explain why I expect arbitration awards under FINRA to vary in some respects relative to results found in previous employment arbitration studies incorporating AAA data (for instance, Colvin, 2011; Colvin & Gough, 2015).

For one, the FINRA system covers a different population of employees from other ADR programs. All registered securities employees are covered by the FINRA system: these are all individuals registered with the Securities and Exchange Commission (SEC) who are able to execute customers' buy-and-sell orders. These employees are required to arbitrate any disputes that might arise within this system as a condition of registering with the SEC, except in cases involving employment discrimination (Mandatory arbitration was a requirement for discrimination claims as well until 1999).

Other systems are broader in coverage. AAA, for example, administers arbitration services within an array of employment disputes. This makes AAA more representative of all workers (not merely those in a single industry), but it means that AAA competes with other private dispute resolution service providers for business, whereas FINRA operates as a monopolistic service provider. The only competition FINRA faces comes from the court system, when discrimination is alleged or from class-action lawsuits.

The most significant difference between FINRA and AAA, though, relates to arbitrator selection. Under the FINRA system, arbitrators are randomly assigned to cases (in earlier years, including the vast majority of those studied in this article, arbitrators followed a rotational pattern of case assignment). AAA follows a simpler striking and ranking system. The filing party gives AAA various criteria that the provider uses to populate a list of potentially acceptable arbitrators. After the disputants receive this list, unacceptable names are struck and the remaining group is ranked according to party preferences. Although this system has been modified slightly over the years and now includes two options, one of which involves AAA taking a more active role in helping to facilitate the selection process, the concept is largely the same as when it was first introduced in 1996. I maintain that AAA therefore gives the disputant parties considerably more control over the list formation and arbitrator selection process than does FINRA. Although this AAA pattern has many positives, one potential negative is that it more easily presents the opportunity for repeat parties (namely, employers) to be matched with the same arbitrator on multiple occasions. The FINRA system is less prone (though not immune) to this possibility.

## HYPOTHESES

The first expectation is that firms with greater mean levels of experience in the FINRA system should perform better than less-experienced companies (Hypothesis 1). As discussed, companies with more experience in a system are also likely to be larger, when compared against firms with less experience. A securities employer like Prudential averages far more arbitration cases than a small brokerage company, for instance, and I anticipate that the Prudentials of the world will perform better in securities arbitration than smaller firms because of their time-invariant characteristics.

It may also be the case that as an organization grows in experience within the FINRA system it will learn from its past experiences and will therefore improve its performance relative to its own prior cases

(Hypothesis 2). This view is predicated on the concept of organizational learning, which argues that firms learn from experiences as well as from their institutional characteristics (see Huber, 1991 as a starting point in this literature). Whereas Hypothesis 1 can be thought of as the *between-firm* effect of experience, Hypothesis 2 considers the *within-firm* effect of experience. A significant finding at the within-level of analysis would raise greater concerns regarding systemic bias in arbitration than would a significant between-level result. Large and well-resourced firms are likely to be more successful in any adjudicative environment simply because they can avail themselves of these resources when compared with other companies. However, if a firm can learn how to adapt to the arbitration system in such a way that it receives relative advantages as it enters into the system repeatedly, the system itself may be at least partially at fault for failing to provide a level playing field for all disputant parties.

The third expectation is that having access to more experienced counsel will benefit both employers and employees (Hypothesis 3). Similar to the treatment of firms, I decompose representation into between- and within-effects. Relative to less-experienced attorneys, those with more experience in FINRA might also have better reputations, might be more adept at handling arbitration complaints, and might have an array of resources upon which they can draw to get their clients the best deal possible. For instance, the most frequently used employee-side attorney in the sample is Jeffrey Liddle, a graduate of Cornell University's School of Industrial and Labor Relations and New York University's Law School and founding partner at Liddle & Robinson, LLP. Liddle has been featured prominently in books and newspaper articles detailing securities arbitration, and his website provides links to significant monetary awards he has won on behalf of clients in arbitration. It is expected that the Jeffrey Liddles within the sample will receive higher awards on average than an attorney with no prior experience in the FINRA system (this can be thought of as the between-attorney experience effect). If theories of learning apply to arbitration in the same way as they apply elsewhere, I would also anticipate that Jeffrey Liddle will improve his performance as he moves from his first FINRA case to his most recent one (this can be thought of as the within-attorney experience effect).

I also anticipate that arbitrators with more FINRA experience will award lower amounts to employees than arbitrators with less experience at both the between- and within-levels (Hypothesis 4). One argument for this expectation is that as arbitrators receive more cases under FINRA, they may be less prone to variance in their award amounts. Experienced arbitrators may have developed a consistent standard of proof or a clear threshold for case merit, for instance, while less-experienced arbitrators may be uncertain as to the appropriate standard or threshold. Since employee awards are always truncated at zero but have a conceivably infinite upper limit, greater variance in awards among inexperienced arbitrators may result in higher awards to employees.[3]

A less positive but equally plausible explanation for arbitrator experience effects would be that experienced arbitrators favor employers in order to signal to firms that they are employer-friendly or that these arbitrators continue to remain on the selection lists due to their more firm-favorable positions either within or outside the FINRA context. FINRA arbitrators earn relatively small amounts of money per case (currently around $300 per session), and it would be conceivable that an arbitrator might use FINRA as a platform upon which he or she might base a future, more lucrative practice outside the securities context. If this were the case, and similar companies used both FINRA and non-FINRA forums for arbitration, arbitrators might use FINRA as a low-cost mechanism by which they could signal their employer-friendly positions to clients in these other forums. If these arbitrators were effective in their signaling behavior, repeated selection in FINRA might proxy for the repeated selection of employer-friendly arbitrators in forums outside the FINRA context.

Though I am unable to directly test this signaling theory of arbitrator behavior, FINRA has in the past admitted to a perception that, under the rotational system used from its inception through the early 2000s, arbitrators appearing with greater frequency than others might be pro-employer. Indeed, the most experienced arbitrator in the sample, Robert D. Herschman, has been accused of industry bias (though it should be noted that these accusations stem from claimant-side lawyers). In a *Newsweek* article from 2004, a lawyer named Jacob Zamansky noted about Herschman, "There's no way [he] will hand a big award to [a claimant]. He's not going to bite the hand that feeds him" (Gasparino, 2004, quoting Zamansky, p. 56). If the Herschmans in the sample do indeed award more favorable outcomes to employers, this should be manifested in both the between- and within-effects. That is, more experienced arbitrators will on average be more employer favorable both relative to less-experienced arbitrators and to their own prior award behaviors.

A third and related rationale for this hypothesis relates to selection effects. FINRA makes its awards public. An effect of the publicizing of awards may be that, if an employer knows it is headed to arbitration with an arbitrator who has favored firms over employees in the past, it might be less willing to settle prior to award issuance, whereas the opposite would be true where a company faces a more employee-friendly or neutral arbitrator. I attempt to control for this possibility by including a measure of settlement in the models.

An additional consideration is that the same arbitrator and employer could function together multiple times. This has been used by previous studies, namely Bingham (1997) and Colvin (2011), as a way of measuring possible bias within employment arbitration. Both Bingham and Colvin found that, where employers and arbitrators are paired more than once, arbitrators are less likely to issue awards favorable to employees. Using matched employer-arbitrator pairs as a proxy for bias is problematic in the FINRA setting, however. Because of the system's closed nature, experienced employers and arbitrators might just as likely be paired simply because they enter into the FINRA system more frequently and therefore have a higher chance of being conjoined. This may indeed indicate bias, or it may indicate that a company like Prudential and an arbitrator like Robert Herschman frequently share common usage of the system but are not deliberately selecting each other multiple times. I therefore control for matched employer-arbitrator pairings but believe that, in the FINRA setting, assessing variation in the between- and within-level effects of experience is a more useful method for modeling different considerations of the role of experience in arbitration outcomes.

## DATA AND METHODS

To test the hypotheses, I turn to data consisting of all employment arbitration decisions rendered within the securities industry between 1988 and 2008. I model the dependent variable (arbitrator award) in three ways. First, I consider whether arbitrators found any merit at all in the employee's claim. This measure is binary (meritorious vs. non-meritorious) and includes all awards. Second, among meritorious cases only (i.e., nonzero awards), I consider both the total amount awarded to the employee and the percentage of claimed compensation awarded. Total award is deflated to 1991 dollars, and the percentage awarded includes only claimed compensation, which is typically tied to things like lost wages or back-pay owed.

The key independent variables are the experience levels of the respondent, the employee and employer attorneys, and the arbitrator. Each experience variable is measured continuously and is derived by creating a sequential count of matching names of individuals (or firms) by filing dates. I estimate the effects of experience both within and across subjects by introducing a modified random-effects (REs) model. Where traditional RE models capture a combined estimate of within- and between-subject effects in recording a single regression coefficient, the modified approach, sometimes called a hybrid model (Allison, 2009), partitions estimates into two distinct components. The within-subject estimates produce results that are similar to a fixed-effects (FE) model, but including these coefficients inside a broader RE framework allows for a less limiting analysis than the traditional FE approach (Bell & Jones, 2015).

In order to capture aggregate (between) and individual (within) experience effects, I produce two distinct values for each of these variables. The first takes the mean experience level of any given entity across all its cases and predicts variations in this mean score against outcomes. So, when looking at employer experience, a company like Prudential, the most frequent user of arbitration in the sample with 114 distinct outcomes over the 20-year period, would receive a mean experience score of 57.5 across all its cases. This mean score (and that for all other employer groups) is predicted against arbitration awards, with the expectation that companies averaging higher overall experience levels will perform better. The same approach is taken for attorneys and arbitrators to calculate their between-effects.

The second value produced is the within-subject experience effect, which controls for the time-invariant characteristics of the party of interest (employer, attorney, or arbitrator) and explores the effects of increasing experience within each entity. This measure is captured by taking the subject's experience level at any given arbitration point and subtracting from this value the subject's mean experience score. This produces a firm's deviation from its average, which varies from negative to positive across all its arbitration cases. So, returning to the Prudential example above, within-subject experience would range from −56.5 at Prudential's first case $(1 - 57.5 = -56.5)$ to 56.5 at its final case $(114 - 57.5 = 56.5)$. Again, the same method is applied within each employer, attorney, and arbitrator.

I also include controls for several other possible influences on outcomes. I condition all results on location, which accounts for uncodified geographic characteristics that might influence awards, as well as the possibility that disputants' choice of venue influenced outcomes (Choi & Eisenberg, 2010). A control for the number of hearing sessions enables me to consider complicated cases on the assumption that more complex claims are likely to involve a larger number of hearing sessions (Choi, Fisch, & Pritchard, 2014). I also include measures of case strength, including the initial amount demanded by the employee, whether punitive damages were claimed or awarded, any motions to dismiss, and requests for expungement of disciplinary records (Choi et al., 2014). I account for arbitrator professionalization by including a dichotomous measure identifying arbitrators licensed to practice law (Colvin, 2011; Colvin & Gough, 2015). Recent studies of employment arbitration in the securities industry have also offered that the charge brought against the employer may be influential on arbitration awards (Government Accountability Office, 2003; Lamare & Lipsky, 2015), as may personal characteristics of the parties (Lipsky, Lamare, & Gupta, 2013), so I include controls for allegation (discrimination claims, other statutory claims, or contractual claims) as well as employee, attorney, and arbitrator gender. Finally, I include year fixed effects in addition to location and employer fixed effects. Including year fixed effects accounts for changes made to the FINRA system and any other time-variant external influences on arbitrator behavior.

## DESCRIPTIVE RESULTS

Table 1 provides descriptive information for the key variables in the sample. Under FINRA, employees won at least some amount of damages in just over 60 percent of cases. This win rate comports with prior research into FINRA (Government Accountability Office, 1992, 2000) although it is higher than the 48.9 percent win rate found in Choi and Eisenberg's (2010) FINRA study. That study includes non-employment disputes, though. The win-rate figure matches well with previous employment arbitration studies by Howard (1995), Bingham (1998a), Bingham and Sarraf (2000), Eisenberg and Hill (2003), and Oppenheimer (2003), all of which find results higher than the 21.4 percent win rate reported by Colvin (2011), which uses AAA data. In total, employees successful in arbitration were awarded, on average, 37.2 percent of the amount they demanded. The mean monetary amount awarded to employees also fits with previous studies. On average, victorious employees received $189,190 in compensation using 1991 dollars. In an earlier study comparing securities industry arbitration awards with litigated outcomes, Delikat and Kleiner (2003) found a mean award of $236,292.

***Table 1.*** Counts, Findings of Merit, Compensation Ratios, and Award Amounts.

| | All Cases | | Meritorious Cases Only | |
| --- | --- | --- | --- | --- |
| | $N$ | Finding of merit (%) | Compensation ratio (%) | Amount awarded ($) |
| Total | 3,118 | 60.2 | 37.2 | 189,190 |
| *Employer experience in FINRA arbitration* | | | | |
| One | 1,016 | 67.0 | 43.6 | 109,992 |
| Two to nine | 983 | 62.2 | 37.0 | 240,219 |
| Ten to twenty-nine | 468 | 56.0 | 28.0 | 230,246 |
| Thirty to sixty-nine | 322 | 48.8 | 34.8 | 180,602 |
| Seventy or greater | 329 | 50.8 | 29.5 | 269,109 |
| *Employee attorney experience in FINRA arbitration* | | | | |
| One | 1,761 | 60.4 | 35.7 | 203,684 |
| Two to four | 470 | 61.9 | 32.0 | 150,683 |
| Five to nine | 116 | 66.4 | 24.9 | 206,136 |
| Ten or greater | 96 | 65.6 | 30.2 | 981,465 |
| *Employer attorney experience in FINRA arbitration* | | | | |
| One | 1,732 | 59.6 | 34.9 | 200,094 |
| Two to four | 728 | 59.5 | 34.1 | 168,655 |
| Five to nine | 195 | 52.3 | 28.0 | 280,045 |
| Ten or greater | 89 | 61.8 | 34.5 | 509,192 |
| *Arbitrator experience in FINRA arbitration* | | | | |
| One | 1,899 | 61.9 | 38.2 | 157,508 |
| Two to four | 961 | 57.2 | 35.0 | 244,508 |
| Five to nine | 165 | 60.6 | 37.7 | 258,515 |
| Ten or greater | 45 | 57.8 | 27.4 | 311,013 |

*Notes*: Total monetary awards are deflated to 1991 dollars. Although experience is grouped into categories for the descriptive statistics, continuous measures are used throughout the regression analysis.

The mean award number is above that of Colvin (2011), who found that victorious employees were awarded $109,858 on average in 2005 dollars under the AAA system. As Colvin notes, the disparity between his results and others regarding win rates and total compensation may be due to the high general pay within the securities industry. This disparity, when taken in conjunction with overall win rates, may also be reflective of systemic differences in the designs of the two programs' arbitration systems.

More experienced employers received better win rates than less-experienced companies. Employee claims were deemed meritorious in 67 percent of cases when the employer had only one experience in the system. Among employers with multiple experiences, however, this number dropped, falling to a low of 50.8 percent where the company experienced a FINRA arbitration 70 or more times. (Only a handful of companies fell into this category of experience: Prudential, Merrill Lynch, Shearson Lehman Hutton, Paine Webber, AG Edwards, and Citigroup.) There is also some evidence that employer experience lowered the relative amount arbitrators awarded to meritorious claimants (i.e., the proportion of claim awarded), but there is little evidence that employer experience affected total monetary award amounts.

Employees hiring more experienced counsel improved their chances of success in arbitration. A single-experience attorney earned his or her client some monetary award 60.4 percent of the time. This number climbs to 65.6 percent among attorneys who had taken FINRA claims to award 10 times or more. No clear trends emerge, however, when considering the compensation ratios of successful cases. Hiring one of the few attorneys who handled 10 or more cases in FINRA, though, yielded a high average monetary award of $981,465 deflated to 1991 dollars.

A different tale emerges when considering employer attorneys. Generally speaking, there is little evidence that more experienced company counsel received more favorable awards than less-experienced counsel. In fact, the highest monetary payouts for successful employees occurred when the most experienced corporate counsel were involved.

Finally, there is some evidence that more experienced arbitrators favored employers. The most experienced arbitrators found merit in employees' claims 58 percent of the time, while inexperienced arbitrators found for employees in 62 percent of cases. Similar results were found for compensation ratios. However, total monetary awards given to employees in meritorious cases were higher as arbitrators became more experienced in the FINRA system. Absent controls, the descriptive information regarding employer, attorney, and arbitrator experience tells us little about awards, however. In addition, it is impossible to disentangle between-subject effects from within-subject effects using this information alone. That is, although the Prudentials of the world may perform better than other companies in terms of win rates alone, without accounting for other factors, it is unclear whether a company like Prudential learns from its prior experiences and uses this knowledge to improve its performance in FINRA arbitration. To answer these questions, multivariate regression models are needed.

# REGRESSION ANALYSIS

The regression outcomes for both between- and within-group effects included in a single hybrid regression model are shown in Table 2.[4] They reveal that, when compared against other employers, those firms with higher average FINRA experience receive significantly better outcomes

***Table 2.*** Regression Analysis (Main Effects).

|  | Finding of Merit (All Cases) | Compensation Ratio (Meritorious Cases) | Amount Awarded (Meritorious Cases) |
|---|---|---|---|
| *Between-group (random effects)* | | | |
| Employer experience | −.007*** | −.115 | −.007*** |
|  | (.002) | (.078) | (.001) |
| Employee attorney experience | −.018 | −.269 | −.040*** |
|  | (.011) | (.456) | (.007) |
| Employer attorney experience | −.013 | .275 | −.037** |
|  | (.030) | (.571) | (.017) |
| Arbitrator experience | −.096*** | −1.004 | −.051** |
|  | (.037) | (.884) | (.025) |
| *Within-group (fixed effects)* | | | |
| Employer experience | .000 | .054 | .000 |
|  | (.002) | (.056) | (.001) |
| Employee attorney experience | .009 | −.163 | −.006 |
|  | (.017) | (.321) | (.009) |
| Employer attorney experience | .011 | −.690 | .030 |
|  | (.033) | (.695) | (.019) |
| Arbitrator experience | −.023 | −.373 | .008 |
|  | (.045) | (.966) | (.025) |
| N | 2,081 | 1,230 | 1,324 |
| Full controls | Yes | Yes | Yes |
| Year fixed-effects | Yes | Yes | Yes |
| Location fixed-effects | Yes | Yes | Yes |
| Model type | Logit | OLS | Negative binomial |

*Notes:* Total monetary awards are deflated to 1991 dollars. In addition to year and location fixed effects, all regressions control for: discrimination, statutory non-discrimination, and contractual claims; employer-arbitrator, employee attorney, and employer attorney matched pairings; employee, attorney, and arbitrator gender; whether the arbitrator is a lawyer; any arbitrator dissent; deflated claim amounts; case complexity; claims or awards of punitive damages; requests for expungement; motions to dismiss the case; motions for summary judgment; and full- or partial-settlements. Full regressions are available as supplemental information.
***$p < .01$; **$p < .05$; *$p < .10$.

with regard to arbitrators' findings of merit ($p < .01$). Predicted probabilities (extrapolated based on the regression coefficients reported in the table) indicate that employees receive win rates of 81.7 percent when facing single-experience companies. Win rates fall to 75.3 percent if the company has been involved in an average of 10 awards. This number continues to decline as average firm experience climbs (falling, for instance, to 46.9 percent if a firm has been involved in 50 awards on average). Once merit has been determined, mean employer experience does not affect award outcomes in relative terms but similar negative patterns are found in terms of absolute award amounts as mean firm experience increases. Conversely, within-employer experience does not affect findings of merit by arbitrators. As a firm becomes more familiar with FINRA, this familiarity does not affect employee win rates.

Employee attorney experience effects are somewhat more muted than employer experience effects. Hiring a more FINRA-experienced attorney does not affect overall win rates or the percent of claim that arbitrators award to meritorious employees. However, surprisingly, more experienced attorneys provide their clients with lower total monetary sums after merit has been assigned than do less-experienced attorneys ($p < .01$). Yet an individual employee attorney does not experience greater success the more he or she partakes in the FINRA system.

Whereas more experienced employers fare significantly better than less-experienced employers in the FINRA system, the same cannot generally be said for their counsel. Employer attorney experience does not significantly benefit employers in terms of arbitration awards, except where merit is found — when arbitrators allocate award amounts, employers using an experienced attorney are ordered to pay smaller amounts to employees than are those employers who have inexperienced representation. Again, there is no evidence that employer attorneys learn to perform better within the system over time relative to their prior experiences.

Finally, the between-group effects of arbitrator behavior indicate that more experienced arbitrators favor employers relative to less-experienced arbitrators, at least in terms of findings of merit ($p < .01$). Predicted probabilities suggest that single-experience arbitrators award employees positive outcomes 74 percent of the time, but that win rates fall to 64.9 percent among two-experience arbitrators and continue to decline at similar rates. An individual arbitrator does not differ in awards as he or she gains experience relative to that arbitrator's own prior behavior. Therefore, arbitrator effects are strictly limited to the between-group at the point of assignment of merit.

## DISCUSSION OF MAIN EFFECTS

The regression outcomes indicate strong evidence that experience effects in FINRA arbitration stem exclusively from differences between subjects and not from within-subject changes. This leads to three broad conclusions. First, experience does indeed help shape outcomes in securities employment arbitration. Second, experience effects are not uniform across all groups: employer experience yields very different outcomes from attorney experience, for instance. Third, evidence indicates that the so-called repeat-player effect, at least in the securities industry, is closer to a "well-resourced player" effect and has very little to do with parties' learning how to adapt to the arbitration system to improve performance over time.

More experienced employers do hold clear advantages in arbitration relative to less-experienced companies. These advantages go beyond simply being able to hire higher quality attorneys and are entirely independent of representation effects, which are accounted for in the data. It is possible that firms with characteristics that lead to their appearing often in FINRA arbitration are more likely to settle unwinnable cases before they reach arbitration. In tests not shown, though, further regressions indicate that employer experience does not predict settlement rates in the data. However, the settlement variable likely underreports the full array of settlements, and it is conceivable that unobserved choices to not pursue claims all the way to arbitration might be more common at more experienced firms. Indeed, it remains possible that any of the reasons offered by Galanter (1974) in his logic toward distinguishing effects of repeat players from one-shot players could explain the outcomes for companies (with the exception of representation considerations). The notion that repeat players improve their performance *relative to their prior outcomes* as they return to FINRA arbitration, however, which would raise greater concerns about bias and embedded inequities in the system, is unsupported by the main results.

Employees might believe that they can counterbalance employer experience effects by hiring experienced attorneys, but the main effects evidence does not support this notion. Hiring a more experienced attorney will change neither the likelihood that an arbitrator will find merit in the case nor the percent of the initial claim that will be awarded to a claimant. In fact, the results indicate that experienced attorneys may earn lower monetary awards for meritorious employees. These findings are subject to outlier influences, however, a few of the most experienced attorneys received lower awards when their clients had meritorious claims, resulting in outcome skew. Thus, the results can be interpreted more comfortably to indicate that, generally speaking, between-attorney experience is not a useful predictor of arbitration awards. Finally, there is no evidence that employee attorneys learn as they move through the process, that the Jeffrey Liddles of the FINRA system learn how to manipulate the system to their advantage.

Employers who hire experienced attorneys garner very little benefit in FINRA arbitration after accounting for the other employer experience characteristics that might yield success. Only when considering the total money awarded in meritorious employee cases do we see evidence that claims involving more experienced employer attorneys lead to lower employee outcomes. On the whole, the broad nonsignificance of employer attorney effects indicates that other employer characteristics are more crucial in determining awards than the choice of representation, though more experienced employer attorneys do appear to be more adept at limiting the total damage that might occur when employees bring meritorious claims to arbitration.[5]

Finally, I find evidence that more experienced arbitrators are less likely to find merit in employees' cases than are less-experienced arbitrators, but that an individual arbitrator does not become more or less employer-friendly as he or she is selected repeatedly. As hypothesized, it may be the case that experienced arbitrators, who are familiar with the FINRA system, might have a better comprehension of typical resolution standards for cases built around similar foundational characteristics. These arbitrators would likely award in narrower bands than would inexperienced arbitrators, who may be less sure what the appropriate resolution standard ought to be in a particular case. To explore this further, I have performed some basic tests within the data, which indicate that the most highly experienced arbitrators also provide the lowest range of award outcomes, whereas a far wider range of outcomes is found among less-experienced arbitrators.

It remains possible that this result might also be explained by two more troubling considerations from a distributive justice perspective. The first is that arbitrators are using the FINRA system as a vehicle to earn employer business outside the system. As noted, an arbitrator is not a FINRA employee — he or she is an independent contractor hired to hear a single case. Arbitrators on average hear only a few employment cases within this system. This speaks to the notion that these arbitrators need business outside the confines of the FINRA employment setting. The second consideration is that experienced arbitrators might not be as "neutral" as less-experienced arbitrators because of their experience as products of the history of the FINRA system. FINRA has gone to great lengths to eliminate the problems inherent when panels of so-called industry arbitrators decide cases. The most experienced arbitrators may have become involved in FINRA when it was common to have cases heard by those with close ties to the industry, however. This explanation is supported qualitatively. Many of the most experienced arbitrators in the data set have ties to the securities industry, including one arbitrator, Robert Shiffra, who was president and majority owner of Tempo Securities while he served as chair arbitrator in 13 employment cases between 1993 and 2002. (Incidentally, Shiffra was called before the SEC in 2007 for his role in securities fraud at his company.)

It is also clear, however, that arbitrators do not become *more* employer favorable as they grow in experience within FINRA. In other words, the Robert Shiffras (or Robert Herschmans discussed earlier) of the FINRA world may be less neutral than an inexperienced arbitrator or might take a more employer-positive position than arbitrators with less experience on the whole for any number of reasons, but they do not change their behavior relative to their own past. This lends credence to the notion that, although arbitrator experience results might be reflective of more or less sinister issues in securities arbitration, there is little evidence that arbitrators make an effort to adjust their behaviors from one case to the next.

## TESTING FOR HETEROGENEITY

The main effect results establish that although experience matters in the FINRA system, concerns that parties learn to exploit the system to their benefit by appearing repeatedly is largely unfounded. However, questions remain regarding the homogeneity of these results. In particular, do experience effects vary by allegation types? Prior work indicates that discrimination claims fare worse in arbitration (Lamare & Lipsky, 2016). Therefore, I believe there is value in assessing whether firm, attorney, and arbitrator experience effects differ according to whether it is a discrimination charge that is filed. Since no theories of which I am aware have linked experience and allegation, I present the following results as a way of exploring parameters unobserved by looking at the main effects alone. For space considerations, I limit my discussion to statistically significant outcomes regarding arbitrator findings of merit.

Although I do not find evidence of between-entity moderation by claim type, I do in fact find some differentiation in within-entity effects according to whether the case dealt with discrimination or not. Fig. 1 shows the

*Fig. 1.* Heterogeneity of Experience Effects by Allegation Type (within-Employer).

results of heterogeneity in within-employer outcomes crossed with allegation. There is no evidence that within-firm experience affects outcomes in
FINRA arbitration when handling contractual claims, but firms do appear
to learn as they repeatedly face discrimination claims. As a company like
Prudential becomes more experienced in facing discrimination complaints,
it appears to learn how to resolve these cases in its favor. It may be the
case that, as companies face more and more similar claims involving Title
VII and other civil rights charges, they develop better defenses against these
allegations. Alternatively, it may be the case that, as a firm is presented
with more discrimination claims, it might better identify and settle potentially high-award complaints that may result in negative publicity. A firm
that learns to behave in this manner would probably take only those cases
it views as winnable to arbitration over time.

Figs. 2 and 3 reveal the heterogeneity of awards by claim type according
to within-attorney experience for employee and employer representatives,
respectively. As Fig. 2 shows, within-employee attorney experience does
not influence findings of merit for non-discrimination cases, but when
discrimination is involved, employees are made significantly better off as an
attorney continues to take cases within the system. Somewhat surprisingly,
though, Fig. 3 shows that as an employer attorney takes more discrimination cases to arbitration, respondents fare worse.

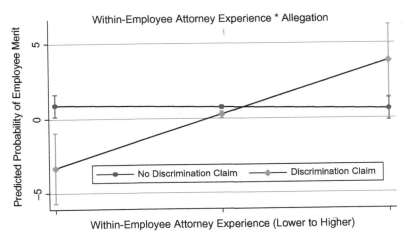

*Fig. 2.* Heterogeneity of Experience Effects by Allegation Type (within-Employee Attorney).

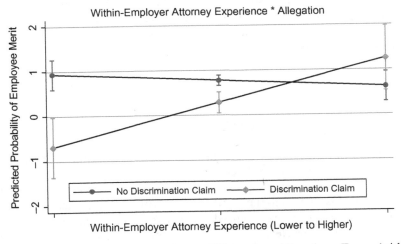

*Fig. 3.* Heterogeneity of Experience Effects by Allegation Type (within-Employer Attorney).

From these findings, two implications emerge. First, a lawyer like Jeffrey Liddle might not improve his performance as he takes more contractual claims to arbitration, but he does become better if the case deals with discrimination. This suggests that, as a lawyer like Jeffrey Liddle gains experience, he might learn which types of civil rights claims will be well received by arbitrators and will take these to resolution, while refusing to take on cases that he believes lack merit. The same learning may not apply to contractual claims, which are far more variegated in their composition than are discrimination cases. Additionally, the surprising result that employer attorneys fare worse as they gain experience in discrimination cases may reflect the possibility that, in instances where employers are unable to settle meritorious and potentially high-profile discrimination claims, these firms call upon their most experienced representatives. Therefore, a lawyer who was highly successful in the early stages of his career in favorably handling discrimination complaints might, as a consequence of this success, take on cases that are increasingly difficult to win over time. Finally, this result might occur only among discrimination claims since a firm might only use a specialist lawyer to deal with civil rights complaints.

Unfortunately, given the lack of theoretical foundation and the limitations of a non-experimental research design, it is difficult to do more than present these results and speculate as to their interpretation. I encourage researchers to more holistically study heterogeneity in experience effects on arbitration outcomes, particularly where discrimination has occurred, so that we might better understand the differentiated results by allegation type.

## CONCLUSION

The ambition of this analysis has been to move beyond the current literature to take a more nuanced account of the role of experience in arbitration. In doing so, I have recast the repeat-player effect as in fact consisting of two elements: between-player effects and within-player effects. Between-player effects separate experienced players from inexperienced players in terms of such characteristics as size, resources, culture, and the like. Within-player effects look at a single entity and explore the extent to which that entity improves its performance as it gains experience. I believe that the repeat-player terminology, while useful as a starting point in weighing the importance of experience in arbitration, lacks the adequate level of depth needed to more fully capture experience effects. Galanter's (1974) original notion of repeat players fits much more closely with a between-player effect than a within-player effect, though the literature has not, as far as I am aware, accounted for the distinction between these effects when modeling experience.

I have explicitly differentiated between-player effects from within-player effects using longitudinal data and hybrid RE and FE models. I employ a robust data set to measure these effects in employment arbitration and can overcome many of the methodological limitations associated with other studies into experience effects. The results indicate clear evidence of a between-player experience effect but very little evidence of a within-player effect outside of discrimination complaints. This suggests that, although securities arbitration may be prone to resource imbalances between employers and employees, parties are not often able to improve their performance within the system over time relative to their entity-specific starting points.

I find some evidence that experience does not affect arbitration outcomes homogenously across all cases. Employer and attorney experience effects are moderated by allegation type, though arbitrators do not generate different patterns of behavior depending on the kind of claim they face. Again, these results indicate that the simple repeat-player versus single-player dichotomy used thus far in the literature is inadequately shallow. Researchers should account for moderation as well as main experience effects, and, as noted, I encourage scholars to develop theories more fully that might govern the heterogeneity effect uncovered within the study.

This work is not without limitations. First, although I use longitudinal fixed- and RE models, the data may still suffer from omitted variable biases. For instance, although employer FE account for any time-invariant firm characteristics, there may be time-variant characteristics (i.e., changes to firm size, culture, resources) for which I cannot account. My conditioning on year helps to overcome this concern, but I cannot fully rule out omitted variable issues.

Similarly, this study, like all observational analyses of employment arbitration, suffers from problems of selection biases. For instance, since the data cover only awards rendered by arbitrators, I cannot easily account for the possibility that certain types of cases were settled prior to award issuance, which would bias the sample in a variety of ways. Like other arbitration studies (Choi et al., 2014; Colvin & Gough, 2015), I attempt to overcome this issue by accounting for settlement, but it remains likely that the data understate the actual settlement rate since this is a self-reported figure provided by arbitrators who issued rulings even after settlement occurred.

Finally, the results may not be generalizable beyond the securities setting. On the one hand, I argue that the particularities of the securities system help to inform some of the differences I find between my data and those used in studies of other systems, like the AAA. Also, understanding the securities system is important in its own right, given that this system governed the Supreme Court's expansion of arbitration in the non-union employment setting, and the Court has had no issue in generalizing outside this system in its subsequent decisions. On the other hand, though, it is unlikely that many securities cases look identical in characteristics to non-securities cases, and I therefore recommend that scholars replicate the more nuanced account of experience in other employment arbitration settings.

On the whole, this study adds to the literature in several ways. I find evidence that, although resources and power imbalances may matter in securities arbitration, parties do not generally learn how to adapt to the system in order to perform better as they become more experienced. I also find some evidence that experience effects are not always uniform across parties and case types. In light of the results, I conclude that the effects of experience on employment arbitration are multifaceted and complex. I do not interpret the results to indicate that the FINRA system is biased toward employers, but neither do I believe that power imbalances in arbitration should be ignored.

## NOTES

1. In 2007, the National Association of Securities Dealers, Inc. (NASD) and the New York Stock Exchange (NYSE) merged their securities arbitration systems into one forum, which became known as FINRA. Prior to this, NASD and NYSE administered separate systems, which together accounted for 99 percent of securities industry arbitrations. These systems were materially identical in their policies and coverage, so I have combined them in the data set.

2. Although I am able to account for more explanatory factors than previous research into this topic, the study does not overcome all concerns related to omitted variables. I discuss this limitation later in the chapter.

3. The FINRA data provide some support for the line of reasoning suggesting that as arbitrators grew in experience, ranges tightened. Those arbitrators with the highest mean number of cases produced maximum awards of about $2 million, while the most inexperienced arbitrators were willing to award as much as $5 million to employees.

4. Similar results can be found using separate random-effects and conditional fixed-effects models rather than the hybrid model used in this chapter, though the separate models are more restrictive on the data and combine both within- and between-results under the random effects model.

5. One concern that emerges from the employee and employer attorney outcomes is that a different unit of analysis might be needed. It may be the case that law firms, not individual attorneys, are better predictors of awards. To address this

concern, I have run regressions (in tests not shown but available on request) substituting firm experience for attorney experience. I find materially equivalent effects across the board. Therefore, I am comfortable concluding that the results do not differ irrespective of the level at which representation is measured.

# REFERENCES

Allison, P. D. (2009). *Fixed effects regression models.* London: Sage.
Bell, A., & Jones, K. (2015). Explaining fixed effects: Random effects modeling of time-series cross-sectional and panel data. *Political Science Research and Methods, 3*(1), 133–153.
Bingham, L. B. (1997). Employment arbitration: The repeat player effect. *Employee Rights & Employment Policy Journal, 1,* 189.
Bingham, L. B. (1998a). An overview of employment arbitration in the United States: Law, public policy and data. *New Zealand Journal of Industrial Relations, 23*(2), 5–19.
Bingham, L. B. (1998b). On repeat players, adhesive contracts, and the use of statistics in judicial review of employment arbitration awards. *McGeorge Law Review, 29*(2), 223.
Bingham, L. B., & Sarraf, S. (2000). *Employment arbitration before and after the due process protocol for mediation and arbitration of statutory disputes arising out of employment: Preliminary evidence that self-regulation makes a difference.* Presented at the Proceedings of the N.Y.U. 50th Annual Conference on Labor, New York.
Choi, S. J., & Eisenberg, T. (2010). Punitive damages in securities arbitration: An empirical study. *Journal of Legal Studies, 39,* 497–546.
Choi, S. J., Fisch, J. E., & Pritchard, A. C. (2014). The influence of arbitrator background and representation on arbitration outcomes. *Virginia Law & Business Review, 9*(1), 43–90.
Colvin, A. J. S. (2011). An empirical study of employment arbitration: Case outcomes and processes. *Journal of Empirical Legal Studies, 8,* 1–23.
Colvin, A. J. S., & Gough, M. (2015). Individual employment rights arbitration in the U.S.: Actors and outcomes. *ILR Review, 68*(5), 1019–1042.
Delikat, M., & Kleiner, M. M. (2003). An empirical study of dispute resolution mechanisms: Where do plaintiffs better vindicate their rights? *Dispute Resolution Journal, 58,* 44–51.
Eisenberg, T., & Hill, E. (2003). Arbitration and litigation of employment claims: An empirical comparison. *Dispute Resolution Journal, 58*(4), 44–55.
Galanter, M. (1974). Why the haves come out ahead: Speculations on the limits of legal change. *Law & Society Review, 9,* 95–160.
Gasparino, C. (2004). Judging wall street. *Newsweek, 144*(10), 56.
Government Accountability Office. (1992). *Securities arbitration: How investors fare.* GAO-92-74.
Government Accountability Office. (2000). *Securities arbitration: Actions needed to address problem of unpaid awards.* GAO-00-115.
Government Accountability Office. (2003). *Recommendations to better ensure that securities arbitrators are qualified.* GAO-03-790.
Hill, E. (2003). AAA employment arbitration: A fair forum at low cost. *Dispute Resolution Journal, 58*(2), 8–16.
Howard, W. M. (1995). Arbitrating claims of employment discrimination. *Dispute Resolution Journal, 50,* 40–50.

Huber, G. P. (1991). Organizational learning: The contributing processes and the literatures. *Organization Science, 2*(10), 88–115.

Lamare, J. R., & David, B. L. (2016). *Resolving discrimination complaints in employment arbitration: An analysis of the experience in the securities industry.* Working Paper.

Lamare, J. R., & Lipsky, D. B. (2016). *Resolving discrimination complaints in employment arbitration: An analysis of the experience in the securities industry.* Unpublished manuscript.

Lipsky, D. B., Lamare, J. R., & Gupta, A. (2013). The effect of gender on awards in employment arbitration cases: The experience in the securities industry. *Industrial Relations, 49*(4), 616–639.

Oppenheimer, D. B. (2003). Verdicts matter: An empirical study of California employment discrimination and wrongful discharge jury verdicts reveals low success rates for women and minorities. *U.C. Davis Law Review, 37,* 511–566.

Sherwyn, D., Estreicher, S. S., & Heise, M. (2005). Assessing the case for employment arbitration: A new direction for empirical research. *Stanford Law Review, 57,* 1557–1591.

Wells Fargo Advisors, LLC, v. Watts. 5:ilcv48.

# NETWORKED DISPUTE RESOLUTION: THE NATIONAL IMPLEMENTATION BODY IN IRISH INDUSTRIAL RELATIONS

William K. Roche and Colman Higgins

## ABSTRACT

Purpose — *The purpose of this chapter is to examine the genesis, operation, and effects of a dispute resolution body known as the National Implementation Body (NIB). The NIB was established by employers, unions, and the State in Ireland and was active between 2000 and 2009. It recorded significant success in resolving major disputes. A distinctive feature of the NIB was its networked character: the body involved key employer and union leaders and senior public servants, who exerted informal pressure on the parties in dispute to reach a settlement either within the NIB process itself or in the State's mainstream dispute resolution agencies.*

Research Methods — *The research draws on case studies of disputes and interviews with key members of the NIB.*

Managing and Resolving Workplace Conflict
Advances in Industrial and Labor Relations, Volume 22, 161–188
ISSN: 0742-6186/doi:10.1108/S0742-618620160000022007

Findings — *The findings reveal how the NIB mobilized networks to resolve a series of major disputes that threatened to derail national pay agreements or cause significant economic disruption.*

Originality/value — *The chapter examines the operation of networked dispute resolution in detail and considers the wider implications of networked dispute resolution in both Continental European and other Anglo-American countries.*

**Keywords:** Conflict resolution; disputes; ADR; networked dispute resolution; Irish industrial relations

This chapter begins by locating networked dispute resolution in the context of more "orthodox" forms of dispute resolution. It then outlines the background of the emergence of the NIB, the types of disputes in which it became engaged, and its mode of operation. A series of case studies of NIB interventions are then presented to identify the nature of the dispute resolution mechanisms used by NIB agents. The final section presents conclusions and considers the more general significance of the NIB as a network-based dispute resolution agency.

# NETWORKED DISPUTE RESOLUTION

Third-party involvement in dispute resolution, whether provided by public dispute resolution agencies, private practitioners, or persons who intervene at the behest of governments, takes many forms. Those most widely used, however, are easy to understand and, local differences aside, are internationally quite generic. In the Anglo-American world, various forms of facilitation, conciliation, mediation, arbitration, and adjudication dominate the practice of dispute resolution in industrial relations (Acas, 2009; ILO/Thompson, 2010; ILO, 2013; Lipsky & Seeber, 2006). These practices and the manner in which they may combine into multi-step procedures are clearly and formally set out in organizations' dispute resolution procedures. They are also codified in the principles governing the intervention of public dispute resolution agencies or in the terms of reference of privately engaged or government-appointed facilitators or arbitrators. The providers of dispute resolution services are typically specialist public servants or independent experts. Not infrequently, independent experts have had prior experience in industrial relations, stemming from professional backgrounds in public dispute resolution agencies, human resource management, or trade unions. Nonetheless, like their public service counterparts, they are expected to operate as neutrals, without a direct stake or vested interest in the terms by which disputes are resolved. Unions, employers, and other interests are also sometimes formally involved in the governance of dispute resolution agencies like Acas in the United Kingdom and the Labour Relations Commission in Ireland.

In recent decades, mainly again in the Anglo-American world, conventional dispute resolution practices have been augmented by a range of alternative dispute resolution (ADR) practices, such as assisted bargaining, med-arb, interest-based negotiations, and conflict management systems (ILO/Steadman, 2003; Lipsky, Seeber, & Fincher, 2003; Roche & Teague, 2012; Roche, Teague, & Colvin, 2014). While ADR practices modify conventional dispute resolution practices in significant respects, primarily by prioritizing interest-based over rights-based solutions to disputes, they continue to be provided by specialist and neutral practitioners with no current vested interest in the outcomes of the resolution. The handling of dispute resolution has also been significantly affected by the decentralization of collective bargaining and the "privatization" of dispute resolution in countries such as Australia and New Zealand (Rasmussen & Greenwood, 2014; Van Gramberg, Bamber, Teicher, & Cooper, 2014). Again, however, new models of delivery of dispute resolution services have not radically affected the basic character of the dispute resolution process.

Other than public agencies and independent practitioners, "troubleshooters" of various kinds may also play a role in resolving industrial disputes. Particularly where serious strikes threaten or occur, governments or the parties in dispute have sometimes mandated experts to seek the basis for a settlement and possibly also to investigate how industrial relations might be improved in the longer term. Recent examples of this longstanding practice in some countries are provided by the Independent Review of the Fire Service conducted in Britain by Bain (2002), an investigation of a union-recognition dispute in the low-cost airline Ryanair, which closed Dublin airport for several days in 1998 (EIRO, 1998), and a report on a dispute at Dublin bus in 2013 (*Industrial Relations News*, October 17, 2013). While little independent research exists on initiatives of this kind, their basic underlying methods appear to involve various combinations of investigation, conciliation, and adjudication, conducted by non-partisan specialists. In these ways, they seem little different at the level of basic process to more mainstream dispute resolution.

Table 1 summarizes the main features of standard or orthodox dispute resolution and provides a means of distinguishing this from what we term network-based or networked dispute resolution. Standard dispute resolution processes derive their mandate from laws or disputes procedure, whether within firms or at sector or national levels, or from the voluntary initiatives of disputing parties to seek the intervention of public dispute resolution agencies or independent practitioners. Dispute resolution practices, which may also be codified in procedures, typically involve intensive efforts and focus on some combination and sequence of conciliation or mediation, investigation, arbitration, or non-binding adjudication. These processes are "confined" in the sense that dispute resolution practitioners

***Table 1.*** Features of Networked Dispute Resolution.

| Conventional Dispute Resolution | Networked Dispute Resolution |
|---|---|
| *Mandate for dispute resolution* <br> Laws, disputes procedures or the invitation of the parties in dispute trigger intervention by dispute resolution agencies or professionals. | *Mandate for dispute resolution* <br> Disputes or impending disputes can be notified by disputants' federations; dispute resolution body may intervene at its own discretion, or disputants may invite involvement. |
| *Dispute resolution processes* <br> Intensive effort is focused on immediate parties to disputes through conciliation/ mediation, investigation, and arbitration/ adjudication. <br> Process is "confined" and heavily reliant on the professional skills, techniques, and neutrality of conflict resolution professionals and agencies. <br> Parties are assisted in moving from opening positions and converging on settlement terms or in avoiding adopting positions (some forms of ADR). <br> Stages of process and links between conciliation/mediation, arbitration/ adjudication parties, and agencies are clearly codified. | *Dispute resolution processes* <br> Informal and simple procedures are a preliminary to mobilizing network pressures to achieve settlement or (re)direct disputes into formal procedure. <br> Process is "expansive" and heavily reliant on political skills, the stature and authority of senior figures and on peer pressure within a network, where mutual obligation and ongoing exchange may be important contributors toward achieving settlement. <br> Procedures (re)entered through network pressure provide a basis for settlement or parities are otherwise guided toward settlement. <br> "Extra-procedural" networking among different conflict resolution parties and agencies are a feature of conflict resolution initiatives. |

focus their efforts intensively on reconciling the parties in dispute, relying heavily on well-established professional skills and techniques, backed by the neutrality of those involved. Stages in the dispute resolution process and any progression between or across agencies are also codified in procedure.

The terms *networks* and *network-based* have entered scholarship in industrial relations mainly through the literature on "new social pacts" in Europe since the 1980s and the role of pay coordination in agreements of this kind. Commentators have observed that the social pacts between employers and unions (and sometimes governments) found in a number of European countries since that time appeared to rely less on imperative coordination within peak federations of unions and employers, or on state coercion, than had centralized bipartite or tripartite agreements of previous eras (Avdagic, Rhodes, & Visser, 2011; Baccaro, 2000, 2003; Higgins & Roche, 2013; Molina & Rhodes, 2002; Traxler, Blaschke, & Kittel, 2001). Under new social pacts, networks within and across peak associations, and sometimes also involving the state as a third-party, substituted in major respects for hierarchical controls and operated quite differently from market mechanisms in influencing pay fixing and behavior in industrial relations.

We wish to develop the idea of networks central to this literature to distinguish a mode of dispute resolution that developed under the NIB and that had a major impact on social partnership in Ireland but that may also have had wider resonance. As summarized in Table 1, in networked dispute resolution the mandate for dispute resolution activity is more diffuse, multi-faceted, and discretionary. While procedure agreements may guide the intervention of dispute resolution agencies where disputes occur, union and employer federations have the discretion to seek settlement themselves or to refer disputes for settlement to public dispute resolution agencies. Possible or emerging disputes may also be considered, where employer or union peak associations, or state authorities, assess that there is a significant risk that such disputes might result in damaging outcomes for pay and competitiveness, or cause economic disruption or dislocation. In this sense, professional and personal networks, involving larger and more diverse organizations and responsive to their separate and mutual interests, play a pivotal role in the dispute resolution process. In consequence, the dispute resolution process may be "expansive" rather than "confined" and draw heavily on the political and brokerage skills of the key parties involved. Leaders of employers' organizations, union confederations, individual unions, senior public servants, and political leaders may bring pressure to bear within their networks on the parties to disputes, obviating, overriding, or possibly supporting the more confined processes and skills used by specialist conflict resolution agencies and professionals. As the dispute resolution process becomes subject to networks and their dynamics, these leaders may become embedded within the social exchange between the parties to networks. In this way, the resolution or avoidance of any individual dispute may be crucially affected by wider dealings between the parties to networks and the mutual favors, obligations, and commitments they enter into in their ongoing dealings with each other. Union and employer leaders may be prepared to trade off support for intervention in a dispute in anticipation of gaining "capital" to be used in another dispute in the future, or because it may be advantageous in their more general dealings with professional interlocutors. Firms or unions faced with pressure from senior public servants or political leaders may have to weigh the potential costs of refusing to come to heel, even if those costs may not be directly or explicitly articulated in the processes through which network pressures are brought to bear. Finally, in networked dispute resolution, linkages and contacts between dispute resolution agencies or across the stages of dispute resolution may be "extra-procedural" and based on personal and professional contact as much as, or more than, formal dispute resolution procedures.

We do not claim that networked dispute resolution activities never arise in conjunction with conventional dispute resolution activities, but only that these tend, at most, to be of marginal significance in the normal work of public dispute resolution agencies or of independent professionals. In the case of the NIB, as will be examined later, networked dispute resolution complemented conventional dispute resolution rather than substituting for the work of public agencies in the field.

## THE GENESIS AND OPERATION OF THE NIB

From 1987 onwards unions, employers, and governments in Ireland were party to a series of tripartite social partnership programs. Each of these programs contained agreements, up to the early 2000s, of approximately of 36 months' duration, providing for phased general pay rises. Successive social partnership agreements were of progressively wider scope, encompassing tax reform, fiscal and economic policy, and a raft of social and labor market policies (Hastings, Sheehan, & Yeates, 2007). The advent of social partnership agreements was associated with both pay discipline — pay drift was very limited during the period up to the early to mid-2000s

(Higgins & Roche, 2013) — and a significant reduction in industrial conflict. As the Irish economy recovered from the deep recession of the 1980s and reached record growth levels and near full employment around the turn of the millennium, employers became more concerned about pay drift and the prospects of growing union pressure on agreed pay norms backed by industrial action. In the public service, a series of disputes had resulted in a cycle of industrial action, as unions used a local bargaining clause in the prevailing national pay agreement to push for pay rises well above the original pay limit for local pay agreements. An unanticipated spike in inflation in the late 1990s resulted in demands by unions for the renegotiation of the then current national pay agreement in the *Programme for Prosperity and Fairness (PPF)* (www.taoiseach.gov.ie/upload). As a quid-pro-quo for agreeing to revise the agreement to take account of inflation, employers insisted on the creation of a new dispute resolution body, the NIB.

The NIB consisted of three parties: the Government (effectively senior civil servants from the Department of the Taoiseach (Gaelic for Prime Minister)), the main employers' association, the Irish Business and Employers' Confederation (IBEC), and the trade union confederation, the Irish Congress of Trade Unions (ICTU). Each of the parties to the NIB assigned at least two people to conduct its work. The NIB was chaired by the Secretary General of the Department of the Taoiseach — the Department's most senior public servant — who was also Secretary General to the Government. Another senior public servant who participated in the NIB's work also acted in a secretarial capacity for the NIB, which had no professional or full-time staff. The NIB's formal proceedings took place in the imposing surroundings of Government Buildings in central Dublin, where the business of the Irish Cabinet and negotiations on social partnership program also occurred. Many NIB figures were people who had negotiated the social partnership agreements that the NIB was in part expected to uphold. The clause of the revised *PPF* agreement that established the NIB stated the following:

> A National Implementation Body representing Government, IBEC and ICTU will meet quarterly to ensure delivery of the stability and peace provisions of PPF. Where particular difficulties arise or are anticipated, the group can be convened at short notice. (Department of the Taoiseach, 2000)

While directed at pressures on the current pay agreement, the establishment of the NIB also reflected an industrial relations legacy stretching back over many decades. Ad hoc dispute resolution initiatives involving senior employer and union officials had been undertaken in response to serious disputes earlier in the era of social partnership. Before that, during the

1970s and early 1980s, when nine successive bipartite or tripartite national wage agreements were negotiated, an institution known as the National Employer Labour Conference (NELC) played a role in policing wage increase norms. This role was in some respects similar to that of the NIB. Originally established in the early 1960s as a forum for employer and union discussions on economic policy and industrial relations, the NELC had become defunct, but it was reestablished in 1970. The reconstituted NELC involved senior officials of employer associations, representatives of the state as an employer, and senior trade union officials. The secretariat of the NELC was also provided by the State (Hardiman, 1988, p. 51; Hillery, 1987, p. 9). The NELC was the forum in which national wage agreements were negotiated until the demise of national pay bargaining in the early 1980s led to the disappearance of the joint body.

The parallel with the NIB arose from the various policing functions of the NELC under the national wage system. A Steering Committee considered matters affecting national agreements, an Interpretation Committee provided rulings on clauses of national agreements, and an Adjudication Committee examined actions by employers or trade unions alleged to have breached the terms of agreements. The main scholar of national wage agreements has written that in addition to the quasi-judicial interpretation and judicial functions discharged by the NELC, the body's Steering Committee often informally influenced parties to alleged infractions and helped resolve cases through drawing their attention to a problem, providing advice, and signaling that an issue might proceed to formal interpretation or adjudication (O'Brien, 1981, p. 215). Activities like these hold parallels, as will emerge later, with some of the dispute resolution activities subsequently engaged in by the NIB. From descriptions of the work of the NELC and its various committees it also appears that the body refrained from the types of direct intervention in disputes that were to become the hallmark of much NIB dispute resolution activity. O'Brien's assessment of procedural experimentation under the NELC's committees also highlights the limited success of the body in restricting breaches of the wage agreements and in particular in curbing a growing wave of "above-the-norm" claims lodged and conceded on grounds of productivity and pay anomalies (O'Brien, 1987, p. 113).

## Profile of NIB Disputes

No definitive register or list of disputes in which the NIB intervened exists. To compile the fullest possible list and profile of disputes involving the NIB, we began by requesting that the NIB provide a list of all disputes for which it retained a record and we cross-referenced and extended this list by examining all reports of disputes involving the NIB in the weekly specialist publication, *Industrial Relations News (IRN)*. The NIB provided a list of 47 instances from 2001 to mid-2009 in which NIB interventions involved the issuing of public statements. The list did not include interventions made on an informal basis. When these cases were compared with all instances of NIB interventions reported in *IRN* a final list of 63 cases was obtained, which is as near as possible to a definitive list of NIB interventions in threatened or actual industrial disputes between 2000 and 2009. In a small number of these instances the NIB issued general interpretations of clauses of national agreements or assisted in the development of protocols relating to clauses in these agreements.

*IRN* reports of NIB disputes also made it possible to identify the trend in NIB interventions and the main issues involved in most of the disputes in which the NIB became involved. Fig. 1 shows the trend in NIB activity over the period 2001−2009. By the time the NIB came into operation, the peak of Ireland's economic boom had passed and economic conditions were becoming more uncertain, initially as a consequence of the dot-com crash and then as a result of the 9/11 attacks in 2001. During its early years the NIB's interventions often dealt with pay claims that threatened to breach national pay agreement norms. The NIB's activity peaked around the middle of the decade during a period in which much of its business was concerned with disputes arising from often complex change and restructuring activities. These types of disputes remained an important feature of the NIB's work until 2009. Pensions and outsourcing issues were concentrated in the latter stages of NIB activity.

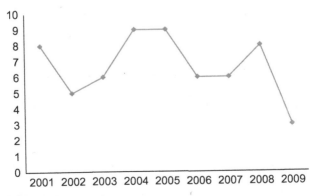

*Fig. 1.* Trend in NIB Interventions in Disputes.

Tables 2 and 3 present an analysis of the sectoral distribution of NIB disputes and of the main issues involved. As shown in Table 2, the incidence of NIB disputes is about even between the private and public sectors. Certain firms and organizations and also particular unions in both sectors were the focus of multiple NIB interventions. Table 3 shows that while pay rises that threatened national pay agreements were a significant focus of the NIB's work, many other issues were also involved in disputes in which the NIB intervened. In particular, the NIB often dealt with disputes that arose from restructuring and change initiatives and from severance or redundancies and outsourcing. The "other issues" category in Table 3 comprised a wide variety of subjects that included promotion, allowances, overtime, safety, and flexible working time.

## The NIB's Dispute Resolution Practices

In order to understand the operation of the NIB, we conducted four interviews during 2009 with prominent employer, union, and public servant members of the NIB. This section draws heavily on these interviews,

**Table 2.** Sectoral Distribution of NIB Disputes.

|  | % |
| --- | --- |
| Public services | 31.7 |
| State-owned firms | 19.1 |
| Manufacturing | 15.9 |
| Services | 22.2 |
| Construction | 7.9 |
| Clarification of national agreements | 3.2 |

**Table 3.** Issues in NIB Disputes.

|  | % |
| --- | --- |
| Pay increases above/outside national agreements | 15.9 |
| Change/restructuring plans | 19.1 |
| Payment of basic rises under national agreements | 11.1 |
| Severance/redundancies/outsourcing | 15.8 |
| Pensions | 4.8 |
| Other issues | 20.6 |
| Not known | 12.7 |

supplemented by documentation on the activities of the NIB. The interviewees represent over half of the NIB's members. While up to eight individuals participated in the NIB from time to time, three senior officials — one each from IBEC, ICTU, and the Department of the Taoiseach — discharged the core functions of the body. They oversaw most of the NIB hearings in the earlier years.

In the later years, several other officials came to deputize for them on occasion. We interviewed each of them. We also interviewed one of the other NIB members, a key official in IBEC, who had extensive experience with dispute resolution. Two other officials of the ICTU were occasionally involved, depending on whether a dispute had arisen in the public or private sector, as was one other senior official of the Department of the Taoiseach. In effect, these other NIB members deputized on occasions for the principals on the NIB.

The key senior officials interviewed remained in situ for the duration of almost all of the NIB's work. Given their centrality to the process and the more intermittent involvement of other members of the NIB, the interview data they provided can be viewed as providing a valid overall picture of the workings of the NIB.

The NIB was added to a dispute resolution framework already well provided with specialist and widely respected state-operated agencies, primarily the Labour Relations Commission (LRC) and Labour Court. National pay agreements stipulated procedures that would use the LRC for conciliation, referring on to the Labour Court for adjudication if necessary. Some areas of the public service had similarly structured conciliation and arbitration procedures. The NIB possessed no statutory or legal powers and could not compel any party to appear before it or comply with any of its decisions or proposals. Under the agreement of the NIB operating procedure, individual employers or unions could not bring a dispute to the NIB by themselves. Instead, they had first to bring it to the attention of either IBEC or the ICTU, who would then refer it to the NIB. If a dispute posed a threat to the national agreement, however, or threatened significant economic damage and disruption, the NIB could intervene on its own initiative.

The NIB did not always hold meetings, particularly if it already felt familiar with the background to a dispute. If a meeting (also sometimes referred to as a *hearing*) took place, the NIB's members would be supplied with background information from IBEC and ICTU. At such a meeting, the role of the NIB would be explained to the parties, clarifying that it was not an adjudicative body. Then the NIB would meet separately with each party, and the parties would provide oral submissions and would respond to questioning from the NIB. Two of the interviewees estimated that meetings with the parties to disputes took place more often than not, but a significant minority of cases (30 percent according to one interviewee) had involved only a meeting of the NIB, itself, after which a statement or recommendation had been issued to the parties. Another interviewee said that meetings became more frequent in the later years of the NIB, particularly in public sector disputes or if the union brought shop stewards along, which added a level of formality in such cases. The decision on whether or not to hold a meeting with the parties would center on the complexity of the dispute and the level of information already available to the IBEC and ICTU members of the NIB. In some cases, where the appropriate procedural step for a dispute was very clear, the NIB itself might not even have met, but might instead have discussed the issue through phone calls and the exchange of draft NIB statements. Even in these cases, however, there would have been substantial contact with the parties.

When disputes were considered, the senior public servant, acting as the NIB's chair, drafted the statement outlining the NIB's view on how the dispute should be settled, based on a consensus among all the parties to the NIB. When a common approach to the dispute was determined by NIB members, IBEC and ICTU would "sound out" their respective "clients." These soundings sometimes altered the NIB's approach. After that stage, a final NIB recommendation would be provided to the parties – within 24 hours if the matter was urgent. If the issue was less pressing and more complex, however, that could take several days or longer and might even involve the NIB commissioning a report on the employer's financial position. The recommendation was often released as a publicly available statement, unless the issue was localized or very specific to one company. Often NIB statements consisted of less than a page, but considerable work went into each one. The NIB's pronouncements contained recommendations on terms, processes, or mechanisms by which disputes might be resolved, putting back "on track" disputes that had become "lost" procedurally.

While the Labour Court was not allowed to hear a dispute a second time, other than to clarify a recommendation, the NIB was not restricted in this way, which allowed it to intervene at various stages in disputes when deemed necessary. But the NIB was careful not to act as a "Supreme" Labour Court, which it felt would add a further layer to the State's third-party dispute resolution agencies. It tried not to usurp or cut across existing dispute resolution agencies, but rather to (re)channel disputes into them. Acting in this specific manner, the NIB could be described as a traffic policeman, directing disputes down what it deemed the proper procedural route. The NIB could not avoid dealing to some extent with substantive issues, though, which could sometimes lead to professional tension between the NIB and the LRC or Labour Court. However, such tensions were kept in check by the NIB cooperating strongly, if informally, with the LRC and Labour Court by sharing information, particularly if the dispute had already been before either of these agencies. For example, several members of the NIB could have had direct contact with senior LRC and Labour Court officials to clarify a conflict of evidence between the parties before the NIB.

A major feature of the NIB's *modus operandi* highlighted by interviewees was to "mobilize the channels of influence" within each of the social partnership bodies. Each side was relied upon to exert influence on behalf of the NIB, employers by IBEC and unions by ICTU. Occasionally, senior officials from the Department of the Taoiseach would contact the parties to a dispute directly. The lack of any statutory powers meant that ultimately the NIB relied on "moral force" or "good offices," as various interviewees described it. The interviews suggested that outright rejection of NIB recommendations by either unions or employers was relatively rare. Where recommendations were rejected, though, the NIB was able to do little, but it was generally felt that because extensive contact with the parties had gone into the crafting of most NIB statements, they were likely to "travel" with the parties to a dispute.

For Congress and also for IBEC, much of the work involved in mobilizing the channels of influence meant senior officials talking to the individual parties involved, to persuade them that the NIB approach was the best way to resolve their dispute. Most individual unions and employers would at least listen to what a senior official from their particular representative body had to say at the NIB's behest. In many cases, the individual employer or union would have originally come to that same union or employer body seeking a solution. One member of the NIB was of the impression that ICTU had somewhat more influence over its members than IBEC because unions were part of a "broader movement" with its own rules, whereas IBEC members simply and more instrumentally paid a subscription for a service from that organization. The Executive Council of Congress, as a peer group, "would exert quite a lot of pressure on its members" around NIB activities, mindful, as well, that many employers had more than one union and that the actions of one could affect others.

Another interviewee said that engaging with an employer might involve pointing out that the NIB was offering "a different way in which you can achieve your end result, but in a way that is seen to be procedurally compliant." Employers tended to be "less besotted" by "one procedural route versus another," as their main concern was "getting to an end result they can stand over commercially." The process of persuading employers might involve one or more meetings held in their own offices or at IBEC offices, perhaps with the assistance of the local IBEC official who normally worked with that employer. It was also important to ensure that the NIB was dealing with the right people within individual companies in dispute. Much of the process of persuasion involves providing information on the possible scenarios for that employer and outlining the possible consequences of any decisions. A key factor in the search for solutions was emphasizing the NIB's primary concern with observing procedures rather than the merits of a case — something that often needed to be explained in particular to expatriate managers of multinational firms.

The NIB's ability to focus the power of the social partner organizations and the government was a key tool, with the combined weight of senior individuals from employer and union organizations and officials representing government having a strong effect on the parties. Here, the government's role in particular could prove crucial. One interviewee said that the NIB succeeded because it brought "everybody within the maw of the government." Another spoke of a sense that there was "a national structure, national policy, and you're being called in because you're not complying with it." NIB members believed that the very fact of being brought into Government Buildings could influence individual participants in a dispute. One remarked:

> The march into Government Buildings — there's no doubt psychologically it had ... a very significant impact. It mightn't have such a big impact on the union practitioners, or some of the employer representatives that are in and out there regularly. But [for] shop stewards, managers of companies, who've never been inside the gates before, the whole thing [had] a fairly daunting image to it. Government Buildings is an impressive, authoritative domain to be wheeled into.

The effect on individual employers and their management could also be significant: a NIB member commented that "employers [tended] to want to justify themselves in the eyes of the government." One interviewee suggested that if a multinational subsidiary was trying to sell the NIB recommendation to its parent company, it helped that the recommendation could be "articulated in a way that emphasises this is a consensual approach that has Government imprimatur." Another NIB member noted however that some employers had no fear of Government. He cited the case of an Irish international newspaper and media concern, Independent Newspapers, which had ignored a NIB statement in 2004, adding that some multinational employers who had a relationship with state development agencies remained unconcerned about the NIB. Public sector employers were more concerned about incurring the wrath of Government, as it was the ultimate employer, but even here some county managers in local authorities were likened to "bishops" — understanding themselves to be supreme in their own domains in their attitude toward central government. In some disputes Government took a direct role and statements were issued by ministers and at times even by the Taoiseach. The NIB saw decisions on such interventions as resting with politicians themselves, but pronouncements from them could be "welcome and helpful."

In summary, NIB interventions in significant disputes were complex and multi-faceted and involved the brokerage of settlements or of procedural routes to settlements. This involved the mobilization of industrial relations networks within social partner organizations and sometimes also of political networks. In these cases, the NIB's deliberations in Government Buildings were simply surface activities around which a more intensive, wide-ranging, and expansive process of brokerage occurred. This involved senior and lower level officials within union and employer associations and sometimes senior public servants expending capital to persuade affiliated unions and firms to comply with NIB proposals. The weight and reputation of the senior figures involved and knowledge that the parties were within the "maw of the government" were significant assets in this process. Extra-procedural networking between key figures in the NIB and state conflict resolution agencies also contributed.


# CASE STUDIES OF THE NIB'S INVOLVEMENT IN MAJOR DISPUTES

In order to complement our examination of the dispute resolution practices of the NIB at the central level, we undertook case studies of the NIB's involvement in major disputes at the firm and sector level based on reports in *Industrial Relations News* and other media, on interviews with NIB members, HR managers and union officials, and on documents. Five case studies are reported here. They were chosen to represent different sectors, issues, and stages of the NIB's life-cycle. The details of each case, derived from the sources outlined, are summarized in Table 4.

*Table 4.* Case Studies of NIB Involvement in Major Disputes.

| Case Details | NIB Mobilization Mechanisms | Outcomes |
|---|---|---|
| Dispute over a claim by IBOA and SIPTU in June 2001 – quantified at 6 percent in SIPTU's case – to compensate members working in banking for the changeover to Euro notes and coins in January 2002. The claim if conceded might have spread to retailing and beyond. | Claim referred to NIB by IBEC and then publicly criticized by the Taoiseach (Prime Minister) and Minister for Finance. A meeting of parties within NIB resulted in refusal of SIPTU head office to support the claim of its Dublin services branch and to apply sufficient pressure on the branch for it not to proceed. The NIB's objective was to "kill off" any perception that a claim for co-operation with the Euro changeover might be successful. Unions in retailing responded by not backing calls from members to lodge similar claims. | Euro changeover claim not proceeded with and pressure for similar claims denied legitimacy and not lodged. |
| In 2007, the retail union Mandate lodged a claim on the UK retailer Argos for a pay rise of €1 above the national wage agreement for the sector. Strike notice served and a one-day stoppage occurred, despite a call from the NIB to refer the claim to the LRC. A further planned one-day stoppage was deferred. | IBEC referred claim to NIB after strike notice served. The NIB issued a statement that was seen by members as galvanizing opposition to union's pay campaign on the part of other unions and employers. The NIB operated via union and employer federations to deny the claim cover and support by other unions. Mandate officials feared exclusion from the ICTU and being denied influence over the wide bargaining agenda pursued in talks on successive national pay agreements. Combined Government and employer pressure steeled the employer against conceding the claim. | Having deferred the second planned one-day strike, the union and employer returned to talks at the LRC and agreed to a pay increase for long-service staff in a settlement substantially below the original claim. |

Following months of negotiations and mediation by different parties, guided at critical points by the NIB, the dispute was resolved without any disruption to the airport or to operations at other Irish airports. Agreement was reached on severance terms and outsourcing, with guarantees for employees transferring to the new outsourcing firms and further guarantees on union recognition.

The dispute was resolved at the LRC, with agreement reached on a phased introduction of new flexi-time bands with agreement on management's plan to implement a new time and attendance system.

The NIB initially resisted direct involvement, instead channeling the dispute back to the LRC and Labour Court. Following the subsequent failure of the parties post the Labour Court investigation to reach a settlement, in spite of many meetings and mediation by an independent facilitator, the NIB brokered the involvement of the CEO of the LRC in talks with a definitive timetable and indicated that it would continue to monitor the dispute closely.

The NIB intervened twice to prevent serious disruption to a major social service by channeling the dispute into the LRC. This was a new departure in that public service unions and employers had usually not resorted to the LRC but instead referred disputes to the public service conciliation and arbitration process. A shift to the LRC and Labour Court was favored by civil service unions, but had not been formally agreed. Access to the LRC, at the behest of the NIB, responded to a clear preference of the CPSU that the dispute be channeled to these agencies.

In 2005–2006, a protracted dispute developed at Shannon Airport over plans to cut 200 of the 550 jobs at the airport and over the outsourcing of airline catering. With the LRC engaged, the union, SIPTU, referred the dispute to the NIB. The NIB sought to persuade the parties to engage at the LRC and Labour Court. The Labour Court criticized the parties for failing to engage fully around the issues in dispute but no further progress ensued, as the firm prepared to implement the job cuts. The NIB again intervened and called on the parties to enter talks mediated by the Chief Executive of the LRC, within a definitive deadline, which resolved the dispute.

In 2008, a dispute arose in the Department of Social and Family Affairs in local talks subsequent to a clause in a 2001 civil service agreement over the extension of flexi-time bands for staff. As the dispute escalated, the union, CPSU, withdrew lunchtime cover in all social welfare offices and threatened an overtime and phone ban. The NIB intervened and brokered the involvement of the LRC. The talks failed and industrial action ensured. The NIB again intervened and channeled the dispute back to the LRC at which settlement was reached.

*Table 4.* (*Continued*)

| Case Details | NIB Mobilization Mechanisms | Outcomes |
|---|---|---|
| In 2009, a dispute developed at the aircraft maintenance firm Lufthansa Airmotive Technik Ireland over company proposals to change work practices and overtime arrangements. LRC conciliation and an investigation by the Labour Court failed to resolve the dispute and the form issued protective notice to its 450 employees. The NIB intervened and nominated a team of two facilitators drawn from ICTU and IBEC to facilitate agreement. The team's proposals were accepted by a majority of the unions, SIPTU, Unite and the TEEU. A subsequent dispute over the implementation of agreed proposals led to the firm again issuing protective notice. The NIB responded by issuing clarification of the proposals and by recommending a strengthening of consultative arrangements at the firm. | Following representations to the government by the plant's German parent company, the NIB met the parties to the dispute. The NIB channeled the dispute to a forum with the potential to find a resolution, subsequent to the failure of LRC and Labour Court involvement. This was done following talks with the parties involved and led to direct ICTU and IBEC involvement under the auspices of the NIB. In effect, the NIB itself was central to finding a solution through officials of its constituent organizations. | The dispute was resolved and jobs at the company saved by the NIB-instigated team's work in "clarifying" the terms of the recommendation by the Labour Court and by further clarifications issued by the NIB when the implementation of these proposals ran into difficulty. |

The cases concern a 2001 dispute over a union claim for compensation for changeover to the Euro; a 2007 dispute over pay in the retailer Argos; a 2005–2006 dispute in Shannon Airport over job cuts and outsourcing; a 2008 dispute in the Department of Social and Family Affairs, which administers social welfare, over the revision of flexi-time bands and associated attendance monitoring; and a 2009 dispute over work practices and shift work arrangements in the aircraft maintenance firm Lufthansa Airmotive Technik. Our focus was on identifying the mechanisms used by the NIB to mobilize networks in pursuit of solutions to these disputes – all significant either because settlements had the potential to spread to other firms and sectors, potentially undermining national agreements (the Euro changeover and Argos disputes) or settlements involving regionally sensitive firms had the potential for economic disruption (Shannon Airport), disruption to an important social service (Department of Social and Family Affairs), or disruptive loss of high-skilled jobs (Lufthansa Airmotive Technik).

The cases reveal that five overlapping mechanisms were employed by the NIB to mobilize networks for the purpose of resolving disputes. These are summarized in Fig. 2 and also discussed below, drawing on evidence from the case studies.

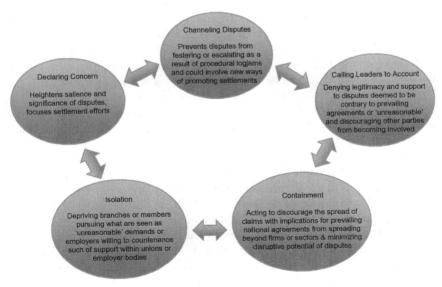

*Fig. 2.* The NIB's Network Mobilization Practices.

*Declaring Concern*

Through its public statements or private contact with the parties to disputes, the NIB commonly declared concern that a dispute had become of
major public significance and threatened pay agreements, economic disruption, or significant numbers of jobs. Such declarations of concern might on
occasion have become the platform for expressions of concern or view-
points by Government figures. On other occasions, the NIB refrained from
issuing public declarations but nevertheless impressed on the parties to a
dispute and their respective social partner organizations that serious concern had arisen among NIB members, not the least the Government,
regarding the course of a particular dispute. The NIB's declarations heightened the salience and significance of the disputes and also the urgency of
reaching settlements, focusing the efforts of both the parties directly
involved and their social partner organizations to resolve the disputes.

In the Euro changeover dispute, IBEC had referred the union's claim
to the NIB, concerned that the claim had the potential to spread across
other sectors. Although the NIB refrained from a public declaration, its
decision to intervene highlighted the significance and potential seriousness
of the issue in dispute and led to the underlying claim being viewed as
"unreasonable," thereby depriving the claim of support from the union's
leadership (Interview with union official). NIB's involvement also became
the platform on which the Taoiseach and the Minister for Finance publicly
criticized the claim. Another union, MANDATE, which represented members in retailing and might otherwise have been drawn into supporting
the claim, refrained from providing support as a consequence of both the
NIB's and senior politicians' actions (Interview with union official). In
the case of the Argos dispute, the NIB issued a public declaration that,
while not preventing a work stoppage was seen as galvanizing opposition
to the union's claim — which was seen as a threat to the prevailing national
pay agreement among both unions and employers. In the Shannon Airport
dispute, the NIB became involved at the behest of the union because the
parties were unable to agree even on what they should be discussing and
had run out of options. The dispute had already been addressed by the
LRC and Labour Court. The NIB declared its concern as to the significance of the dispute and in the process recreated momentum toward a settlement by rechanneling the dispute back to these agencies and again later
by putting pressure on the parties to "make a final effort" toward settlement. In the dispute involving social welfare staff, the NIB on two occasions sought to prevent serious disruption to a major social service but

refrained from issuing public declarations. In the dispute at Lufthansa
Airmotive Technik, the subsidiary's parent firm had instigated NIB involvement. That led to talks at Government Buildings between the parties
directly involved, including the German parent firm, at which the seriousness of the issues involved, including the threat to jobs at the plant, was
highlighted.

NIB declarations of concern, whether made publicly or privately to
those involved and their wider social partner organizations, highlighted the
seriousness of disputes and the urgency of finding a settlement. Their
declarations focused attention or added momentum to focusing attention
on settlement efforts and sometimes in effect marked out claims as unreasonable, thereby depriving them of wider union or employer support.

### Channeling Disputes

A standard NIB activity was to channel or rechannel disputes into the public dispute resolution agencies, as provided for in local procedures or those
contained in national pay agreements. Channeling sometimes involved
working behind the scenes to "tee-up" or fast-track a dispute to the LRC
or Labour Court and sometimes involved moving disputes in new directions, if expedient to the process of reaching settlement. In this way disputes that might otherwise have festered or escalated for loss of momentum
toward settlement were kept within procedure and contained. By channeling disputes the NIB in effect acted extra- or supra-procedurally, sidestepping the fact that these disputes had already exhausted procedure and
could not strictly be presented again for conciliation or for further investigation by the Labour Court. The NIB also sometimes brokered new
approaches to dispute resolution that had not been envisaged in existing
local dispute resolution procedures.

In the Argos dispute, the NIB sought to channel the dispute back into
the LRC in line with an earlier recommendation by the Labour Court. In
Shannon Airport, the NIB responded to a union request for intervention to
break a procedural logjam also by referring the parties back to the LRC. A
subsequent intervention by the NIB provided for immediate access to mediation by the CEO of the Labour Relations Commission, with a stipulation
that the talks be concluded within a tight timeframe. This channeled the
dispute back through conventional procedure, but at the highest possible
level and in the shortest possible timeframe. In the social welfare and
aircraft maintenance disputes the NIB broke new procedural ground in

dispute settlement. In the social welfare dispute, CPSU, the union involved, expressed a preference for the dispute to be resolved within the LRC—Labour Court process rather than through the civil service conciliation and arbitration process, as provided for under prevailing procedure. This request reflected a more widely declared preference by civil service unions for access to the LRC and the Labour Court, which had not been formally established. On grounds of expedience the NIB brokered the involvement of the LRC in settling the dispute, departing from formally agreed procedure. In the case of Lufthansa Airmotive Technik, the NIB similarly nominated a team of two officials from IBEC and the ICTU to address settlement options, rather than pressing the "reset button" by channeling the dispute back to the main state agencies.

### Calling Leaders to Account

The NIB sought to call leaders of union and employer bodies to account for their prior consent to enter into local or national agreements, including procedural agreements. This practice involved reminding senior figures in the firms and unions involved and in ICTU and IBEC that they had entered into, and were expected to adhere to, collective agreements. This practice was focused on denying "cover" to unions' intent on or engaged in industrial action in pursuit of unreasonable claims and on stiffening the resistance of employers to such claims. This practice was particularly important in disputes that threatened national agreements or were intended to ratchet pay up across the economy with similar effect. In the Euro changeover dispute, the NIB's activities were seen to have distanced national leadership of one of the unions from the claim of their branch and to have denied the dispute support and legal cover by the union's leaders. A NIB member identified the body's aim in this case as to "try to kill off any notion that ongoing increase for cooperation with the Euro changeover was in any way credible or sustainable" (Interview with NIB member). In the case of the Argos dispute, the NIB's activities resulted in other unions "circling the wagons" and denying Mandate wider support, even raising the prospect of expulsion from ICTU. On the employer side, the NIB's support for the prevailing national agreement was seen to have "steeled the company to hold fast to its position" in resisting the claim (Interview with employer official). No national agreement was at issue in the case of Shannon airport, but the NIB called leaders to account for their "lack of progress over a protracted period" and to remind them of their obligations in line with good industrial relations practice to "make a final effort" to find a solution.

## Isolation

The practice of calling leaders to account was sometimes closely related to the practice of "isolation." The NIB's activities were sometimes geared to isolating activists or union branches pursuing, supporting, or tolerating claims seen as unreasonable. Isolation involved applying enough pressure on union head offices and on employers to weaken the momentum behind claims without publicly castigating or humiliating the parties involved, which would have been counterproductive. In the Euro changeover dispute, the union branch that had instigated the claim was in effect isolated by being denied head-office support. No explicit or public rebuke was involved and the branch was not even requested formally to abandon the claim. In the Lufthansa Airmotive Technik dispute, NIB activities appeared to have been instrumental in reducing the influence of a group of union members strongly opposed to proposals that would have cut high levels of overtime on their lines. Strong leadership from a union official was seen as instrumental in mobilizing the majority of the workforce behind the NIB's ICTU-IBEC team's settlement proposals.

## Containment

An important feature of the NIB's activities was to preclude claims and resulting concessions from spreading beyond firms or sectors in which they had originated and, in the process, threatening prevailing national pay agreements or provoking economy-wide pressure on pay and conditions. This was evident in the Euro changeover and Argos disputes, where the NIB explicitly sought to contain disputes and settlements that could have upset national precedents and norms across sectors. The NIB showed a limited degree of tolerance of local or sectoral settlements seen to depart from national norms, however, provided that these could be insulated or contained within the firms or sectors directly involved. In the case of the Shannon Airport and social welfare disputes, containment was focused more on preventing or minimizing any disruption to key public utilities or social services.

## CONCLUSIONS AND DISCUSSION

The NIB played a key role in dispute resolution in Ireland from 2000 to 2009 through what we have described as a networked mode of dispute resolution that was different from, if also supplementary to, standard dispute resolution as practiced by state dispute resolution agencies or independent practitioners. Its primary modus was to mobilize networks within and across employer and trade union confederations and dispute resolution agencies, within "the maw of government," to find solutions to the most serious disputes that occurred during the period in which it operated. Much of its work was informal or extra-procedural in that it was not covered by formal procedural agreements or arrangements and might indeed have been more effective for this reason, allowing a complex of pressures and inducements to be brought to bear on disputes and disputants. The main mechanisms of NIB involvement were identified on the basis of case studies of five major disputes in which the body became involved. These mechanisms went beyond and often appeared quite different from the repertoire of dispute resolution practices deployed by dispute resolution professionals. In particular, the NIB sometimes sought to shape the internal dynamics of union and employer associations' engagement with disputes by highlighting the public significance of disputes, holding leaders accountable, bolstering senior officials, and isolating activists seen as acting unreasonably. In these ways, the NIB innovated in conflict resolution through instituting what we have described as networked dispute resolution.

The NIB ceased to function when social partnership collapsed after the advent of the Irish financial and economic crisis. Though the institution itself is no more, echoes of the NIB continue to be heard in Irish industrial relations. In 2010, for example, unions and employers in the private sector concluded a protocol on collective bargaining and dispute resolution, which contained provision for a NIB-like body to handle major disputes. The body was not brought into being, seemingly because Government hesitated to become party to arrangements that harked back to the social partnership era. In some serious disputes, such as a dispute that disrupted Dublin Bus services in 2013, an ad hoc NIB-like arrangement was established to resolve the dispute. The parties involved from IBEC, ICTU, and the senior public service opted to act through a two-person investigative team, as the NIB itself had done on occasions. A similar mechanism was established in March 2014 to deal with the long-running pensions issue at the airline Aer Lingus and the state-owned airports. As such, the possibility of the NIB being reinstituted in some form, when the economy recovers and the labor market tightens, cannot be ruled out. That aside, the operation of the NIB provides an interesting example of an innovative form of conflict resolution with distinctive networked features that added a further dimension to the dispute resolution activities of public agencies and their specialist practitioners.

When considering the wider implications of the Irish experience with networked dispute resolution it needs to be recognized that the international literature is of little assistance. This literature focuses either on the legal and structural features of formal dispute resolution agencies (Valdes Dal-Re, 2002; Weltz & Kauppinen, 2005) or on changes in conflict resolution practices within organizations (Roche et al., 2014). A case could be made that Ireland has been exceptional in the extent to which networked dispute resolution prevailed under social partnership. Such exceptionalism could in turn be attributed to the small economy; to interlocking state, employer, and union elites; to a consensus that social partnership was a key element of the Irish "economic miracle"; and to an institutional heritage that inclined the parties toward a networked approach to resolving serious disputes. But, as suggested earlier in the chapter, the Irish experience may have a wider resonance given the role of networks in promoting wage coordination and in underpinning "new social pacts" in a number of European countries from the 1980s and 1990s. Indeed, some scholars have suggested that networks were *the* defining or distinctive feature of new social pacts, providing the glue that bound employers and unions to various kinds of wage coordination policies (Baccaro, 2002, 2003; Molina & Rhodes, 2002; Traxler, 2003; Traxler, Brandl, & Glassner, 2008; Traxler et al., 2001). Yet, seldom has the recent literature on wage coordination and social pacts moved beyond highly abstract and general portrayals of how networks operate to coordinate wage bargaining or contain pressure on pay norms. It is not surprising, therefore, that this study is the only one that has so far addressed the role of networks and associated mechanisms in responding to disputes and threats of economic dislocation. Given the supposed importance of networks in recent European industrial relations, the present study may shine a light on an area worthy of further and more concrete investigation in the countries that have concluded social pacts during recent decades (Avdagic et al., 2011; Pochet & Fajertag, 2000).

Whether networks play a role in conflict resolution in countries in the Anglo-American world, without a tradition of social pacts, is more open to question. Strike activity and collective conflict have declined sharply across the developed world. Anglo-American dispute resolution agencies have often responded by redefining their missions and shifting their focus to more proactive and earlier modes of involvement in conflicts (Roche et al., 2014). There are indications that some new forms of "proactive mediation" in collective bargaining may involve coalitions and networks that extend beyond the employers and unions immediately involved in disputes. Networks may be mobilized and coalitions built to gain settlements and to diffuse them more widely. In the United States, the FMCS has initiated a program of early intervention and proactive facilitation in the private and public sectors. This sometimes involves working with stakeholders at multiple levels. The stakeholders can range from the employers and unions involved in disputes − the locus of conventional conciliation − to industry or sector groupings, public agencies, boards, and government (Cohen, 2011). In similar vein, Cutcher-Gershenfeld (2014) has observed that the future of collective bargaining as an institution may now rest to some degree on its capacity to incorporate the interests of multiple stakeholders as well as the public interest (Cutcher-Gershenfeld, 2014). As dispute resolution agencies shift their focus and recalibrate their methods in these ways, various forms of network-based dispute resolution, albeit different in character to the Irish NIB model, could have a vibrant future in the wider world.

# REFERENCES

Acas. (2009). *The alchemy of dispute resolution − The role of collective conciliation.* Acas Policy discussion papers. Acas, London.

Avdagic, S., Rhodes, M., & Visser, J. (Eds.). (2011). *Social pacts in Europe: Emergence, evolution and institutionalization.* Oxford: Oxford University Press.

Baccaro, L. (2000). Centralized collective bargaining and the problem of 'compliance': Lessons from the Italian experience. *Industrial & Labor Relations Review, 53,* 579−599.

Baccaro, L. (2002). The construction of democratic corporatism in Italy. *Politics and Society, 30,* 327−357.

Baccaro, L. (2003). What is alive and what is dead in the theory of corporatism? *British Journal of Industrial Relations, 41*(4), 683−706.

Bain, G. (2002). *The future of the fire service: Reducing risks, saving lives.* London: Department for Communities and Local Government.

Cohen, G. H. (2011). *A new model for managing labor-management conflicts with early third-party intervention.* Paper presented to the International Agencies Meeting, Cardiff.

Cutcher-Gershenfeld, J. (2014). Interest-based bargaining. In W. K. Roche, P. Teague, & A. Colvin (Eds.), *The Oxford handbook of conflict management in organizations.* New York, NY: Oxford University Press.

Department of the Taoiseach. (2000). *IBEC/ICTU/government agreement on the PPF.* Dublin: Department of the Taoiseach.

EIRO. (1998). *Ryanair dispute closes Dublin airport*. Dublin: Eurofound. Retrieved from http://www.eurofound.europa.eu/eiro/1998/03/inbrief/ie9803224n.htm

Hardiman, N. (1988). *Pay, politics and economic performance in Ireland 1970−1987*. Oxford: Clarendon Press.

Hastings, T., Sheehan, B., & Yeates, P. (2007). *Saving the future: How social partnership contributed to Ireland's economic success*. Dublin: Orpen Press.

Higgins, C. (2013). Dublin bus report backs binding arbitration. *Industrial Relations News*, October 17.

Higgins, C., & Roche, W. K. (2013). Networked pay coordination and the containment of second-tier pay bargaining: Social partnership at the height of the economic boom. *Economic and Industrial Democracy*, *35*(4), 667−93.

Hillery, B. (1987). 'An overview of Irish industrial relations' in department of industrial relations, university college Dublin. In W. A. Kelly, T. Murphy & B. Hillery (Eds.) *Industrial relations in Ireland: Contemporary issues and developments*. Dublin: Department of Industrial Relations, University College Dublin.

International Labour Office. (2013). *Labour dispute systems: Guidelines for improved performance*. Geneva: ILO.

International Labour Office, Steadman, F. (2003). *Handbook on alternative dispute resolution*. Geneva: ILO.

International Labour Office, Thompson, C. (2010). *Dispute prevention and resolution in public service labour relations: Good policy and practice*. Sectoral Activities Programme Working Paper. ILO, Geneva.

Lipsky, D., & Seeber, R. (2006). Managing organizational conflicts. In J. Oetzel & S. Ting-Toomey (Eds.), *The sage handbook of conflict communication*. Thousand Oaks, CA: Sage.

Lipsky, D., Seeber, R., & Fincher, R. D. (2003). *Emerging systems for managing workplace conflict: Lessons for managers and dispute resolution professionals*. San Francisco, CA: Jossey-Bass.

Molina, O., & Rhodes, M. (2002). Corporatism: The past, present and future of a concept. *Annual Review of Political Science*, *5*, 305−331.

O'Brien, J. F. (1981). *A study of national pay agreements*. Dublin: Economic and Social Research Institute.

O'Brien, J. F. (1987). 'Pay determination in Ireland' in department of industrial relations, university college Dublin. In W. A. Kelly, T. Murphy & B. Hillery (Eds.) *Industrial relations in Ireland: Contemporary issues and developments*. Dublin: Department of Industrial Relations, University College Dublin.

Pochet, P., & Fajertag, G. (2000). A new era for social pacts in Europe. In G. Fajertag & P. Pochet (Eds.), *Social pacts in Europe − New dynamics*. Brussels: European Trade Union Institute.

Rasmussen, E., & Greenwood, G. (2014). Conflict management in New Zealand. In W. K. Roche, P. Teague, & A. J. Colvin (Eds.), *The Oxford handbook of conflict management systems*. New York, NY: Oxford University Press.

Roche, W. K., & Teague, P. (2012). Do conflict management systems matter? *Human Resource Management*, *51*(2), 231−258.

Roche, W. K., Teague, P., & Colvin, A. J. (Eds.). (2014). *The Oxford handbook of conflict management systems*. New York, NY: Oxford University Press.

Traxler, F. (2003). Coordinated bargaining: A stocktaking of its preconditions, practices and performance. *Industrial Relations Journal, 34*(3), 194–209.

Traxler, F., Blaschke, S., & Kittel, B. (2001). *National labour relations in internationalised markets: A comparative study of institutions, change and performance.* Oxford: Oxford University Press.

Traxler, F., Brandl, B., & Glassner, V. (2008). Pattern bargaining: An investigation into its agency, context and evidence. *British Journal of Industrial Relations, 46*(1), 33–58.

Valdes Dal-Re, F. (2002). Synthesis reports on conciliation, mediation and arbitration in the European Union countries. In V. Dal-Re (Ed.), *Labour conciliation, mediation and arbitration in European Union countries.* Madrid: Ministero de Trabajo y Asuntos Sociales.

Van Gramberg, B., Bamber, G., Teicher, J., & Cooper, B. (2014). Conflict management in Australia. In W. K. Roche, P. Teague, & A. J. Colvin (Eds.), *The Oxford handbook of conflict management systems.* New York, NY: Oxford University Press.

Weltz, C., & Kauppinen, T. (2005). Industrial action and conflict resolution in the new member states. *European Journal of Industrial Relations, 11*(1), 91–106.

# TOWARD A SYSTEM OF CONFLICT MANAGEMENT? CULTURAL CHANGE AND RESISTANCE IN A HEALTHCARE ORGANIZATION

Paul L. Latreille and Richard Saundry

## ABSTRACT

Purpose — *This chapter reports on attempts to develop a more integrated and strategic approach to managing conflict within a large state-owned provider of healthcare in the United Kingdom that goes beyond more conventional offerings such as workplace mediation.*

Methodology/approach — *It adopted a detailed four-stage mixed-methods organizational case study approach, with the findings reported here drawing primarily on semi-structured interviews with a range of stakeholders, including line managers.*

Findings — *The data suggest that a systematic and integrated approach to identifying conflict and a range of coordinated interventions involving key organizational stakeholders can begin to embed a culture of resolution. There is resistance to such innovation, however, rooted in perceptions that it potentially weakens the authority of front-line managers.*

Managing and Resolving Workplace Conflict
Advances in Industrial and Labor Relations, Volume 22, 189–209
Copyright © 2016 by Emerald Group Publishing Limited
All rights of reproduction in any form reserved
ISSN: 0742-6186/doi:10.1108/S0742-618620160000022008

Originality/value — *The research reported here provides the first UK evidence for the adoption of an Integrated Conflict Management System and for the potential of such strategic choices and approaches to effect culture change in the manner sought by policy-makers.*

**Keywords:** Workplace conflict; mediation; conflict management system; resolution; manager and culture

A dominant theme within the conflict management literature is the extent to which organizations have adopted coordinated and strategic approaches to the resolution of workplace conflict. The potential of integrated conflict management systems (ICMSs) to transform organizational culture rather than simply manage disputes has received significant attention in the United States (Lipsky, Seeber, & Fincher, 2003; Lynch, 2001, 2003). Furthermore, there is evidence that "bundles" of conflict resolution practices are increasingly found within U.S. corporations (Lipsky, Avgar, Lamare, & Gupta, 2012).

In the United Kingdom, although organizations have tended to resolve disputes through conventional rights-based disciplinary and grievance procedures, the potential of alternative dispute resolution (ADR) has become a central focus of public policy. Greater emphasis has been placed on early managerial responses to conflict and the increased use of workplace mediation, in particular. Notably, the UK government has seen mediation as having the potential to transform organizational culture (BIS, 2011), but this rhetoric has as yet had limited empirical foundation: mediation is used in a relatively small minority of workplaces (Wood, Saundry, & Latreille, 2014), more likely in larger, public sector workplaces. Thus far, there is little sign of the broader range of practices found in the United States (Teague, Roche, & Hann, 2012).

Perhaps most significantly, evidence from both the United Kingdom and the Republic of Ireland has found that senior managers and HR practitioners tend to view conflict management as a transactional and not a strategic issue, limiting the diffusion of innovative approaches. Furthermore, an important source of resistance to integrated approaches to conflict management is the reluctance of managers to cede authority over decisions relating to employee conduct and performance (Saundry et al., 2014; Teague & Doherty, 2011).

This chapter examines the case of Trustorg, a state-owned healthcare provider and part of the UK's National Health Service (NHS), that has attempted to develop a coordinated and strategic approach to the management of workplace conflict over the last seven years. Trustorg employs approximately 9,000 staff, operates nine hospitals, and is responsible for a wide range of community care services. The findings draw on over 50 semi-structured interviews with mediators, HR practitioners, front-line managers, and trade union representatives that sought to begin to answer a number of key research questions: To what extent did the approach adopted by Trustorg represent an ICMS? What were the key drivers of the change in the Trust's approach? What has been the impact? What role have managers played in the development of conflict management at Trustorg? And what does this case tell us about the potential for such innovation in the UK?

Our chapter is structured as follows. We first examine the extant literature in this area before setting out the methods used in this research. The findings are then presented chronologically, charting the development of conflict management within Trustorg. The implications of the findings are then discussed and conclusions are drawn.

# MEDIATION AND SYSTEMS OF CONFLICT MANAGEMENT

Growing concerns over the cost and impact of workplace conflict in the United Kingdom have brought increased attention to ADR and, particularly, to workplace mediation. Proponents of mediation have long argued that it offers demonstrable advantages over slow, complex, and adversarial grievance and disciplinary procedures, which tend to focus on rights as opposed to interests (Pope, 1996; Reynolds, 2000). In the United Kingdom, data suggest resolution rates (full or partial) of around 90 percent (or more) (Latreille, 2011; Saundry, McArdle, & Thomas, 2013; Saundry & Wibberley, 2012), mirroring U.S. evidence that also points to high levels of participant satisfaction with both process and outcome (Bingham, Hallberlin, Walker, & Chung, 2009; Kochan, Lautsch, & Bendersky, 2000; McDermott, Obar, Jose, & Bowers, 2000). In addition, there may be an impact beyond the specific disputes that are mediated: a range of studies in the United Kingdom have suggested in particular that mediation training and participation in mediation can have a positive impact on conflict-handling skills (Saundry & Wibberley, 2014).

The extent to which UK organizations have embraced mediation is unclear: there is some evidence that while its use has increased, that use is limited to a relatively small minority of organizations. The number of individual mediations conducted annually by Acas has risen from 35 in 2004–2005 to 256 in 2013–2014 (Acas, 2006, 2014). Analysis of the recent 2011 Workplace Employment Relations Study revealed that around 15 percent of workplaces that had experienced a dispute in the last 12 months had used mediation by a third party (Wood et al., 2014).

The UK government's promotion of workplace mediation has extended to claims that its use can transform organizational cultures and provide the basis for high-trust relationships (BIS, 2011). Commentators in the United States, however, have argued that mediation alone may be insufficient, and that wider benefits are more likely to be realized when organizations introduce complementary ADR practices (Bendersky, 2003) as part of an overall strategic approach. It is argued that ICMSs represent a new "philosophy of organizational life" (Lynch, 2001, p. 208) and a change in organizational "mind-set" in regard to conflict management (Lipsky & Seeber, 1998, p. 23. Accordingly, ICMSs create a "conflict competent culture where all conflict may be safely raised and where persons will feel confident that their concerns will be heard, respected, and acted upon ..." Lynch, 2001, p. 213) and where "managers are expected to prevent, manage, contain and resolve all conflict at the earliest time and lowest level possible" (Lynch, 2003, p. 212).

While an ICMS may be made up of a range of different components Lipsky and Avgar (2010; see also Lipsky et al., 2003) set out five broad characteristics: first, the system should be broad in scope, providing access for all employees; second, it should underpin a culture of tolerance and early resolution in which employees should feel able to challenge and raise any issues; third, the system should have multiple options for resolution, including both rights- and interest-based processes that employees should be able to access at any point. Finally, the system should be underpinned by strong support structures. Lynch (2003) argues that the participation of stakeholders both in the development of the system and ongoing implementation, oversight, and governance is critical, while capacity should be built by creating awareness and understanding of the system and developing conflict competence among key leaders through training and conflict coaching. This notion in turn is founded on "corporate commitment" through which conflict management is not only championed by senior leaders but also accepted as a core competence and integrated within strategic objectives, communications, and policies.

In the United States, Lipsky et al.'s (2012) study of Fortune 1000 companies suggests organizations are increasingly adopting more strategic and proactive approaches to managing conflict. One-third of the corporations in the sample had adopted features associated with ICMSs. Furthermore, there was evidence of a wide range of practices beyond mediation and arbitration, such as early case assessment and peer review (a process by which disputes are adjudicated by a panel of coworkers). In the United Kingdom and the Republic of Ireland, however, there is little evidence of organizations adopting more integrated approaches that locate conflict management as a central element of HR strategy (Roche & Teague, 2011). Research points to an antipathy among managers to the idea that conflict is an inevitable feature of organizational life (Teague & Doherty, 2011). A succession of studies have in fact found the attitudes of line managers to represent a major barrier to the spread of ADR, viewing mediation as both an admission of failure and a threat to their authority (Saundry & Wibberley, 2012; Seargeant, 2005), and reflecting what Lipsky and Avgar have characterized as the "traditional approach to workplace conflict" (2010, p. 41).

It is interesting to consider the reasons for the different rates of diffusion of integrated and strategic approaches to conflict management in the United Kingdom and the United States. Lynch has argued that ICMSs may be triggered by a crisis, the need for regulatory compliance, or a desire to reduce cost. They may also be driven by the pursuit of cultural transformation in order to underpin broader strategies and to seek competitive advantage (Lynch refers to these as the 5Cs.).

It could be argued that in both the United Kingdom and the United States, compliance and cost have shaped organizational approaches to conflict resolution. In both countries, the erosion of collective regulation and increased reliance on individual employment rights have seen an increased emphasis on employment litigation (Colvin, 2003; Lipsky & Seeber, 1998; Saundry et al., 2014). Nonetheless, while it is important not to exaggerate the threat of litigation (Colvin, 2012), the cost of litigation through the U.S. civil court system is substantially higher than that of the equivalent Employment Tribunal system in the United Kingdom. Colvin (2014, p. 176) characterizes the U.S. system as "high risk, high reward" and reports studies showing median damages in employment cases ranging from $150,000 to $300,000. In contrast, while employer groups in the United Kingdom have criticized the burden of the employment tribunal system, the median award for equivalent claims ranges between $7,000 and $10,000. It could be argued, therefore, that the incentive for U.S. organizations to innovate is substantially higher than for their UK counterparts.

Another key driver of ADR in the United States has been union substitution as employers have sought to ward off organizing campaigns through the introduction of conflict resolution mechanisms (Lipsky & Seeber, 2000). Interestingly, however, data from the Fortune 1000 study suggest that the extension of ADR and the development of conflict management systems to complement existing provisions in unionized workplaces by extending ADR to non-union workers may be a more powerful influence (Lipsky et al., 2012). But key differences with union-management relations in the United Kingdom weaken or in some way reshape these stimuli. First, grievance and disciplinary procedures are widespread across both unionized and non-unionized workplaces (Wood et al., 2014) and tend to have similar forms, although procedures in unionized workplaces may be more detailed and offer greater protection for employees. Second, grievance and disciplinary procedures in the United Kingdom are essentially managerial procedures within which managers make final decisions and also hear appeals. Therefore, the only chance most employees have for a complaint to be adjudicated by a third party has traditionally been through litigation, whether the employee is a union member or not. And third, in both unionized and non-unionized workplaces, employees have a legal right to be accompanied to a disciplinary or grievance hearing by a trade union representative.

Accordingly, it could be argued that there is little need to use ADR either to substitute for, or complement, unionized approaches to conflict resolution. Indeed, in the United Kingdom the introduction of in-house mediation schemes has tended to occur in the public sector, in which union membership and organization are concentrated. Although unions in the United Kingdom may have traditionally worried that ADR was "a way of undermining the role of the union in representing members" (Bleiman, 2008, p. 15) case study research has suggested that union representatives who experience workplace mediation see it as a way of delivering results for members that conventional rights-based approaches, in which managerial authority is embedded, often fail to secure (Saundry & Wibberley, 2014). This reflects Lipsky and Seeber's contention that "ADR systems can extend the authority and influence of a union into areas normally considered management prerogatives" (2000, p. 45). Moreover, as Bleiman (2008) argues, unions may have an important role to play as enablers, securing the informed consent that is fundamental to mediation uptake and success.

In addition, the experience of the United States suggests that integrated and innovative approaches (such as peer review) are more likely to be found in "high road" organizations, which see conflict management as part of human resource strategy designed to maximize employee engagement and maintain competitiveness (Colvin, 2004). In such organizations, therefore, the development of conflict management systems may be aligned and integrated with their existing strategy and culture (Lipsky & Avgar, 2010). However, the link between the strategic management of conflict and employee engagement is, to date, notably absent from managerial discourse in Great Britain and Ireland. Instead, conflict management remains associated with the administration of disciplinary and grievance procedures and is consequently stereotyped as a low value and essentially transactional element of the management function. The fact that research points to an aversion among managers – and particularly senior managers – in UK organizations for even accepting that conflict is an issue might therefore militate against the development of more strategic approaches. This in turn highlights the importance of more detailed examination of the role that managers play in the diffusion of conflict management practices and systems in terms of both leadership and front-line application.

Overall, while there is growing evidence that explains the diffusion of ICMSs in the United States, we know less about the antecedents of similar strategies in the United Kingdom. This is in part because there are so few examples. In this chapter, therefore, we look at the case of one organization that has attempted to develop an integrated and strategic approach to conflict management.

## METHODOLOGY

The setting for this research is an NHS Foundation Trust (Trustorg) that manages the provision of hospital, community health, and adult social care services to over half a million people. It is one of the largest employers within its region, with almost 9,000 staff. As a Foundation Trust, the organization has a large degree of managerial autonomy, but as part the UK's NHS it relies on a share of central government funding and follows a range of nationally decided or agreed-upon protocols, policies, and agreements. In addition, trade unions are recognized for collective bargaining purposes at the national level and within each NHS Trust. Trade union density is also typically high, with 56 percent of workers in the UK public sector being members of a trade union compared to 14 percent in the private sector.

Therefore, this case is not representative of organizations in the UK as a whole. Nonetheless, it provides a valuable setting for this research for a number of reasons. The NHS is one of the largest employers in the world, having had approximately 1.39 million staff in 2014. Consequently, it plays an influential role in relation to employment relations policy and practice in the United Kingdom. Furthermore, the publication of the Francis Report in 2013 which investigated major failings at a large UK hospital has placed increased focus on the link between staff well-being and engagement and patient care and, in particular, on the importance of developing cultures in which staff are able to raise issues without fear of retribution. Indeed, Francis subsequently recommended that "consideration should be given at an early stage to the use of expert interventions to resolve conflicts, rebuild trust or support staff who have raised concerns" (Francis, 2015, p. 15). This focus on conflict resolution provides this case study with particular salience.

The data reported in this chapter were generated as part of a detailed organizational case study that used a mixed-methods approach to provide both a broad overview of conflict management and a deeper examination of the way in which managers and employees interact within different processes of dispute resolution.

The first stage of the research involved the examination of existing documentation regarding individual dispute resolution. This included policies and procedures relating to grievance, discipline, capability, and bullying and harassment. In addition, we analyzed data regarding disciplinary and grievance cases between 2008 and 2014 and NHS staff survey data between 2005 and 2013. We also studied mediation records that included details of case types, durations, and outcomes and anonymized evaluations completed by participants between 2006 and 2014.

The second stage of the research focused on interviews with a sample of mediators, HR practitioners, and trade union representatives. We designed the interviews to provide an overview of the key issues and explore the nature of conflict resolution; the introduction and operation of the mediation service; and the extent to which this had shaped the way in which conflict was, and is, managed. In total, 16 interviews were conducted, each lasting between 35 and 90 minutes.

The third stage contained an online survey that sought to explore line managers' and supervisors' experiences of, attitudes toward, and approaches for dealing with work conflict. We received 237 completed responses, an estimated response rate approaching 50 percent.

Finally, we interviewed operational managers (of all grades) and mediation participants. Some interviewees were selected because they had been involved in mediation service interventions or worked in areas that had faced particular challenges in respect to workplace conflict. Others were chosen because they had indicated on their questionnaire that they were prepared to take part in an interview to discuss their views in greater detail. Overall, 35 such interviews were conducted, each lasting between 20 and 90 minutes.

The findings in this chapter, which draw on the qualitative data outlined above, are organized in four main sections: first, the development of conflict management at Trustorg; second, the key drivers for change; third, the impact of these changes; and, finally, the role of managers both in leading, and also responding to, this new system.

# FINDINGS

*Developing ADR at Trustorg — Toward an Integrated System?*

Like most large, public sector organizations in the United Kingdom, Trustorg's traditional approach to workplace conflict revolved around the operation of written policies and procedures.[1] Separate procedures dealt with disciplinary matters, employee grievances, and dignity at work issues (largely accusations of bullying and harassment). These had developed over time and were subject to joint negotiation with trade unions, although they applied to all employees. Importantly (as is typical in the United Kingdom), there was no provision for independent third-party intervention; decisions, including appeals, rested with Trust managers.

The first major change to this approach came with the establishment of an internal mediation service. Initially, a cohort of 12 staff was trained, drawn from a range of posts within the organization, including consultants, managers, nurses, HR staff, and trade union representatives. This reflected a deliberate attempt to embed the service in different areas of the organization. An additional seven mediators were trained in 2011.

Importantly, existing procedures and processes were also revised to include mediation as an option. Perhaps more significantly, the Dignity at Work Policy, which sought to deal with complaints of bullying and harassment, was redesigned to not only include mediation but also acknowledge the importance of resolving conflict at work through early intervention.

Critically, this revision acknowledged the limitations of existing rights-based procedures:

> Conflict in the workplace can have an adverse effect on employees' morale and team relationships … formal procedures such as the Grievance Policies very rarely lead to an improvement in the working relationship and may serve to escalate the problem. The key to dealing with conflict or working relationship difficulties is early identification of issues and where possible informal resolution and not through the Grievance Procedure. (Trustorg Dignity at Work Policy)

This placed dignity at work issues in the wider context of conflict management and provided a clear and demonstrable link with resolution processes. Furthermore, it represented a significant break with adversarial union and management roles implicit in rights-based organizational procedures.

The extent to which the role of the mediation service was intertwined with broader approaches to managing conflict and its consequences was not limited to policy and procedure. Occupational health psychologists, who coordinated Trustorg's mediation service, also played a central role in addressing the issue of workplace stress more widely. They developed a structured and systematic approach to identifying stress "hotspots" by analyzing a range of key indicators (referred to as "dashboard data"), including absence rates, turnover, counseling referrals to occupational health, the number of formal disciplinary and grievance cases, the number of violent incidents, conflict, and the existence of organizational change.

It is important that this information was considered by a Health and Well-being Steering Group that included senior managers; staff from HR, Occupational Health, and Health and Safety; consultants; and staff-side representatives. The coordinator of the mediation service chaired the Group. Thus, the management of conflict within Trustorg was not simply a management strategy but was underpinned by a partnership approach. It was notable that all union respondents were fully committed to the work of the Steering Group and saw no contradiction between participation in this and their role in defending their members' interests.

Once hotspots were identified, a range of interventions was considered. This could include a stress risk assessment within the part of the organization identified and potentially followed up by individual mediation, targeted training, team facilitation, and conflict coaching. Team facilitation involved groups of staff discussing issues that were leading to conflict. This was normally facilitated by members of the mediation service and also often involved HR and more senior managers. This process was not voluntary, though, and was therefore distinct from individual mediation.[2]

In addition, trained mediators were sometimes used to facilitate discussions between two staff members over issues when full-blown mediation was not deemed necessary. Another example could have included conflict coaching, or working closely with individual managers to develop their confidence and capability in handling difficult issues.

In our research we found examples of many such interventions. Of course, these did not preclude the use of formal rights-based disputes procedures whenever they were appropriate. Nonetheless, there was clear evidence of the development of a strategic approach to the management of conflict and a combination of rights- and interest-based processes typical of ICMSs (Bendersky, 2003; Lipsky et al., 2003).

Two other types of training were also available: training in relation to conflict resolution within teams (offered through the occupational health psychologists) and training in handling difficult conversations (being rolled out to line managers by the HR department but designed and delivered by one of the more experienced workplace mediators and senior HR managers) in Trustorg. This was a critical and central aspect of the HR strategy.

## *Drivers for Change*

Respondents identified two main drivers for change. The first was the perceived failure of conventional rights-based procedures and the consequent costs incurred by the organization. Trustorg's procedures were designed to provide consistency, equity, and legal compliance, but according to respondents from both management and unions at Trustorg, they were complex, time-consuming, and stressful for all involved, and they rarely led to resolution:

> ... we were probably pretty poor in all that sort of stuff, so it used to get embroiled in formal process. We'd have grievances that went on for ages because we were trying to solve interpersonal relationships with grievance investigations, where all you end up with is "he said, she said" on a bit of paper. (HR practitioner)

Both management and union representatives were skeptical that these processes produced outcomes that were positive for the parties involved. The following comment was typical of respondents' views of grievance procedures, and it highlighted the ambiguity of resolutions, which in itself could exacerbate workplace conflict:

> If you, say, put in a grievance against someone because you have been bullied ... after the investigation they've no feedback, you don't get any feedback in terms of what

actually happened to that person. So yes the process would have been carried out appropriately but the end result might not be satisfying to the victim ... They end up with nothing to say this has been addressed ... It gets dragged out a lot and it brings in a lot of people and it is quite expensive. (Manager)

A mediator made a similar point that participants rarely felt that grievances produced a satisfactory outcome:

The problem with the grievance, you've normally got to come down on one side or the other ... The person that was unsuccessful in the grievance always felt as though they hadn't been heard, not listened to, and it was a divisive action. (Mediator)

Secondly, there was evidence that prior to the introduction of the mediation scheme, workplace conflict was becoming an increasing problem for the organization. A significant number of cases involving relationship problems between colleagues were being referred to Trustorg's counseling service, for example, while staff survey results suggested that bullying and harassment was an issue for a sizeable proportion of employees. In 2005, 18 percent of employees reported experiencing bullying and harassment from other staff and 42 percent reported workplace stress. This was above the national average for similar organizations within the NHS.

This also reflected an increased emphasis on cost reduction and efficiency within public services as a whole, with workforce reductions and reorganization evident across the NHS (see inter alia Pownall, 2013). At Trustorg, more proactive approaches to the management of performance and staff absence could lead to tensions between line managers and team members, with the latter perceiving the approach taken by the managers as bullying and unreasonable.

... the majority that I've been involved in ... there are some underlying performance issues. When you're trying to manage performance, you inherently get complaints of, "I'm being bullied and harassed, I'm being victimized, I'm being picked on," or they go off sick and you have to manage them through a process then. (Mediator)

Therefore, action to address and resolve issues at an early stage could lead to an increase in observable conflict by bringing matters into the open that might have otherwise been left at rest and ignored.

More broadly, the way in which the organization responded to these challenges reflected a proactive and strategic choice (Lipsky et al., 2003, 2012); from the start, there was intent to change the culture of conflict management reflecting strategic rather than transactional priorities:

... It was about culture change I think, we thought that really from the outset, that it wasn't just about getting a group of people trained in Mediation skills, and providing a

Service, it was about looking at embedding informal Conflict Resolution into the whole organization (Consultant Occupational Health Psychologist)

## *Changing the Culture of Conflict Management?*

A wide range of respondents reported that the developments outlined above had positive impacts. In a direct sense, workplace mediation was seen as being more effective than conventional grievance processes and was more likely to resolve issues and restore employment relationships relatively quickly and cost-effectively. Of the 60 cases that were mediated, 54 (90 percent) were completed with agreement. Perhaps more importantly, our research also pointed to a number of indirect impacts. First, those respondents who were trained as mediators believed that this had wider benefits for themselves and the organization. These new skills had helped them to deal with and manage issues more effectively outside the mediation room. One mediator who also managed a team explained the impact on his own practice:

> It's been useful for the Trust but it's actually been useful to me ... I (1) address things early; and (2) communicate with the team especially on how you're expecting them to work and address performance issues as soon as possible before they get out of hand. (Mediator)

Second, most managers who had been through mediation had consequently reflected on the way they dealt with difficult issues and improved their practice accordingly. For example, one manager who had been involved in an unsuccessful mediation had nevertheless changed the way he responded to conflict:

> I was probably more a person that would reach for the policies and procedures and wait necessarily until someone wanted to make it a formal process. Not any more ... I'd spend twenty minutes with someone who's upset ... but it doesn't matter, it nips it in the bud, the person has been listened to and we discuss what their options are and what they want to do. (Manager)

Furthermore, a respondent who was a mediator and a manager argued that mediation could have a powerful impact on the participants:

> I usually find that it is the first time that those people will have had an actual chance to sit and talk to each other face to face and the emotion in the rooms ... is really very powerful ... It's a realization that you know what they think maybe is just speaking at work is having a really dramatic effect on somebody in their home and personal life ... (Mediator)

At the level of the organization, there was certainly evidence that awareness of ADR had increased, with mediation becoming part of the toolkit for most managers in Trustorg:

> [Managers] think ... this is probably a better alternative than going down ... an official path, which takes up such a lot of time. So I think culturally, people now see it as just part of the tool kit they've got as a manager to deal with conflict and difficulty, whereas they didn't before ... (Manager)

This had also filtered through to management—union relationships — the emphasis on mediation meant that trade union representatives and senior managers tended to look for solutions to problems without recourse to formal rights-based processes:

> I regularly say to Managers where there's conflict within a team, why don't we just organize a team meeting, I'll come along, we'll get HR to come along and we'll just have a discussion about what the concerns are as opposed to leaving it until the wheels come off. (Trade union representative)

Moreover, there was a sense from the data that the work of those involved within the mediation service in developing a range of interventions and the role of the Health and Well-Being Steering Group had created an environment in which early and less formal approaches to conflict resolution were encouraged:

> I think over the time the mediation service has been running, the organization has really made lots and lots of efforts about culture ... [Trustorg] is in a really good place at the moment, so it's one cog of a lot of cogs; I think that has really improved the atmosphere in the field ... (Mediator)

In addition to targeted interventions such as stress risk assessments, facilitated meetings, and conflict coaching, there was increased emphasis on the importance of developing people management skills and competencies. Respondents argued that changes to recruitment were particularly significant in creating a culture of resolution. Several noted a clear shift away from recruitment and development based on clinical skills toward broader competencies and core values. This shift was unusual and was contrary to CIPD (2012) evidence that more technical skills often constitute the prime criteria, with a management and leadership deficit evident. Senior managers and clinicians therefore had to demonstrate a much wider and more people-oriented skill set. An HR practitioner explained that senior clinical staff had to go through an assessment centre ... you have to have a thirty minute role play about a performance management issue with a member of staff so they're not just recruited on the fact that they're a consultant. (HR practitioner)

Critically, this did not just reflect an acceptance within the Trust that managing conflict is a key strategic issue but that the ability of managers to address and resolve difficult issues was central to organizational performance and patient care:

I feel if we get the staff experience right, then do you know what? We'll never have to worry about the patient experience .... (Manager)

### Champions and Challenges

There is little doubt that senior managers played a critical role both in developing a more integrated approach to conflict management and in embedding it within the organization. There was in fact an identifiable champion of these changes (Lynch, 2001), a consultant clinical psychologist in Trustorg's occupational health department. In addition, however, there was also palpable commitment from the Director of Human Resources and the Chief Executive.

A number of respondents cited the importance of clear leadership in driving a more integrated approach to conflict management that began to link conflict with productivity and performance:

... Our occupational [health] psychologist is absolutely the key person in all of this ... After she joined us, we really started to talk about conflict and how we can manage conflict and link between the conflict and things like sickness absence ... If you manage conflict you don't have people who are going off work who are stressed, that you can improve your productivity ... I would say those two [Trustorg] people have been pivotal to saying this is important, pushing it through and making it key to the HR strategy. (HR Practitioner)

In addition to having two key management supporters, having a number of HR managers serve as mediators helped to strengthen the centrality of conflict resolution within the HR strategy. A more key factor, however, was the fact that the scheme coordinators were located in the occupational health psychology department and outside the HR department. Conflict was thus identified more closely with well-being than with compliance. In addition, since the health psychologists were viewed as genuinely impartial, this was argued to increase the access of stakeholders to the system.

However, the research also revealed a number of barriers to embedding a culture of conflict management within Trustorg. The main challenge revolved around managerial attitudes. While most managers were positive about mediation, in line with previous studies (Latreille, 2011; Saundry & Wibberley, 2014), a number admitted to being resistant to taking part in mediation when it was first suggested. Some felt that agreeing to mediation or referring a case to mediation was an admission of failure of some kind. One senior manager explained this as follows:

> Well I'm a senior manager, why haven't I been able to do this myself? That didn't help. Because, in my head I should've been able to do that without mediation … Why didn't I pick up on that before? (Manager)

Another manager expressed frustration that a case they had been dealing with reached mediation:

> … There is a sense of frustration that you … that I didn't necessarily have all the skills to see this particular issue through to fruition. (Manager)

Perhaps most acutely, though, mediation could be seen as a threat to managerial authority, particularly in relation to the management of performance. Front-line managers felt that they were expected to address issues of conduct and capability, but that if employees objected to this, instead of being backed by senior managers they were instead encouraged to resolve the issue through mediation. For some, this implied an acceptance that they were at fault and, consequently, they felt undermined.

Accordingly, front-line and middle managers, while supporting the principle of mediation, felt that it could be used as a default option for staff when they challenged managerial decisions. The managers felt that, while mediation might resolve any personality differences, the performance or conduct issue would still have to be dealt with. These concerns were encapsulated by the following comment from a line manager who had been asked to attend a mediation session:

> I don't think that I'll get anything out of it, I don't want to go to mediation, I don't even know what the issues are so I don't know what I am going to hear. Which I think is hard because I think if it's going to be something personal then, about you know, that I'd like to prepare myself for it. I think that the performance issues are still there and have to be dealt with so I am not sure if that is going to resolve anything in that way … but I'll go and do it and I think that the member of staff will find it beneficial. (Manager)

A broader concern expressed by managers was that they often had very little information as to the complaint made against them or the nature of the issues that had led to the mediation. This increased uncertainty, anxiety, and potential resistance to the process. One manager explained the experience as follows:

> I got a phone call ... from [a senior manager] saying I need to see you now ... he said that communication has broken down ... She suggested the way forward was mediation ... I felt quite traumatized by the whole thing because what she said was not actually true or factual. But no-one investigated that, it was all based on her word alone. (Manager)

Therefore, while management resistance to mediation was related to a fear over a loss of authority, this was not simply caused by managers clinging to their traditional role and status within conflict management (Lipsky & Avgar, 2010). Instead, attitudes toward mediation and the culture of conflict resolution that had developed at Trustorg were affected by the wider organizational context and, particularly, by increasing pressure to improve performance.

## DISCUSSION AND CONCLUSION

Given the lack of evidence for the development of integrated and strategic approaches to conflict management within the United Kingdom, this research is significant in three respects: first, it provides a clear example of an ICMS; second, it provides useful insights into the factors that potentially promote the development of such approaches; and, third, it provides insights into the role played by management both in terms of leading and resisting, innovative approaches to workplace conflict.

The approach adopted by Trustorg highlighted a number of key attributes and characteristics of ICMSs (Lipsky & Avgar, 2010; Lipsky et al., 2003; Lynch, 2001). Critically, from the outset, the organization sought not simply to revamp dispute resolution but to use conflict management as a route to cultural transformation. This involved the development of a range of rights- and interest-based processes with multiple points of entry. Furthermore, rights-based processes were overhauled to incorporate mediation and to provide a focus on early and informal resolution. Critically, conflict-handling skills were not only valued but conflict management was seen as linked to strategic imperatives in terms of both staff well-being and the delivery of effective patient care. Currently, there is evidence of the development of a conflict-competent culture: informal and early resolution appears to be embedded within the organization, and the role of the mediation service is accepted and well understood.

But why has this approach developed in this case and what does this tell us more generally about the drivers for innovation in conflict management? There is little evidence that this was a response to either the threat of litigation or an attempt to undermine or provide a substitute for union representation. Indeed, trade unions were both supportive and directly involved in the introduction, development, and implementation of the system. It is also difficult to argue that the changes were driven by external regulatory or environmental pressure, as the development of the strategy predated the increasingly intense media and governmental spotlight on patient care (Francis, 2015).

Instead, the changes were triggered by a belief that existing practices and processes were unable to cope with conflict that had its roots in the increased pressure faced by staff within Trustorg and the NHS as a whole. Furthermore, it was argued that this could have a direct impact on performance and patient care. In short, this was a strategic choice (Lipsky et al., 2012), which was in turn dependent on the actions of key organizational leaders. The importance of champions in leading the development of ICMSs has been previously identified (Lipsky et al., 2003; Lynch, 2001), but a distinctive feature in this case was the pivotal role played by a consultant occupational health psychologist. This had two important effects: first, it located effective conflict management as a central pillar for employee well-being rather than reacting to difficult and costly disputes; and, second, it provided a degree of separation between the HR and managerial functions of the organization and conflict resolution, which arguably increased access and engendered trust in the system from employees and trade unions.

The study also suggests that transforming the culture of conflict management is not straightforward, however, and is critically related to the nature of managerial authority and the dynamics of workplace relations. As suggested above, the development of conflict management at Trustorg was, in part, a response to broader changes in the management of work. Increasing pressures on managers to increase efficiency and improve performance arising from austerity measures by the UK government created an environment in which conflict was inevitable.

The most significant barrier to embedding the new culture of conflict management was the attitude of managers themselves. In particular, frontline managers were less convinced than their more senior colleagues as to the use of mediation and other conflict management initiatives. This reflected a tension between the operational pressures faced by managers and the emphasis on less formal and more collaborative approaches to conflict. Moreover, for some managers, the enthusiasm of the organization for resolution through mediation threatened to hamper their ability to identify and address issues of conduct and capability.

These findings have a number of wider implications. They provide additional evidence of the potential of integrated and strategic approaches to conflict management to embed cultures of early resolution. They also underline the importance of the involvement of organizational stakeholders and particularly trade unions. However, in adding to evidence that strategic choice rather than structural factors are central in driving such developments, this research suggests that the prognosis for the diffusion of ICMSs is likely to rest on senior managerial leaders accepting not only that conflict is an inevitable part of organizational life but also that the way that it is managed shapes employee well-being, engagement, and, consequently, performance. Unfortunately, the evidence to date suggests that in the United Kingdom, at least, this is the exception rather than the rule.

## NOTES

1. These often came in response to legal claims via Employment Tribunals: see Earnshaw et al. (1998).
2. Trustorg does not provide group mediation, but it offers voluntary individual mediation for issues involving two or three persons. Team facilitation, in contrast, can be any size group of four upwards and is mandatory.

## ACKNOWLEDGMENTS

The authors are grateful for the financial support of the UK government's Advisory, Conciliation and Arbitration Service (Acas) in conducting the research on which this chapter is based, but they acknowledge that the contents represent their views, not those of Acas or its employees. The authors would like to thank the editor and referees for their helpful comments on earlier drafts.

## REFERENCES

Acas. (2006). *Annual report and accounts, 2005–2006*. London: Acas.

Acas. (2014). *Annual report and accounts, 2011−2012*. London: Acas.

Bendersky, C. (2003). Organizational dispute resolution systems: A complementarities model. *Academy of Management Review, 28*(4), 643−656.

Bingham, L. B., Hallberlin, C., Walker, D., & Chung, W. (2009). Dispute system design and justice in employment dispute resolution: Mediation at the workplace. *Harvard Negotiation Law Review, 14*, 1−50.

Bleiman, D. (2008). *Should I try mediation?* A discussion paper for trade union members, mimeo. Retrieved from http://www.scottishmediation.org.uk/downloads/Mediation unionmemberdiscussion.pdf. Accessed on December 22, 2008.

CIPD. (2012). *CIPD annual learning and talent development survey report*. London: CIPD.

Colvin, A. (2003). Institutional pressures, human resource strategies and the rise of nonunion dispute resolution procedures. *Industrial and Labor Relations Review, 56*(3), 375−392.

Colvin, A. (2004). Adoption and use of dispute management practices in the non-union workplace. *Advances in Industrial and Labor Relations, 13*, 71−93.

Colvin, A. (2012). American workplace dispute resolution in the individual rights era. *The International Journal of Human Resource Management, 23*(3), 459−475.

Colvin, A. (2014). Grievance procedures in non-union firms. In W. Roche, P. Teague, & A. Colvin (Eds.) *The Oxford handbook on conflict management in organizations*. Oxford: Oxford University Press.

Department of Business, Innovation and Skills [BIS]. (2011). *Resolving workplace disputes: A consultation*. London: BIS.

Earnshaw, J., Goodman, J., Harrison, R., & Marchington, M. (1998). *Industrial tribunals, workplace disciplinary procedures and employment practices*. Employment Relations Research Series, No. 2. London: Department of Trade and Industry.

Francis, R. (2015). *Freedom to speak up − An independent review into creating an open and honest reporting culture in the NHS*. Retrieved from https://freedomtospeakup.org.uk/ wp-content/uploads/2014/07/F2SU_web.pdf. Accessed on April 14, 2015.

Kochan, T., Lautsch, B., & Bendersky, C. (2000). An evaluation of the Massachusetts commission against discrimination alternative dispute resolution program. *Harvard Negotiation Law Review, 5*, 233−274.

Latreille, P. L. (2011). W*orkplace mediation: A thematic review of the Acas/CIPD evidence*. Acas research paper 13/11.

Lipsky, D., & Avgar, A. (2010). The conflict over conflict management [Electronic version]. *Dispute Resolution Journal, 65*(2−3), 38−430.

Lipsky, D., Avgar, A., Lamare, J., & Gupta, A. (2012). *The antecedents of workplace conflict management systems in U.S. corporations: Evidence from a new survey of Fortune 1000 companies*. Ithaca, NY: Institute on Conflict Resolution, Cornell University.

Lipsky, D., & Seeber, R. (1998). *The appropriate resolution of corporate disputes: A report on the growing use of ADR by U.S. corporations*. Ithaca, NY: Institute on Conflict Resolution. Retrieved from http://digitalcommons.ilr.cornell.edu/icr/4

Lipsky, D., & Seeber, R. (2000). Resolving workplace disputes in the United States: The growth of alternative dispute resolution in employment relations. [Electronic version]. *Journal of Alternative Dispute Resolution, 2*, 37−49.

Lipsky, D., Seeber, R., & Fincher, R. (2003). *Emerging systems for managing workplace conflict: Lessons from American corporations for managers and dispute resolution professionals*. San Francisco, CA: Jossey-Bass.

Lynch, J. (2003). *Are your organization's conflict management practices an integrated conflict management system?* Retrieved from http://www.mediate.com//articles/systemsedit3. cfm. Accessed on April 15, 2013.

Lynch, J. F. (2001). Beyond ADR: A systems approach to conflict management. *Negotiation Journal, 17*(3), 207–216.

McDermott, P., Obar, R., Jose, A., & Bowers, M. (2000). *An evaluation of the equal employment opportunity commission mediation program.* U.S. Equal Employment Opportunity Commission. Retrieved from http://www.eeoc.gov/eeoc/mediation/report/. Accessed on March 14, 2013.

Pope, S. (1996). Inviting fortuitous events in mediation: The role of empowerment and recognition. *Mediation Quarterly, 13*(4), 287–295.

Pownall, H. (2013). Neoliberalism, austerity and the health and social care act 2012: The coalition government's programme for the NHS and its implications for the public sector workforce. *Industrial Law Journal, 42*(4), 422–433.

Reynolds, C. (2000). Workplace mediation. In M. Liebmann (Ed.), *Mediation in context.* London: Jessica Kingsley.

Roche, W. K., & Teague, P. (2011). Firms and innovative conflict management systems in Ireland. *British Journal of Industrial Relations, 49*, 436–459.

Saundry, R., Latreille, P., Dickens, L., Irvine, C., Teague, P., Urwin, P., & Wibberley, G. (2014). *Reframing resolution—Managing conflict and resolving individual employment disputes in the contemporary workplace.* Acas Policy Series.

Saundry, R., McArdle, L., & Thomas, P. (2013). Reframing workplace relations? Conflict resolution and mediation in a primary care trust. *Work, Employment and Society, 27*(2), 221–239.

Saundry, R., & Wibberley, G. (2012). *Mediation and informal resolution – A case study in conflict management.* Acas research paper 12/12.

Saundry, R., & Wibberley, G. (2014). *Workplace dispute resolution and the management of individual conflict—A thematic analysis of 5 case studies.* Acas research paper 06/14.

Seargeant, J. (2005). *The Acas small firms mediation pilot: Research to explore parties' experiences and views on the value of mediation.* Acas research paper 04/05.

Teague, P., & Doherty, L. (2011). Conflict management systems in non-union multinationals in the republic of Ireland. *International Journal of Human Resource Management, 21*(1), 57–71.

Teague, P., Roche, B., & Hann, D. (2012). The diffusion of workplace ADR in Ireland. *Economic and Industrial democracy, 33*(4), 581–604.

Wood, S., Saundry, R., & Latreille, P. (2014). *Analysis of the nature, extent and impact of grievance and disciplinary procedures and workplace mediation using WERS2011.* Acas research paper 10/14.

# TREATING CONFLICT: THE ADOPTION OF A CONFLICT MANAGEMENT SYSTEM IN A HOSPITAL SETTING

Ariel C. Avgar

## ABSTRACT

Purpose — *This chapter explores the adoption and implementation of a conflict management system (CMS) in a hospital setting. In particular, it uncovers the different motivations and challenges associated with a CMS across various stakeholders within the organization.*

Methodology/approach — *The chapter is based on qualitative research conducted in a large American hospital that adopted and implemented a CMS over the course of 15 months. The author conducted extensive interviews with stakeholders across the organization, including top management, union leaders, middle managers, clinicians, and frontline staff. Findings are also based on an array of observations, including stakeholder meetings and conflict management sessions.*

Findings — *The case study demonstrates the centrality of underexplored, generalizable, and industry-specific pressures that may lead organizations*

Managing and Resolving Workplace Conflict
Advances in Industrial and Labor Relations, Volume 22, 211–246
ISSN: 0742-6186/doi:10.1108/S0742-618620160000022009

*to reconsider their use of traditional dispute resolution practices and to institute a CMS. It also highlights the inherent organizational ambivalence toward the design and adoption, initiation and implementation, and routine use of a CMS and it documents the different types of outcomes delivered to various stakeholders.*

Originality/value — *The chapter provides a nuanced portrait of the antecedents to and consequences of the transformation of conflict management within one organization. It contributes to the existing body of research exploring the 30-year rise of alternative dispute resolution and CMSs in a growing proportion of firms in the United States. The use of an in-depth case-study method to examine this CMS experience offers a number of important insights, particularly regarding different stakeholder motivations and outcomes.*

**Keywords:** Dispute resolution; conflict management system; ombuds; healthcare

# CHALLENGING PREVAILING ASSUMPTIONS

Conflict and its resolution are central phenomena in the study of organizations (Avgar, Lamare, Lipsky, & Gupta, 2013; Barbash, 1984; Cutcher-Gershenfeld, 1991; Kolb & Putnam, 1992; Lewin, 1987, 2001; Lipsky, Seeber, & Fincher, 2003). Over the past three decades, organizational practices and processes designed to resolve workplace conflicts and disputes have undergone a comprehensive and dramatic transformation (Avgar et al., 2013; Lipsky et al., 2003; Rowe, 1997; Rowe & Bendersky, 2003). Specifically, a growing number of nonunion firms have adopted a variety of formalized grievance and alternative dispute resolution (ADR) procedures alongside integrated conflict management systems (CMSs). This expansion of organizational conflict management has provided firms with internal mechanisms that facilitate employee voice on the one hand and the bypassing of external settlement paths on the other (Colvin, 2003; Lewin, 1987; Lipsky et al., 2003; Rowe, 1997).

While conflict is an integral component of organizational life, the responses to conflict are varied, complex, and dynamic. Different approaches to, and methods of dealing with, workplace conflict are likely to produce qualitatively different organizational and individual outcomes (Avgar,

2015; Cutcher-Gershenfeld, 1991). Not unexpectedly, therefore, the rise of ADR in the American workplace and the use of nontraditional conflict management techniques have had significant ramifications for organizations and their employees.

From an organizational perspective, the replacement of traditional authoritarian methods of resolving conflicts and disputes with institutionalized mechanisms that seek to enhance integrative resolution methods has required adaptations to managerial practices, work arrangements, and organizational culture (Avgar, 2015; Bendersky, 2007; Lipsky & Avgar, 2008; Lipsky et al., 2003). In addition, evidence from the union setting suggests that transformed dispute resolution methods can positively affect firm performance and employee commitment to the organization (Colvin, 2004; Cutcher-Gershenfeld, 1991; Katz, Kochan, & Gobeille, 1983; Katz, Kochan, & Weber, 1985).

At the individual level, reconfiguring the existing framework for resolving workplace conflicts and disputes has had clear implications for the ways in which organizational members (employees and supervisors) interact, voice concerns, and perform their work. Different dispute resolution systems have been shown to affect employee attitudes and responses to conflict in different ways (Bendersky, 2007; Mahony & Klaas, 2008; Olson-Buchanan & Boswell, 2008).

The transformation of organizational dispute resolution and its workplace consequences has not gone unnoticed in theory or in practice. Over the past three decades, legal, industrial relations, and organizational behavior scholars have been studying this shift away from the traditional and predominately authoritarian management of conflict and toward an institutionalized proactive approach (Avgar et al., 2013; Bendersky, 2007; Colvin, 2003; Eigen & Litwin, 2014; Ewing, 1989; Fuller, 1978; Lewin, 1987; Lipsky & Avgar, 2008; Lipsky, Avgar, & Lamare, 2014; McCabe, 1988; Westin & Feliu, 1988). This research has contributed greatly to existing knowledge about this consequential phenomenon by documenting the transformation and providing an in-depth portrait of its contours and inner workings.

Nonetheless, a number of research questions related to the adoption and implementation of these practices have remained relatively underexplored. A great deal is still unknown, for example, about the different drivers that lead organizations to adopt and implement a host of new practices and procedures (for exceptions see Avgar et al., 2013; Colvin, 2003). Research has not yet fully explored the rationales and strategic considerations that have motivated a growing proportion of firms to abandon their traditional models and to replace them with institutionalized internal mechanisms.

A recent stream of research has begun to examine the strategic underpinnings driving organizational adoption of different practices (Avgar, 2015; Avgar et al., 2013; Lipsky, Avgar, & Lamare, 2014). This research suggests that such decisions are, among other factors, a function of a strategic orientation regarding the benefits that are likely to accrue as a result of this new approach. What this research has not yet fully explored is the different considerations and motivations across multiple organizational stakeholders. My chapter builds on this strategic perspective and, with a focus on diverse stakeholder perspectives, attempts to uncover some of the key factors that drive an organization to adopt a new conflict management approach.

A second area of research that needs additional empirical evidence relates to the outcomes delivered to different stakeholders as a result of the adoption of new conflict management practices (for a recent exception see Teague & Roche, 2012). Some researchers suggest that firms adopt these practices with the expectation that they will be associated with certain benefits (Avgar, 2015; Lipsky, Avgar, & Lamare, 2014). Organizations may adopt new practices with the expectation, for example, that this will improve their ability to manage their workforce in a collaborative and integrative manner. Others may adopt new practices in an effort to improve their ability to avoid litigation. Still others may be seeking to advance efficiency gains (Avgar, 2015; Lipsky, Avgar, & Lamare, 2014). To what extent are these expectations being realized? To what extent are different outcomes being delivered to different stakeholders within the organization? To date, there is relatively little empirical evidence regarding the organizational outcomes associated with ADR and CMS.

In an effort to examine adoption drivers and associated outcomes, this chapter describes in detail the experience of one large American teaching hospital (referred to here as Ohio Medical) in designing, implementing, and utilizing a workplace CMS that centered around the office of an ombuds (often called an ombudsman). Employing a case-study methodology, I describe the pressures that led to the system's adoption and analyze the individual and organizational outcomes for the hospital and its multiple stakeholders. This analysis contributes to the conflict management literature by providing a more complex, nuanced, and rich illustration of how such systems play out across a specific organization.

In exploring these research questions, the case study challenges a number of dominant assumptions prevalent in the conflict management literature. First, it challenges the common assumption that, in their decision to adopt new practices, organizations are responding primarily to external environmental pressures, such as litigation and unionization threats. In addition, the qualitative evidence documented here challenges the notion that adoption pressures and drivers operate in a consistent manner across the organization and its different stakeholders. As will be discussed below, the Ohio Medical case study shows that the impetus for the adoption and maintenance of such a system and the corresponding strategy developed are nuanced and multifaceted and are likely to vary across stakeholders.

Second, the traditional analysis of ADR and CMS outcomes, to the extent that they are addressed at all, focuses almost exclusively on the effects that conflict resolution processes have on individual employees or group members. One of the interesting insights gained from the Ohio Medical case study is that the effects of a CMS can be observed across different levels of the organization and, more importantly, that outcomes vary across these different levels.

Third, some of the existing conflict resolution scholarship assumes a congruence between the motivations for adopting conflict management practices and their associated outcomes. The evidence described below presents a striking disconnect between the dominant rationales for taking a proactive conflict management approach at Ohio Medical and the actual benefits of this approach for the hospital and its stakeholders.

Finally, conflict management scholars have placed much of their emphasis on the early adoption process (see most notably Lipsky et al., 2003). According to this perspective, the decision to adopt an ADR or CMS is the key organizational hurdle. Once a system is in place, for the most part, organizational commitment is taken for granted. The case study described below challenges this perspective by exposing the tensions and difficulties encountered in sustaining a CMS after it had been adopted and despite clear and acknowledged benefits. Recognition of ongoing organizational ambivalence toward conflict management programs may help to explain the relatively slow diffusion of such institutions in general and in the healthcare arena in particular. Incorporating a focus on organizational challenges beyond the initial decision to adopt a CMS is, therefore, an important extension of existing research.

## METHODOLOGY AND CASE-STUDY BACKGROUND

Qualitative and quantitative data were collected at Ohio Medical over a period of approximately 15 months. The qualitative methodology included some 75 interviews with employees and managers throughout the hospital, including the chief executive officer (CEO), the chief operating officer (COO), an array of middle managers, and frontline employees from various hospital departments. It also included observations of management meetings, of ombuds office meetings, trainings and dispute resolution sessions, and of the program's Joint Operating Committee (JOC), in addition to the use of archival material, including the hospital newsletter and transcripts from hospital meetings.

Following correspondence with the hospital ombuds, I was granted research access to the hospital and specifically to activities and material dealing with conflict and conflict management across the hospital. I participated in monthly JOC meetings in which important discussions took place regarding the program, and in management and professional meetings, all of which provided important contextual information about the hospital culture, pressing issues and considerations, and the strategic mindset. It was on the basis of this information that a stakeholder perspective emerged. It became apparent that an examination of the repercussions of a CMS on the participating parties to a given dispute is insufficient; it is also necessary to explore the broader organizational stakeholders and their standing vis-à-vis the program.

With regard to quantitative data, I was granted access to archival information on complaints that were filed through the ADR system. In addition, a specially designed survey was used to measure employee attitudes and perception toward the CMS. A comparison of the survey results with documented dispute resolution activity provided an opportunity for an analysis of the extent to which various conflicts were dealt with through different conflict resolution outlets. In sum, access granted by Ohio Medical to both qualitative and quantitative data provided a unique opportunity to study a dispute resolution program in an industry that has received relatively little scholarly attention in this regard.

Lipsky et al. (2003) maintain that since CMSs are, for the most part, private systems and, that since many organizations are reluctant to share detailed information on these programs, there is a significant knowledge gap regarding implementation and internal processes. These authors state "research that has been conducted on conflict management systems has tended to be across rather than within organizations. Thus, we have less knowledge of internal systems than we would like" (p. 263). This chapter will fill in some of the existing knowledge gaps based on a comprehensive and in-depth description of the experiences within one internal system.

Ohio Medical was a unique and convenient setting in which to examine the issues discussed above due especially to the conception, design, and implementation of a dispute resolution system piloted there by the Federal Mediation and Conciliation Services (FMCS) in 2004. Founded in 1914, Ohio Medical is a not-for-profit teaching hospital with 540 beds and a staff of over 1,000 physicians, 3,400 healthcare professionals and support staff, and 500 volunteers. It serves a population of over 1.2 million in the northeast Ohio area. According to *U.S. News and World Report*, the hospital ranks among the 100 best hospitals in the United States. At the time of the CMS adoption and implementation, Ohio Medical was rated among the top 30 hospitals in the nation for heart care and surgery and in the top 50 for respiratory disorders. It has also been ranked among the top 100 hospitals by such healthcare research groups as Solucient and Leapfrog.[1] The hospital's revenue around the time of the CMS implementation was $343 million, with a profit of approximately $27 million.

In the summer of 2003, Ohio Medical was contacted by the FMCS concerning the possibility of serving as a site for a pilot dispute resolution program. The pilot systems initiated in a number of different settings and locations by the FMCS in 2002 included a number of common features. First, they were implemented parallel to at least one collective bargaining agreement that covered a portion of the organization's workforce. Second, each system included the implementation of a number of conflict management options (Robinson, Pearlstein, & Mayer, 2005). This characteristic is in line with the general literature on CMSs (Lipsky et al., 2003). Third, all pilot programs included an interest-based resolution option that focused on the needs and interests of the disputing parties as opposed to contractual or statutory rights (Robinson et al., 2005). Fourth, the FMCS decided that one of the necessary characteristics of a dispute resolution system in a unionized setting was the presence of an internal neutral (such as an ombuds), as opposed to the use of a roster of external neutrals.

Following introductory meetings with labor and management stakeholders, Ohio Medical and the FMCS set up a design team in January 2004. Key and relevant stakeholders were identified during meetings with the unions, top management, and the human resources department. The team included five representatives from management, five representatives from each union, and five representatives from the nonunion hospital workforce. A wide array of additional hospital stakeholders beyond those formally selected were also involved in the design process. This broad and diverse team composition played a key role in both the design process and the implementation field notes, December 2005. Two FMCS mediators facilitated the monthly meetings. At the conclusion of a year-long design process during which the team grappled with issues of structure, division of authority and procedures, an ombuds office and JOC were established. In February 2005, the dispute resolution program, titled AGREE, got underway.

Reflecting the general excitement with which this unique initiative was pursued, the vice president of human resources sent out the following announcement:

> As most of you know, we have had a committee comprised of equal representation from management, non-union non-management, [unionized] employees at work for over a year on the development of an alternative dispute resolution program. We are the first of some 25 employers across the country targeted by the FMCS ... to look at and try to find better ways to deal with conflict. What makes this approach unique is that it has been developed exclusively through collaboration and consensus.... The committee members are coming before you as a group with great enthusiasm to roll out the program.[2]

In the analysis below, I refer to the AGREE program and its ombuds office as a CMS. I do so based on Lipsky et al. (2003) outline of the core characteristics of a CMS: (a) broad scope, (b) tolerant culture, (c) multiple access points, (d) multiple options, and (e) systemic support structures. The AGREE program met the majority of these characteristics. First, the hospital ombuds was given a very broad mandate and the flexibility to address a wide array of organizational conflict. Second, despite the challenges associated with the implementation of a CMS described in more detail below, the hospital did attempt to leverage the hospital ombuds and the design process that led to its creation in an effort to establish a more tolerant conflict management culture. Third, given the flexibility, broad mandate, and informal nature of the hospital ombuds, there were multiple access points into the system and multiple resolution options afforded to employees and supervisors. Finally, the hospital invested considerable resources in establishing the hospital ombuds and, despite the ambivalence described below, demonstrated a commitment to providing this program with systemic support and appropriate structures to help give it both legitimacy and the capacity to deliver on its conflict management objectives.

### Pressures to Innovate: Adoption Drivers Revisited

Much of the research on conflict management practices in nonunion settings has examined the external environmental pressures that lead organizations to abandon traditional authoritative methods of dealing with conflict. One of the most detailed frameworks for understanding ADR adoption and use by U.S. and Canadian companies is set forth by Colvin (1999, 2003). Colvin's research on dispute resolution in the telecommunications industry demonstrates that companies facing a perceived threat in terms of employee litigation were more likely to adopt an arbitration-based program than other ADR procedures. Firms that faced a perceived threat of unionization, on the other hand, were more likely to adopt a peer review-based program. Lipsky et al. (2003) expand the array of pressures affecting organizational adoption to include additional environmental pressures as well as such internal organizational factors as conflict management strategies.

Research at Ohio Medical demonstrated the complexity of organizational adoption pressures and forces. The study of factors leading to the adoption and implementation of the AGREE program revealed a number of underexplored adoption drivers, both external and internal. Not only did the hospital face a broader and more complex set of pressures than previously recognized in the literature, but also different hospital stakeholders responded to and were motivated by different external and internal factors. This type of evidence is central to the development of a more sophisticated and nuanced understanding of how CMSs emerge and, once they do, how they operate.

## *The Role of Traditional Drivers*

Before examining less documented conflict management adoption drivers, we need to assess the role that traditional drivers played at Ohio Medical. With regard to two of the most prevalent drivers in the literature — the threat of litigation and union avoidance — interviews with top executives suggested that they were far less central than in other documented cases. The consensus among central interviewees was that in considering the adoption of a dispute resolution system, litigation factors had very little, if anything, to do with their decision.

One sign of the fact that a litigation-avoidance strategy was not a dominant driver in the hospital's decision to adopt an innovative conflict management strategy was the minimal contact and communication between the ombuds office and the general counsel's office. For example, when, early on in the program's implementation, the ombuds office contacted the general counsel's office to review and align roles and responsibilities, the latter articulated the position that there was no real overlap between the offices and no need to coordinate.

Since the hospital engaged in collective bargaining with two separate unions that represent almost half of its workforce, the traditional union-avoidance pressures highlighted in the literature are less obvious than they are in nonunion settings. Many of the top managers interviewed denied adamantly that the decision to adopt an ADR system was motivated by a desire to keep unionization at bay. The vice president of human resources, for example, argued that had this been a motivation, the hospital would not have allowed the unions the degree of influence that they had in the design and implementation of the program.

Other informants, however, including those in management positions, depicted a more complex linkage between union considerations and the adoption of the program. Some, such as the director of labor relations, did in fact view the AGREE program as a mechanism for increasing leverage vis-à-vis the unions. Union leaders from both the unions representing clinical and nonclinical employees – the Ohio Nurses Association (ONA) and the United Steel Workers of America, respectively (USWA) also suggested that one of the considerations in adopting the program had to do with the collective bargaining relationship, but neither felt that it was a union-substitution strategy.

Labor and management were both motivated by a desire to overcome adversarial relations. In 2002, one year prior to the agreement to participate in the FMCS pilot program, the hospital was averaging more than 130 grievances each year, a number that was viewed as extremely problematic for both sides. The director of labor relations noted, "the adversarial model was not working and I wanted us to move to a change in labor management relations" (Interview with hospital labor relations director). Unions, and especially the USWA, were also seeking ways to change the relationship with management (Interviews with USWA local president and vice president).

Similarly, both unions and management at Ohio Medical viewed the AGREE program as a mechanism by which some of the adversarial dynamics, manifested in a 12-day nurses' union strike in 2005, might have been alleviated. The strike had a traumatizing effect on both nurses and management, especially human resource managers. Implementation of the CMS was seen as one of the obvious ways to avoid this situation in the future. The hospital CEO maintained that one of the central motivations for adopting the program was a move away from the labor relations dynamic that brought about the strike. He stated:

> The program came about, in part, because we realized [from the strike] that we were just not connecting with our employees. If we are going to continue to provide a higher level of care to our patients, the very first group we need to take care of is our employees. The strike showed us that there was a gap between us and the union and that gap needed to be narrowed.

However, the CEO also noted that:

> You don't adopt a program like AGREE because you want to avoid unions. If you are
> only adopting it to bust the union, employees will see through that and realize that is a
> managerial attempt to keep the status quo.

Given the fact that traditional adoption motivations did not appear to play out in the traditional manner at Ohio Medical, the question of alternate pressures becomes all the more important and interesting.

*Industry-Specific Drivers*
One of the limitations of existing research regarding the adoption of dispute resolution systems is the relative absence of an industry specific or contextual analysis. Much of what is known about organizational dispute resolution drivers fails to incorporate either industry-specific factors or variations across industries. Although Colvin's research (2003) was conducted in a specific industry (telecommunications), his analysis is intended, for the most part, to apply across industries. Lipsky and colleagues studied firms from a variety of industries and did, in fact, categorize industries on the basis of their conflict management strategies, but they did not delineate the factors influencing adoption variation across these industries.

Research at Ohio Medical revealed a number of healthcare-specific pressures that contributed to the original decision to adopt the AGREE program and to subsequent decisions to maintain the program: (a) the hospital accreditation process, (b) the dramatic shortage of nurses and other healthcare professionals, (c) the ongoing efforts to increase patient satisfaction indicators, and (d) the hyper-competitive nature the industry.

*Hospital Accreditation.* One of the forces that shaped the support of Ohio Medical's top management for the adoption of the AGREE program was the potential effect it might have on various hospital accreditation efforts and specifically on the Joint Commission's periodic review. The Joint Commission, which at the time of this study was referred to as JCAHO, was founded in 1951 as a joint initiative of the central healthcare associations (the American College of Physicians, the American Hospital Association, the American Medical Association, and the Canadian Medical Association). It provided an accreditation framework for hospitals and other healthcare organizations at the time of the CMS adoption. The Joint Commission was founded in an effort to improve quality of care in U.S. hospitals by creating standardized criteria by which to evaluate these organizations.

Today, the Joint Commission accredits over 21,000 healthcare organizations and serves as a premier provider of benchmarks for quality and safety within the industry. Hospitals that seek the Joint Commission's highest level of accreditation go through a rigorous and in-depth on-site review at least every three years. In its accreditation process, the Joint Commission assesses nearly every facet of a hospital's operation. The review team examines key performance indicators regarding patient safety, quality of care, and workforce-related criteria.

At the time of CMS adoption and implementation, the Joint Commission had no official requirements regarding workplace dispute resolution, but the influence of this key organization was clearly present in the hospital's decision to adopt the program. First, the Joint Commission had signaled a desire to implement a dispute resolution standard as part of the accreditation process in the future and issued voluntary guidelines regarding appropriate and recommended practices and training. Furthermore, even in the absence of this signal, Ohio Medical hoped that the adoption of the AGREE program would have a favorable effect on ongoing efforts to achieve high accreditation marks.

In interviews with managers, several expressed the hope that voluntarily adopting a mechanism for dealing with employee conflicts would highlight the hospital's commitment to its workforce and, therefore, to quality of care. Ohio Medical, which is not unique in this respect, seemed conditioned to automatically assess the majority of its organizational initiatives and actions from the standpoint of their potential effect on the Joint Commission review process. The Joint Commission's presence loomed large in hospital corridors and departments, management meetings, and hospital innovations, including the AGREE program. Top management saw the dispute resolution system as a program that would make the hospital stand out in the accreditation process.

Accreditation pressures illustrate a relatively unique healthcare issue that appeared to shape the organizational strategy regarding conflict management program adoption. Such a system was perceived by the hospital as having the potential of enhancing not only the actual dynamics between the parties that would make use of the program, but also the appearance of the hospital on a number of broader external fronts. Thus, in some ways, the adoption of a CMS can be seen as the acquisition of legitimacy and the management of external impressions. This pressure may also exist in other settings where accreditation has a strong behavior-modifying effect.

*Workforce Recruitment and Retention.* An additional industry-specific pressure influencing Ohio Medical's decision to adopt a dispute resolution system related to the challenges it, like most U.S. hospitals, faced in the recruitment and retention of medical professionals, especially nurses. Early in my research at Ohio Medical the centrality of recruiting and retaining highly skilled nurses became evident. While negotiating access to the hospital and the program, my contacts, including the hospital ombuds and the COO, stated that they would be very excited if my research could focus on nurses and the problem of turnover. Throughout my research, there was continued interest in the link between the CMS and the hospital's ability to retain nurses.

While scholars have debated the extent to which an actual shortage of nurses exists (Lafer, 2005), many hospitals in the United States operate under the assumption that they must compete aggressively for the recruitment and retention of clinical professionals and especially nurses (Avgar, Eaton, Givan, & Litwin, 2016; for estimates of future nursing shortages see Dall et al., 2013). Hospitals and the healthcare industry as a whole have responded to this apparent shortage of medical professionals in a variety of ways. Most notably, healthcare organizations have been engaged in fierce competition to attract and retain qualified professionals, and especially nurses. Recruitment and retention formed a dominant driver at Ohio Medical and when confronted with the opportunity to implement a dispute resolution system, the possible effects on this crisis were paramount.

Ohio Medical was clearly not alone in its concerns regarding the recruitment and retention of nurses and other healthcare professionals and their efforts to adopt innovative practices that might assist them in overcoming this challenge. One of the industrywide manifestations of this competition is the creation of "magnet" hospital status. Similar to the Joint Commission accreditation process discussed above, the American Nurses Credentialing Center (ANCC), established through the American Nurses Association in 1990, has developed a review process. Through this process, which was implemented in 1994, a hospital could be recognized as an attractive and high-quality employer for nurses — a magnet for highly trained and qualified nursing professionals. At the time of the adoption and implementation of the CMS, approximately 250 hospitals out of over 6,000 operating in the United States had been designated by the ANCC as *magnet institutions*.

At the time of this research, Ohio Medical was not recognized as a magnet hospital. During the period that I conducted research, there was a concentrated effort to attain this status. Interestingly, in the process of applying for magnet status, active steps were taken to highlight the CMS. For example, the hospital submitted documentation regarding the program, the cases it had handled, and the effects it had on nurses. Despite these efforts, Ohio Medical was unsuccessful in passing the review process. Frustrated by this failure, hospital administrators referred to the attainment of magnet status as the "Nobel Prize" of nursing, and they were determined to succeed in future attempts.

As was the case with the the Joint Commission pressure discussed above, the aspirations to achieve this important healthcare credential played a central role in the consideration and adoption of the AGREE program. A nursing director at the hospital stated "if we can show nurses that we take them seriously and pay attention to their issues at work, it may help us get magnet status next time around."

Another manifestation of the competition over skilled clinical professionals was the hospital's drive to receive recognition as an *employer of choice*. Similar to the magnet status, employer of choice is a status granted by an external body based on employment-centered criteria. It is seen as a method by which to recruit and retain staff. The vice president of human resources acknowledged that one of the motivating factors in adopting the AGREE program was the desire to achieve preferred employer status. "Whether it will actually assist us in achieving this objective, time will tell."

*Gaining Advantage in a Hyper-Competitive Industry.* Like most hospitals in the United States, Ohio Medical operated in a state of hyper-competition. The hospital competed aggressively with a number of healthcare providers, but particularly with one of the other large hospitals in the same city (referred to here as Ohio General). The competition with Ohio General was so dominant that it appears to have motivated many of the hospital's decisions and actions. In a general management meeting that I observed, Ohio Medical's track record was consistently benchmarked against the data on Ohio General. Managers took great pride in outranking this competitor on various parameters and were disappointed and frustrated by areas in which they fell behind.

In an interview conducted with the director of the Ohio Medical's cardio-vascular department on the day the department received a very high ranking from *U.S. News and World Report*, I was told that what makes this especially satisfying was that they outranked Ohio General. Similarly, the AGREE program was seen as a way to outdo other hospitals in a highly competitive industry.

## To Treat or Not to Treat Conflict? Organizational Schizophrenia

One of the interesting aspects of dispute resolution in the healthcare arena is that despite the arguable need for such mechanisms, there is relatively slow movement in this direction. Ohio Medical provides a unique lens through which to view the decision to engage in a nontraditional proactive conflict management strategy. The case-study data also provide important insights about subsequent signs of resistance, or at least ambivalence, toward the program on the part of different groups of stakeholders.

Despite the acknowledged benefits of the program, major stakeholders, and particularly top management, were engaged in incessant efforts to assess outcomes associated with the program. The constant effectiveness assessment went beyond the standard and periodic examination of costs and benefits to the organization and appeared to be an attempt to gather evidence that could undermine the program itself and could be used to undercut the program, possibly leading to its demise.

The mixed signals conveyed at various levels of management and the union leadership represent what I will refer to as *organizational schizophrenia* in dealing with conflict. Like the Greek meaning of the term schizophrenia — split mind — Ohio Medical demonstrated a split organizational personality in reference to conflict management in general and its conflict resolution program in particular.

This schizophrenia seems to have stemmed from three primary tensions. First, some of the hospital stakeholders, primarily top and middle management, found it difficult to acknowledge that conflict is an inherent and persistent organizational phenomenon. Second, and more central to the organizational ambivalence, stakeholders struggled in identifying the appropriate outcome measures upon which to assess the effectiveness of the program, leading to an array of inconsistent measures and, more importantly, assessments. Some scholars have attributed this difficulty in measuring effectiveness to the lack of organizational information about the program and its accomplishments (Lipsky et al., 2003). Although research at the hospital provided support for this argument, it also provided other explanations for this fundamental dispute resolution challenge.

The difficulty in assessing conflict resolution outcomes stems, among other things, from multiple and contradictory interests and the fact that different hospital stakeholders appeared to benefit in different ways from the system. Thus, at Ohio Medical, there was a lack of consensus regarding the very criteria for measuring effectiveness. Stakeholders did not lack the necessary information for evaluating effectiveness but, rather, they had a hard time identifying what actually constituted effectiveness.

Finally, one of the consequences of the AGREE program was a relatively dramatic shift in the way hospital stakeholders operated. For example, the program had clear implications for the way in which the human resources department handled employee complaints and disputes and, to some degree, other general functions as well. More than merely changing hospital policies, the CMS altered roles and responsibilities as well as the general approach to workplace conflict. In some respects, these changes benefited human resource managers, but in others the shift was a threat to the traditional boundaries of human resource policies and practices. The perceived threat is likely to have resulted in some degree of resistance from a central and powerful dispute resolution stakeholder.

Similarly, the presence of an ombuds office changed the dynamics between middle managers and their employees. Here, too, the change had positive implications, such as support for the restructuring processes. In other ways, however, middle managers felt the program threatened their managerial prerogatives and that it questioned their competence. The concurrent opportunities and threats associated with the program for different stakeholders help explain the observed organizational schizophrenia.

*Ambivalence at the Top Management Level*

The AGREE program at Ohio Medical was set up largely as a result of support from top management. The support of the hospital CEO and the direct hands-on involvement of the COO played key roles in signaling to the design team, and later to the JOC, that this project was sanctioned by the hospital leadership and, more importantly, was linked to broader organizational objectives. This endorsement, nevertheless, was not without limits and seemed to coexist alongside a healthy dose of hesitation, ambivalence, and frequent reevaluation.

A number of factors may explain these reactions. First, although the costs associated with the adoption of the program were clear and measurable, the expected outcomes were more difficult to identify and quantify. In the absence of tangible outcomes that would provide measures of cost effectiveness, the hospital CEO, COO, and other top executives engaged the ombuds and the JOC in ongoing efforts to produce clear and measurable program results.

For example, the hospital ombuds reported that during each of her encounters with the hospital CEO (formal and informal) she was asked whether employees were more satisfied now that the CMS was in place. The CEO articulated this focus in this comment:

> From my vantage point a key indicator of program success is employee satisfaction. 1,200 employees have taken a survey that I hope will show higher satisfaction levels because this gives us a confidential and objective way to measure what the program is doing.

According to the ombuds, the CEO's measure of program effectiveness was based almost exclusively on increased employee satisfaction, and it was through this lens that he evaluated its viability. But as observed by the ombuds:

> [The] link between my program and employee satisfaction is one that I cannot really make. Sometimes employees that come to my office leave less satisfied; that does not mean that the process has not benefited the parties or the hospital.

Nonetheless, the difficulty in making a clear case for the relationship between the dispute resolution system and employee satisfaction is likely to have weakened the CEO's support for the program.

A second factor that appears to have contributed to top management's ambivalence toward the program stemmed from its effects on the traditional roles of key organizational actors. Specifically, as discussed above, the implementation of the AGREE program clearly affected the human resources department and its organizational mandate. As the director of labor relations said, "My job and the HR department's job is to be both good cop and bad cop The AGREE program pushes me toward the good cop role and I am not sure if that is always good."

Speaking about this tension, the vice president of human resources said that

> Turning the total design and governance of this type of a program over to an entity outside the HR department was very difficult for me. Some of us did have fears regarding how much authority this individual and group [the JOC] would have to transcend the normal rules and boxes regarding what goes on in the work environment.

In keeping with the organizational ambivalence, however, she also acknowledged the ways in which the program enhanced the hospital's ability to deal with conflict beyond the traditional human resource "paradigm."

> In my 35 years in HR I certainly have had to deal with conflict and in many cases as the intervener. But my background is not that of a trained facilitator or mediator. I work with the information I have and with my skills, which I must say are pro-management by virtue of where I sit. It's nice to know that we have this service and that an individual

or department can get individualized impartial and confidential attention. They can get my attention, but it will not be impartial.


## Middle Management Ambivalence

Top management was not the only hospital stakeholder to exhibit a split personality regarding the program. Middle managers, a central stakeholder for the success of the program, showed mixed signs of acceptance and resistance as well. In contrast to top management, however, the order of this ambivalence was reversed: beginning with resistance and followed by parallel signs of support.

Research on the role of middle managers and organizational innovation has demonstrated how central this stakeholder is to the successful implementation of a program (for a discussion, see Batt, 2004). Although top management determines whether a new program will live or die, the support of middle management dictates the quality of the program during its existence.

Middle managers with whom I spoke, especially nursing directors, stated that they were unsure of what the program could do for them and what it could do for their employees. Some felt that use of the program by their employees reflected negatively on them and signaled their lack of managerial skills and abilities. In certain units of the hospital, the ombuds encountered very reluctant managers who either refused to participate at all or did so with little commitment to the process. Middle managers who participated also expressed reservations about paying too much attention to conflict, especially interpersonal conflict, and concerns about taking on additional responsibilities in their already overburdened jobs.

Interestingly, the oscillation from resistance to support among this group of stakeholders seemed to be associated with an increased understanding of the ways in which the program could assist them in their work. One of the program's primary benefits for middle managers was training in dispute resolution-related skills. It was this benefit that led at least some of the managers at this level to recognize the value of the system. Nevertheless, as with top management, the movement from one state of mind (resistance or support) to another did not negate the original attitude. In other words, middle manager support for the program did not necessarily mean resistance had been overcome. One indicator of increasing middle management support for the program was seen in the usage patterns of this stakeholder group. In 2005, 18 (8 percent) of the 222 hospital members who participated in the program were managers; in the first half of 2007, 155 (38 percent) of the 406 participants were managers.

## Union and Employee Ambivalence

The unions operating at Ohio Medical, especially the USWA, were strong advocates for the adoption of the CMS during the design and implementation phases. Nevertheless, they too demonstrated ambivalence toward the use of the system. This ambivalence was especially prevalent, though, within the nurses' union. Despite the emphasis placed by the hospital on engagement in the program, both the nurses' union and its members were reluctant to join fully in the implementation of the program and especially in its use. On many occasions, ONA representatives were absent from JOC meetings and initiatives and both the ombuds and the FMCS facilitator had difficulty engaging the ONA leadership in the program and gaining their support. In addition to weak involvement on the part of the union, the nursing staff itself was slow and hesitant to use the program in order to address conflicts in their units. During its first year of operation, only 8 percent of the 222 employees who made use of the program were ONA members (ombuds archival data).[3]

Low usage and participation by members of the union did not go unnoticed; it received a great deal of attention by the JOC, the ombuds, and hospital leadership. "We built this for them, why aren't they coming?" was a common sentiment expressed by many of the other stakeholders. For top management, especially the hospital COO, these data were of great concern and fueled their own ambivalence to the program. Given that one of their primary adoption drivers was the improvement of nurses' recruitment, retention, and overall satisfaction, if the program could not deliver on this front, some managers wondered whether it was all worth it (Field notes, March 2006).

In a discussion of the factors contributing to ONA's lack of engagement, some felt it was due to internal tensions within the union. Others attributed it to the general culture of self-reliance among nurses. According to this argument, nurses view themselves as resilient and no-nonsense professionals. A program that assists in resolving day-to-day conflict stands in contradiction to this core component of their occupational identity.

However, research at the hospital, including interviews with nurses, did not support this hypothesis. Nurses I interviewed recognized the cost associated with conflict in their units and were eager to have access to mechanisms that alleviated it. What, then, explained ONA leadership and membership resistance to participate in the program? Interviews with the hospital ONA president and members highlighted two main factors. First, as hypothesized by the JOC, internal tensions and problems diverted attention from the CMS. The second and more central reason for ONA reservations, though, seems to stem from a lack of clarity about the ways in which the program would benefit the union as a whole and its membership. In other words, the union and its members' resistance to the CMS can be attributed to outcome ambiguity.

One of the reasons for this ambiguity can be traced to the 2004 nurses' strike that threatened the implementation of the program. As mentioned above, the strike had a traumatic effect on the bargaining parties and on the union members. It also influenced ONA perceptions of the program. In some ways, it seemed that the program was assessed through a collective bargaining lens. The ONA was interested in how the program could improve its standing in the 2007 bargaining round and as long as this link was unclear, so was their support for the program.

In keeping with the overall schizophrenic response to the dispute resolution system, all of the above signals of reservation were countered by other signals of strong support for the program. Union leaders indicated, for example, that they saw the program as an integral part of their collective bargaining structure. In fact, despite relatively low use by ONA members in its first two years, 2007 saw an increase in nurses' participation in the program. Thus, of 406 employees who participated in the AGREE program, 12 percent were ONA members.

# WHAT HAVE YOU DONE FOR ME LATELY? A STAKEHOLDER PERSPECTIVE ON CONFLICT MANAGEMENT OUTCOMES

As described above, each of the major stakeholders at Ohio Medical exhibited mixed receptiveness toward the adoption, implementation, and use of the program. An emerging and consistent theme in this regard was outcome ambiguity. All of the stakeholder groups had a difficult time both identifying and quantifying the potential benefits (for a similar discussion regarding the difficulty in quantifying system outcomes, see Lipsky et al., 2003, p. 307). The centrality of this theme requires an examination of the relationship between the CMS and outcomes for the various stakeholders.

Much of the literature on ADR and CMSs has been limited in its discussion of outcomes. Dispute resolution practices have been assessed, primarily, in terms of their effects on organizational turnover or exit (see, e.g., Batt, Colvin, & Keefe, 2002; for a detailed review see Colvin, Klaas, & Mahony, 2006). Other studies have examined the effects of nonunion dispute resolution procedures on the career progression of the employee who filed the complaint and the employee against whom the complaint was filed (Lewin, 1987). Finally, researchers have examined outcomes from a litigation perspective, such as win rates and ADR-to-courtroom cost comparisons (for a review see Colvin et al., 2006). Except for these general-outcome categories, there is a gap in the research on organizational and individual-level outcomes of ADR strategies.

Where outcomes have been examined, the distinction between different categories of organizational stakeholders has received little attention. With the exception of the distinction in Lewin's research between employees who file complaints and the supervisors against whom the complaints are filed, the literature examines the issue of outcomes in a one-dimensional manner. The Ohio Medical case study allows for the examination of CMS outcomes delivered to four stakeholder groups: frontline employees, middle managers, the hospital unions, and top management.

As demonstrated below, the system had vastly different effects on each of the groups. Although the formal function of a CMS is to resolve microlevel conflicts between individuals, this case study highlights that, in fact, the system provided a mechanism through which broader organizational outcomes, such as communication and coordination, were achieved.

### *Outcomes for Frontline Employees*

Traditionally, conflict resolution research has focused on the effects of a system on actual users, namely frontline employees. Since these systems are put into place to deal with individual-level outcomes, outcome measures have focused on individual usage, individual turnover, and career advancement. Interestingly, the evidence on these outcome measures is also ambiguous and it is in no way clear how such systems actually affect frontline employees.

Research at Ohio Medical highlights three main outcomes for frontline employees: (a) resolution of micro-level conflicts with peers and supervisors, (b) resolution of systemic problems or conflicts, and (c) collective voice for nonunion employees.

### Individual-Level Conflict Resolution

During my research at Ohio Medical, I observed a number of sessions conducted by the ombuds with frontline employees. For the most part, these sessions addressed conflicts arising in a given unit among employees or between employees and supervisors. The ombuds was called in to develop strategies for dealing with conflict and its underlying causes. In such instances, the presence of a dispute resolution system provided an alternate outlet for the unit supervisor through which persistent problems that were usually interpersonal could be addressed.

What the sessions highlighted in particular was the potency of such individual-level conflicts and their dramatic effects on the way frontline employees carried out responsibilities. On several occasions, employees described the effects of conflicts with peers in their unit as unbearable and paralyzing in terms of their ability to conduct routine work. One LPN described it this way:

> There are mornings when the thought of coming into work and dealing with all of this makes me sick. I sometimes need to stop on the side of the road I get so sick. To throw up I mean. I will call in and say, I am going to be late, I had to stop on the side of the road again. It just gets to me that way. I don't know why.

The visceral effect of conflict described by this LPN was not unusual. Employees spoke about spending large portions of their time dealing with conflicts that arose on their floors and of the physical and emotional consequences of these conflicts. At this level, the CMS provided a mechanism for resolving persistent conflicts and, more importantly, provided tools and skills for dealing with such situations. In short, the system represented an institutionalized vehicle through which to confront deep-rooted interpersonal and professional conflicts.

Prior to the implementation of the AGREE program, many of these conflicts were not dealt with at all or were brought to the unit supervisors. Supervisors were not always trained to deal with the issues and often lacked the ability or motivation to confront individual-level conflict. Thus, for example, 39 percent of the conflicts processed by the AGREE program between January 2005 and March 2006 included horizontal or peer-related issues. This is the largest category of conflict addressed by the program during this period. Hierarchical conflict (between employees and their managers or supervisors) represented 32 percent of the conflicts brought to the AGREE program. These categories dominated other organizational issues, such as discrimination, staffing and safety, and compensation.

### Resolution of Systemic Problems
Another way in which the AGREE program influenced frontline employees was by providing an outlet for dealing with unit or department-level issues. The ombuds was called in by employees to assist with a variety of issues, including environmental conditions and the way in which work was structured. In these situations, the ombuds served as a facilitator, convening the necessary parties for the resolution of the broader organizational issue at hand.

### Collective Voice for Nonunion Employees
A third way in which the system affected employees was by providing those who were not unionized with a mechanism through which to organize their own collective voice. For example, "non-bargaining" employees in one of the hospital laboratories used the ombuds office to collectively engage management over a series of issues that had been surfacing for years. Employees were concerned about the treatment they received from supervisors and managers, the way in which shifts and supervisory positions were allocated, and by other work-related issues. By making use of the system, employees were able collectively to rally around issues that had been dealt with at the individual level in the past. One of the employees in the laboratory admitted that "The presence of the program gives me the confidence in our attempts to improve the lab.... Before the program, we would not have met in this way."

Another employee in the same laboratory said, "As non-bargaining employees we had no outlet previously. Using the AGREE program, we raise safety and benefits issues."

Emboldened by the progress they were able to make in this manner, laboratory employees set up a committee designed to "coordinate and *represent*" employee demands to management. In one session in which these employees met with the ombuds to discuss their concerns, they set forth a list of demands regarding the various issues they felt management needed to address. The manner in which the list was generated resembled a collective bargaining framework. Thus, the presence of a CMS seems to have provided employees who lacked a traditional, institutionalized collective voice an alternate voice mechanism. One laboratory employee said,

"Everywhere you go in this hospital you hear 'we are an employer of choice,' but management *has to give* and not just claim employer of choice. We need to see results."

Another indicator of the role the AGREE program played for non-bargaining members is the usage rate by this employee group. Non-bargaining members were, in fact, a leading user of the CMS. In 2005, 69 percent of system participants were non-bargaining and non-management employees. In 2007, 37 percent of system participants were non-bargaining and non-management employees, suggesting that the system was gaining legitimacy among other groups alongside non-bargaining frontline employees.

In one sense, this finding is in line with the goal of certain stakeholders to avoid unionization through a CMS. On the other hand, both the degree and the way in which nonunion employees made use of the system for collective action probably exceeded management's expectations. While top management did not adopt the CMS in an effort to avoid unions, they were also not expecting it to be leveraged as a tool through which employees exercised collective action. Some employees, in fact, expressed the hope that this collective activity would eventually pave the way for unionization. One of the laboratory "organizers," who was also a member of the AGREE JOC, observed, "Management feels that our demands are union demands — and maybe they are."

The director of labor relations for one of the hospital's recently merged rehabilitation centers noted, "The AGREE program is a response to employee needs and provides a voice for good employees under bad managers." He also commented that some managers have viewed this aspect of the program as "giving the employees the keys to the shop."

Finally, the finding that the system provides different outcomes for nonunion as opposed to unionized employees is in line with the stakeholder perspective. It suggests that CMS outcomes vary not only at different hierarchical levels (frontline vs. managerial), but within stakeholder levels as well (union vs. nonunion).

*Outcomes for Middle Managers*

Among middle managers, the dispute resolution program had two dominant effects. First, it served as a coordinating mechanism for managers, primarily with respect to organizational restructuring. Second, it provided managers with specific conflict resolution skills and competencies.

## Coordination in the Midst of Restructuring

Existing literature on hospital restructuring has presented empirical evidence on the consequences associated with this process in terms of conflict and its resolution. Interviews conducted with middle managers at Ohio Medical provided additional support for the claim that structural changes experienced by most hospitals in the United States have had dramatic organizational consequences, particularly for middle management. Thus, for example, the manager of the hospital's practice sites and physician practices stated:

> We are going through a major overhaul and we need buy in. I want to redesign the way we work and implement system changes, but there is tremendous resistance. Restructuring creates mistrust which makes our job in changing things around here very difficult.

In response to employee resistance to the restructuring process, this particular manager turned to the AGREE program for assistance and support. The ombuds was brought in to assist in what became a multiparty restructuring negotiations arena. As the unit's managers found themselves negotiating with the physicians, nurses, and allied professionals over the contours and implications of the unit restructuring, the presence of an in-house neutral proved highly beneficial.

One of the interesting aspects associated with the restructuring of this particular unit was the strong resistance on the part of physicians to the anticipated changes. Although physicians were not active users of the system, in the case of the restructuring of the unit and negotiated change with this strong hospital stakeholder, the dispute resolution program seemed to have extended into their domain. The physician director of this unit referred to the dynamics as follows: "Some people around here have a lot of power in resisting change. If the doctors are not supportive of us, employees will not listen to us. We need the program's help to *negotiate status, power, and control.*"

The administrator of this same unit said. "You are never going to get consensus out of doctors. We need to develop consensus over restructuring and need assistance in this negotiation."

What emerged from this specific example and from interviews with other managers throughout the hospital was the role the CMS played as a coordinating and consensus-building mechanism in the service of managers confronted with the challenges of restructuring. Thus, although the resolution of conflict was integral to this system role, it was not the only component. The ombuds helped managers build alliances and develop trust in the changes necessitated by the restructuring pressures described above.

Often what appears to be interpersonal workplace conflict is actually a problem of coordination that stems from uncertainty regarding organizational structures and roles. In this sense, the CMS not only treated workplace conflicts, but also assisted managers in handling structural issues that might otherwise have led to conflicts. As the ombuds reported:

> One group of employees had been laboring for years under a faulty understanding of their organizational structure. Discussions clarified, for example, who reports to whom. This new information helped them understand behavior about which they had been resentful and angry. They continue to refine their organizational understanding and are moving forward to create an excellent team that provides excellent patient care.

With the increased institutionalization of the AGREE program, the role of restructuring coordination become more prominent. The ombuds was asked to attend a number of unit retreats intended to ease the restructuring process and to discuss the ways in which unit members dealt with the fears, frustrations, and conflicts associated with it. In addition, a growing number of middle managers began turning to the program for assistance in dealing with colleagues and supervisors on restructuring issues.

This coordinating role became especially vital in early 2007, when rumors of a possible merger with another large Ohio hospital became prevalent. Despite attempts on the part of top management to dispel these rumors, employees and middle managers began using the AGREE program as a mechanism to voice and process merger implications. Significantly, those making use of the program in this regard were overwhelmingly middle managers.

In the summer of 2007, the hospital announced that although there were no concrete plans to merge, the two hospitals were engaged in discussions of ways to cooperate. This announcement triggered an even greater usage of the AGREE program by hospital managers. The increase was so dramatic that the ombuds began devoting much of her time to these stakeholder issues at the expense of frontline employee conflict resolution.

## Conflict Management Skills

A second dominant outcome associated with the AGREE program for middle managers was the attainment of conflict management skills and competencies. A number of interviewees felt that top management increasingly expected middle managers to deal proactively with conflict. Given what they perceived as pressure to incorporate conflict resolution into their managerial roles, hospital managers began assessing their capabilities in this domain. Many voiced complaints that were variations on the following

theme: "I was trained as an RN and as a supervisor not as a 'dispute resol-
ver.'" One manager in a cardio-vascular department observed that if she
was going to be evaluated on the basis of her ability to mediate staff conflicts, she needed to develop the skill set to do so. She noted,

> Employee satisfaction in my unit was very low and I wanted to examine how we and I
> could communicate better within the unit. I am trying to convey myself differently and
> to resolve staff conflicts, but I need to improve my conflict resolution abilities. My 360
> evaluation came back with low scores on dispute resolution abilities, so I contacted the
> AGREE program. I need to build these skills.

A nurse supervisor in the cardio-vascular center also articulated this
need, stating:

> Supervisors who have used the system have done so because they felt that it assisted
> them in managing. We all like to think that we can manage in every situation, but
> unfortunately that is not the case. In critical care, we deal with strong, smart, and com-
> petent individuals. It's important for us to have professional dispute resolution training
> and support to deal with conflicts.

Another hospital manager speaking about the use of the program said:

> You can't be all things to all people. We all need help, and there seems to be a greater
> willingness to request help having seen what the ombudsman can do. Interview,
> June 2006.

A large proportion of manager—employee conflicts were addressed
through the AGREE program. Many of these resolution sessions were also
used to engage managers around skills and techniques that in turn could be
used to resolve conflicts internally. Thus, for middle managers, the
AGREE program appears to have served two related managerial
needs — coordination and training. Again, although this stakeholder group
benefited from the actual resolution of workplace conflicts and disputes
between frontline employees, their motivations for using and supporting
the system were distinct.

## *Outcomes for Unions*

One of the unique characteristics of the dispute resolution system implemented at Ohio Medical was the involvement of unions in both its design
and its operation. The dominant outcome for the unions was, in fact, a
dramatic expansion of their organizational roles. Prior to the adoption of
the AGREE program, the state of labor relations at the hospital was

traditional and very adversarial. Hospital management engaged unions exclusively around issues related to collective bargaining. The involvement of the unions on the design and JOCs transformed labor-management relations in a number of ways. Most pronounced was the legitimacy gained by the unions as central organizational actors beyond the scope of collective bargaining. The USWA president described this change as follows:

> Management is more open minded now and understands our position. Before the program we were prototyped as the bad guys, always wanting something for nothing. Now they see us differently. This program has really impacted our CEO and COO and how they relate to us.

In addition to the effect on the unions' role, the program has, for the most part, delivered on the unions' expectation regarding non-contractual conflicts. As mentioned above, one of the adoption drivers for the unions was the belief that an in-house neutral would be able to alleviate the pressures associated with peer and other conflicts. They sought a way to address employee workplace conflicts that were outside of their official jurisdiction.

The AGREE program served this purpose. The USWA president reported a drastic reduction in non-contractual issues and complaints dealt with by her office. She noted that prior to the program the union felt obliged to deal with all issues that were brought to them. Now that an alternative outlet existed, the union felt less pressure to engage management in this way. She said, "We need to service our members. If there is no other place for these conflicts we will deal with them. But, now we refer them to the ombudsman."

## Outcomes for Top Management

As discussed earlier, top management supported the adoption of the AGREE program based on the anticipated effects on employee satisfaction and turnover alongside the role it might play in hospital certification. Very soon after the adoption of the dispute resolution program it became clear that it would serve two other, unanticipated roles — enhancing vertical communication in the hospital and supporting the hospital's espoused organizational culture.

### Strategic Communications
Hospital leadership quickly realized that being vested in the adoption of a CMS had the potential to convey top management communications down

to middle managers and frontline employees and to receive communications from these groups through the ombuds. Of special note in this respect was the COO, who seemed intuitively to sense that the program could be used in this capacity.

On a number of occasions, the COO relied on the AGREE program to disseminate information about leadership goals and vision. This was an important function, given the emphasis that hospital leadership and the COO in particular placed on organizational communication. For example, when asked in a hospital "town hall meeting" what could be done to improve the organization, the COO stated "We need to continue to improve communications and interaction between leadership and direct care providers and support staff." Regarding the program's role in promoting organizational communication, she remarked:

> One of the things that the program does is keep me apprised of the culture, the things that are setting people off, the issues that we need to fix. Having someone who is close to the action and who can help me take the bigger picture approach is very good. It is not that I don't trust other individuals, but they have vested interests.

In addition to articulating leadership messages through the dispute resolution program, top management and especially the COO and vice president of human resources used the program to learn about other stakeholder problems and concerns in a more direct manner. One of the areas where this was clearly exhibited related to fears and frustrations about hospital restructuring. As mentioned above, the program played an important role in both support and coordination, as well as conflict resolution, related to restructuring. When such issues arose, they were routinely communicated to hospital leadership.

Apprehensions regarding a possible hospital merger were a good case in point. Although the CEO and COO may have been aware of the unrest this was causing at all levels, the actual evidence provided by the CMS sensitized them to the extent of the problem. By briefing the hospital COO on emerging issues related to restructuring in various hospital units, the ombuds was able to connect top management to the perspectives and perceptions of managers and employees that may not otherwise have been clearly understood or articulated. Over time, the ombuds office came to recognize its role as a facilitator of organizational communication. The ombuds framed the program's role in the following manner:

> Having a confidential, independent program like AGREE allows employees an avenue for having the kinds of discussions that keep them engaged in change processes. Especially in the hierarchical and fast-paced environment of health care, clear

communication can be compromised even by the best communicators with the best intentions. At [Ohio Medical] maintaining excellent and easy channels for communication is an important goal, not only for employee satisfaction but also for patient safety.

## Organizational Culture

A second outcome associated with the AGREE program for top management was the reinforcement the espoused culture of trust. It is hard to miss the organizational culture sought after by its leadership: large banners and signs boast the trustworthiness of the hospital and its staff. One of the advertised slogans prevalent throughout the hospital states, "Never underestimate the power of trust." Another banner states, "We will never take your trust for granted." Finally, an advertisement for hospital awards includes "Awards are nice, trust is better."

The emphasis on trust as an organizational value was evident throughout my interviews with the hospital CEO and COO. Both articulated the need, especially in a highly competitive industry, to create an environment that fosters trust with patients. Although this emphasis on trust pertained in many ways to the relationship between the hospital and its client base, the culture of trust set forth by management was not solely a hospital–patient attribute. In interviews, I would regularly inquire about the meaning of the trust-focused slogans. Many, including top managers, interpreted these as referring to trust between the hospital and its employees and more specifically between management and frontline employees. One employee explained "You can't expect to have trust with the patients if you don't have trust with the employees."

Although a culture based on trust between different stakeholders was a goal for top management, it was not evenly diffused across the hospital. Some managers and frontline employees treated aspirations for trusting relationships and the slogans that marketed these in a rather cynical manner. Not everyone felt that awards took second place to trust. Furthermore, many of the pressures placed on hospitals and the responses they inspired have been empirically linked to outcomes that are in tension with organizational trust, such as stress, decreased satisfaction, and increased conflict.

In this sense, the AGREE program played an unanticipated role in strengthening both the level of actual organizational trust and perceptions of the hospital as genuinely committed to this core value. AGREE assisted in building trust in four central ways. First, by resolving actual conflicts and disputes, the program assisted in mending relationships and increasing interpersonal trust. Second, it played a central role in facilitating unit and hospital restructuring in a manner that provided employees and managers with more information and tools to confront fears, concerns, and frustrations. In doing so, the program enhanced unit-level trust. By delivering on these two outcomes for frontline employees and managers, the program was also achieving a third outcome – support for the organizational culture. Finally, one of the most dominant ways in which the CMS fostered organizational trust was through the JOC. As discussed above, this committee brought together representatives of most of the hospital stakeholders to discuss and manage the dispute resolution program. In order to achieve this objective, the parties (union leadership, managers, and nonunion employees) had to develop a trusting relationship.

As observed by the USWA president, "Decisions made by the JOC and actions taken have to enhance the trust we have in each other." In a hospital report to the community, the local USWA president is quoted as saying, "Our AGREE program is helping improve communications with each other and to further strengthen our work environment by building a culture of mutual respect and trust." Coming from the union president, this was a strong endorsement of the program's role in advancing a managerial-centered objective and illustrates the broader role played by the dispute resolution system. The very showcasing of the AGREE program in the annual report as a way in which the hospital has been striving to achieve the desired culture further underscores the program's role.

At monthly JOC meetings, the need for trust was a common, if not always fulfilled, objective. Since the JOC members also served in key hospital roles and communicated in this capacity outside their JOC affiliation, trust gained in this setting had important implications for the other arenas. One of the most obvious and central examples for this diffusion of trust from the JOC to other hospital relationships was the June 2007 bargaining round between the ONA and the hospital.

As noted, 2004 bargaining was interrupted by a 12-day strike that had a lasting effect on the parties. Despite some trepidation on the part of all sides, the 2007 negotiations were uneventful and resulted in a contract both parties were content with. This was attributed to the AGREE program in general and to the JOC specifically. In this sense, the operation of the JOC itself was a vehicle through which the hospital worked toward breathing life into the goal of establishing a culture of trust.

# CONCLUSION

The Ohio Medical case study contributes to the discussion of organizational conflict management in two primary ways. First, it presents evidence of a more complex relationship between traditional drivers and the decision to adopt a CMS. As discussed, neither of the traditional organizational motivations − litigation avoidance and union substitution − played as a dominant role as one might have predicted from the literature. The litigation avoidance and reduction motivation did not seem to factor into the top management's decision-making process. Although union-related factors did influence hospital actors, their role diverged from conventional ADR and CMS wisdom. Labor relations actors at the hospital viewed the system as a way to change and improve the collective bargaining process but not as a means of bypassing it, as is often maintained. This suggests the need to incorporate more variation in the discussion of traditional adoption drivers.

Second, the case study highlighted the centrality of other underexplored and generalizable, industry-specific pressures that lead organizations to reconsider conflict management practices and procedures. Such pressures as professional and organizational accreditation, workforce shortages, extreme competition, and patient satisfaction levels were all shown to have played a role in shaping Ohio Medical's strategic decision to restructure the management of conflict.

These findings have both theoretical and practical implications. At the theoretical level, they call for additional research on the organizational motivations for adopting CMSs. From a practical standpoint, the evidence regarding context-specific drivers suggests that organizations need to tailor these systems to address as many drivers as possible. In other words, building on the CMS logic, the specific contours of a system should reflect the original stakeholder expectations and anticipated benefits, among other things.

A second insight provided by the Ohio Medical case study was the ongoing organizational ambivalence toward the CMS even after it was adopted and implemented. In other words, the decision to adopt or not to adopt a system is only the first in a series of many decision points regarding its overall utility. The hospital questioned the system frequently and attempted to establish clear cost−benefit criteria for sustaining the program, despite the difficulty in quantifying the system's benefits. Here too, the findings have implications for researchers and practitioners. First, from a research standpoint, merely focusing on an organization's adoption decision fails to address the relevant processes associated with subsequent implementation. On the practical level, organizations need to anticipate and address ongoing concerns and resistance at various levels and among various stakeholders.

Another of the factors driving the documented organizational ambivalence toward a CMS stems from the difficulty of assessing potential costs and benefits. Although benefits will always be hard to quantify and generalize, research, especially qualitative, can amass additional evidence on the various costs and benefits involved in the adoption and use of a program. Organizations, for their part, may benefit from the creation of internal criteria for assessing a CMS. In other words, they may reduce their ambivalence by articulating a set of system objectives by which they can assess outcomes.

Finally, the Ohio Medical case study illustrates the importance of ensuring that the system is delivering for multiple stakeholders and the consequences associated with the failure to do so. This study highlights three main outcome categories across stakeholders. At the frontline level, the outcomes associated with the program were primarily relational — focusing on the relationships between peers, employees, and their supervisors. At the middle management level, associated outcomes were primarily structural — the coordination of organizational restructuring. Finally, at the top management level, outcomes were primarily related to organizational culture and communication.

Future research should continue to explore the multifaceted costs and benefits associated with ADR and CMS by complementing existing quantitative findings with rich qualitative evidence about the adoption and implementation processes and the motivations of different stakeholders. The past 30 years have seen tremendous advances in the study of internal management of organizational conflict and disputes. Nevertheless, there is still a great deal of work to be done to better understand and document organizational decisions to adopt such practices and the benefits that they deliver or fail to deliver to multiple stakeholders.

## NOTES

1. Both are organizations that conduct benchmarking studies on U.S. hospitals; the first is a for-profit research and consulting firm and the second is a nonprofit health advocacy group.

2. Source is an internal e-mail provided by the hospital in archival materials on the program.

3. There were approximately 900 ONA members out of the 5,900 Ohio Medical employees at the time of this study.

## ACKNOWLEDGMENTS

The author wishes to thank Ryan Lamare and David Lipsky for their very helpful input and feedback. Thanks also to WonJoon Chung for his terrific research assistance. Last but not least, sincere thanks to "Ohio Medical's" employees, union leaders, and administration, and to their extremely dedicated ombudsman. A portion of this chapter appeared previously in Avgar (2011).

## REFERENCES

Avgar, A. C. (2011). The ombudsman's ability to influence perceptions of organizational fairness: Toward a multi-stakeholder framework. *Journal of the International Ombudsman Association, 4*(1), 5–15.

Avgar, A. C. (2015). Internal resolution of employment disputes. In A. Feliu, W. Outten, J. Drucker, B. Winograd, & A. Bloom (Eds.), *ADR in employment* (pp. 45–85). Arlington, VA: ADR in employment. BNA Books.

Avgar, A. C., Eaton, A. E., Givan, R. K., & Litwin, A. S. (2016). Work and employment relations in healthcare: Introduction to a special issue of the industrial and labor relations review. *Industrial and Labor Relations Review*. Only available at http://ilr.sagepub.com/content/early/2016/05/06/0019793916649171.extract

Avgar, A. C., Lamare, J. R., Lipsky, D. B., & Gupta, A. (2013). Unions and ADR: The relationship between labor unions and workplace dispute resolution in US corporations. *Ohio State Journal on Dispute Resolution, 28*(1), 63–106.

Barbash, J. (1984). *The elements of industrial relations.* Madison, WI: The University of Wisconsin Press.

Batt, R. (2004). Who benefits from teams? Comparing workers, supervisors, and managers. *Industrial Relations: A Journal of Economy and Society, 43*(1), 183–212.

Batt, R., Colvin, J. S. A., & Keefe, J. (2002). Employee voice, human resource practiced and quit rates: Evidence from the telecommunications industry. *Industrial and Labor Relations Review, 55*(4), 573–594.

Bendersky, C. (2007). Complementarities in organizational dispute resolution systems: How system characteristics affect individuals' conflict experience. *Industrial and Labor Relations Review, 60*(2), 204–224.

Colvin, A. J. S. (1999). *Citizens and Citadels: Dispute resolution and governance of employment relations.* Unpublished dissertation manuscript, Cornell University.

Colvin, A. J. S. (2003). Institutional pressures, human resource strategies, and the rise of non-union dispute resolution procedures. *Industrial & Labor Relations Review, 56*(3), 375–392.

Colvin, A. J. S. (2004). The relationship between employee involvement and workplace dispute resolution. *Relations Industrielles/Industrial Relations, 59*(4), 681–704.

Colvin, A. J. S., Klaas, B., & Mahony, D. (2006). Research on alternative dispute resolution procedures. In D. Lewin (Ed.), *Contemporary issues in employment relations.* Champaign, IL: Labor and Employment Relations Association Series.

Cutcher-Gershenfeld, J. (1991). The impact of economic performance of a transformation in workplace relations. *Industrial and Labor Relations Review, 44*(2), 241–260.

Dall, T. M., Gallo, P. D., Chakrabarti, R., West, T., Semilla, A. P., & Storm, M. V. (2013). An aging population and growing disease burden will require a large and specialized health care workforce by 2025. *Health Affairs, 32*(11), 2013–2020.

Eigen, Z. J., & Litwin, A. S. (2014). Justice or just between us? Empirical evidence of the trade-off between procedural and interactional justice in workplace dispute resolution. *Industrial and Labor Relations Review, 67*(1), 171–201.

Ewing, W. D. (1989). *Justice on the job: Resolving grievances in the nonunion workplace.* Boston, MA: Harvard Business School Press.

Fuller, L. (1978). The forms and limits of adjudication. *Harvard Law Review, 92*(2), 353–409.

Katz, C. H., Kochan, T. A., & Weber, M. R. (1985). Assessing the effects of industrial relations systems and efforts to improve the quality of working life on organizational effectiveness. *Academy of Management Journal, 28*(3), 509–526.

Katz, C. H., Kochan, T., & Gobeille, K. (1983, October). Industrial relations performance, economic performance, and QWL programs: An interplant analysis. *Industrial and Labor Relations Review, 37*(1), 3–17.

Kolb, M. D., & Putnam, L. L. (1992). Introduction: The dialectics of disputing. In D. M. Kolb & J. M. Bartunek (Eds.), *Hidden conflict in organizations: Uncovering behind the scenes disputes* (pp. 1–31). Newbury Park, CA: Sage.

Lafer, G. (2005). Hospital speedups and the fiction of a nursing shortage. *Labor Studies Journal, 30*(1), 27–46.

Lewin, D. (1987). Dispute resolution in the nonunion firm: A theoretical and empirical analysis. *The Journal of Conflict Resolution, 31*(3), 465–502.

Lewin, D. (2001). IR and HR perspectives on workplace conflict: What can each learn from the other? *Human Resource Management Review, 11*(4), 453–485.

Lipsky, D. B., Avgar, A., & Lamare, J. R. (2014). Conflict resolution in the United States. In W. K. Roche, P. Teague, & A. Colvin (Eds.), *The Oxford handbook of conflict management in organizations* (pp. 405–424). Oxford University Press.

Lipsky, D. B., & Avgar, A. C. (2008). Toward a strategic theory of workplace conflict management. *Ohio State Journal on Dispute Resolution, 24*(1), 143–190.

Lipsky, B. D., Seeber, L. R., & Fincher, D. R. (2003). *Emerging systems for managing workplace conflict: Lessons from American corporations for managers and dispute resolution professionals.* San Francisco, CA: Jossey-Bass.

Mahony, D., & Klaas, B. (2008). Comparative dispute resolution in the workplace. *Journal of Labor Research, 28*(4), 251–271.

McCabe, D. M. (1988). *Corporate nonunion complaint procedures and systems: A strategic human resources management analysis.* New York: Praeger Publishers.

Olson-Buchanan, J. B., & Boswell, W. R. (2008). An integrative model of experiencing and responding to mistreatment at work. *Academy of Management Review, 33*(1), 76–96.

Robinson, P., Pearlstein, A., & Mayer, B. (2005). Encouraging "dynamic adaptive dispute systems" in the organized workplace. *Harvard Negotiation Law Review, 10*, 339–382.

Rowe, M. (1997). Dispute resolution in the non-union environment: An evolution toward integrated systems of conflict management. In S. E. Gleason (Ed.), Workplace dispute resolution: Directions for the 21st century (pp. 79–106). East Lansing, MI: Michigan State University Press.

Rowe, M., & Bendersky, C. (2003). Workplace justice, zero tolerance, and zero barriers. In T. A. Kochan & D. B. Lipsky (Eds.), *Negotiations and change: From the workplace to society* (pp. 117–137). Ithaca, NY: ILR Press.

Teague, P., & Roche, W. K. (2012). Line managers and the management of workplace conflict: Evidence from Ireland. *Human Resource Management Journal, 22*(3), 235–251.

Westin, F. A., & Feliu, G. A. (1988). *Resolving employment disputes without litigation.* Washington, DC: The Bureau of National Affairs, Inc.